# Table of Contents

# INTRODUCTION

Congratulations on preparing to take the first step to becoming an officer in the United States Air Force! The AFOQT is an important exam for many reasons, but mostly because it lets the Air Force know where your strengths and weaknesses lie, and how they can best utilize your abilities. It gives them a glimpse of your raw abilities in a few subjects, but will also test your ability to stay calm under pressure. Some sections, such as Math and Science, will test your raw knowledge and intellect, not to mention how hard you prepared (or not) for the exam. Other sections are deceptively simple, in that the task is something you might think a six year old could do. The catch though is that you have an absurdly short amount of time on these sections and the task is usually designed to seem easier than it is. Their goal, in this case, is to see how you respond when the odds are stacked against you, and you know that you won't be able to finish. Do you panic and make mistakes, or push through diligently and do your best? This study guide will prepare you for both aspects of this challenging exam. The AFOQT is a competitive test, so you need to aim high...no pun intended.

## Sections on the AFOQT

There are 12 sections on the AFOQT and will follow this order:

1) Verbal Analogies – 25 questions, 8 minutes
2) Arithmetic Reasoning – 25 questions, 29 minutes
3) Word Knowledge – 25 questions, 5 minutes
4) Math Knowledge – 25 questions, 22 minutes
5) Instrument Comprehension – 20 questions, 6 minutes
6) Block Counting – 20 questions, 3 minutes
   (10-minute break)
7) Table Reading – 40 questions, 7 minutes
8) Aviation Information – 20 questions, 8 minutes
9) General Science – 20 questions, 10 minutes
10) Rotated Blocks – 15 questions, 13 minutes
11) Hidden Figures – 15 questions, 8 minutes
12) Self-Description Inventory – 220 questions, 40 minutes

As you can see, there are a few sections with minimal time limits, giving you only 10-15 seconds per question in some cases. The only section we will NOT cover in this study guide is the "Self-Description Inventory". This is not a section you can "study" for and there are no tricks here. It is simply a personality questionnaire, so be sure to be totally honest and straightforward in your answers. Don't give answers for what you think 'they want to hear'.

## Scoring on the AFOQT
You will be given scores in five areas:
- Pilot
- Navigator
- Academic Aptitude
- Verbal
- Quantitative

Each score is made up of different combinations of the 12 sections of the AFOQT and each has a different minimum score. In all 5 cases, the scores are percentiles, which range from 1 to 99. An average score would fall in the upper 40's. It is recommended that for those who want to be a pilot, that you achieve a score of 70 or higher across all five categories. Scores in the 85-95 range are considered strong scores. The sections comprising each score and the minimum required score to be considered are listed below for your reference:

- **Pilot**
  - Minimum Score to be pilot: 25
  - Minimum Combined Pilot & Navigator score: 50
    - (Note: Must have a minimum of 10 Navigator Score)
  - Score Comprised of sections:
    - Arithmetic Reasoning
    - Math Knowledge
    - Instrument Comprehension
    - Table Reading
    - Aviation Information

- **Navigator**
  - Minimum Score to be Navigator: 25
  - Minimum Combined Pilot & Navigator score: 50
    - (Note: Must have a minimum of 10 Pilot Score)
  - Score Comprised of sections:
    - Verbal Analogies
    - Arithmetic Reasoning
    - Math Knowledge
    - Block Counting
    - Table Reading
    - General Science

- **Academic Aptitude**
  - No minimum; composite of Math and Verbal sections
  - Score Comprised of Sections:
    - Verbal Analogies
    - Arithmetic Reasoning
    - Word Knowledge
    - Math Knowledge
- **Verbal**
  - Minimum Score for all candidates: 15
  - Score Comprised of Sections:
    - Verbal Analogies
    - Word Knowledge

- **Quantitative**
  - Minimum Score for all candidates: 10
  - Score Comprised of Sections:
    - Arithmetic Reasoning
    - Math Knowledge

## Test Day Procedures

On test day, be prepared for a 3.5 hour test day, including administrative information and instructions. You will have one 10 minute break halfway through the exam. You do not want to waste time reading instructions; you should be totally familiar with those before sitting down. Pencils and paper will be provided, you may NOT use a calculator. No food or drink is allowed during the test.

It is important to note that there is no wrong answer penalty on the AFOQT. Again...

## THERE IS NO PENALTY FOR WRONG ANSWERS!

*This means, under no circumstance, on any section of the entire test, should you EVER leave a question blank even if it is a wild guess.*

## Additional Important Information about the AFOQT

One of the most important factors to take into consideration is that you may only take the AFOQT twice. Never, ever think of the first exam as a "practice round". You need to study diligently and do your absolute best the very first time you take it.

If you decide to take the exam a second time, keep in mind you must wait 180 days (6 months) and your second score will become your official score, even if you do worse! Your most recent score is the only one anyone will see. In some extremely rare circumstances, you might secure a waiver to take the AFOQT a third time, but that is highly unlikely for most candidates.

Finally, it is important to consider that the USAF looks at the whole package you send them. For example, if the average score for candidates who earn a pilot position is 90, just because you might only have an 85 does not mean it is impossible to win a spot. Conversely, just because you have a 99 does not automatically guarantee anything. They will look at your entire application package, including your GPA and the other four scores you receive.

One more time, just to be sure: DO NOT EVER LEAVE A QUESTION BLANK!!!! You will better understand as you work through the different sections just how short the time limits are. Do not allow yourself to be caught off guard with only 5 seconds left and note enough time to fill in any answers before the buzzer. You must maintain situational awareness of the clock, which is best done by practicing under timed conditions.

# Chapter 1: Verbal Analogies

Some relationship objectives are contained on the Verbal Analogies section. With these types of analogies, you must determine the relationship between the words and complete the analogy with the correct choice. There are 25 questions with a time limit of 8 minutes, giving you roughly 20 seconds per question. The key here is to become familiar with analogies and get some practice, and most people will find that 20 seconds is ample. We will first review some of the type of analogies you might run into, and then do a practice test. The concept of analogies is pretty straight forward, but don't brush it off because it is the subtleties that lose points.

## Similarity/Contrast

Most often, similarities and contrasts involve synonyms (words that mean the same thing) or antonyms (words that have opposite meanings). An analogy that involves synonyms is primarily a definition of terms – determining one word that could be replaced with another word. In such a relationship, you must ascertain what a word means and how it is connected to the others in the analogy. An analogy that involves contrasts shows the relationship between a word and its opposite.

Example:
zenith : summit :: vale (a. nadir   b. yang   c. arboreal   d. gorge)

Answer: Choice (D) is correct. Zenith and summit are both words that refer to the highest point of something, like a mountaintop. Therefore, look for the pair of words that are synonyms. Vale and gorge both refer to low points – synonyms – so choice D is best.

## Whole-Part/Part-Whole

This type of analogy denotes the relationship between a whole thing (house, for example) and a part of the whole (room).

Example:
autocracy : individual :: meritocracy : (a. unwise   b. talented   c. multitude   d. indigent)

Answer: Choice (B) is correct. An autocracy is a system in which one individual is rewarded with power. Therefore, look for the answer choice in which the second word is the most important part of the first word. In a meritocracy, distribution of power is based on people's ability and talent.

**Membership**

A membership analogy is very similar to the whole-part analogy. It shows the relationship between a whole group and a member of the group.

Example:
xenophile : foreign :: (a. hippophile   b. bibliophile   c. anglophile   d. oenophile): wine

Answer:  Choice (D) is correct. A xenophile is a person who is interested in foreign cultures, and an oenophile is a person who is interested in wine.

**Object/Characteristic**

In this type of analogy, you must establish the relationship between a person or object and its characteristic.

Example:
carnivore : lion :: piscivore : (a. tiger   b. penguin   c. reptile   d. beetle)

Answer: Choice (B) is correct. A lion is a carnivore, which means it is a meat-eater. Therefore, the relationship between the two words is categorical – lions are a type of carnivore. Choice (B) is correct because penguins are piscivores or fish-eating.

**Cause/Effect**

This type of analogy involves analyzing the relationship between a word and the outcome or result it causes. Occasionally, the analogy may be written with the effect first, and you must determine the cause.

Example:
sycophant : flatters :: raconteur : (a. critiques   b. repels   c. regales   d. leads)

Answer: Choice (C) is correct. In the initial part of the analogy, a sycophant is a person who flatters others. So, in the answer choices, look for the pair in which the second word describes the effect of the first term's behavior.  A raconteur is a storyteller – one who regales others with tales.

**Agent/Object**

This analogy type is one that shows the relationship between a person and a tool or object that he/she uses. You might also see similar analogies that involve a non-living thing – an object – and how it is used.

Example:
codicil : supplement :: condiment : (a. assault   b. pronounce   c. revere   d. flavor)
Answer: Choice (D) is correct. A codicil is an appendix to a will; its function is to supplement or explain further. Therefore, look for the answer choice in which the second term describes the function of the first term. The purpose of condiments is to flavor food. Therefore, choice (D) is correct.

**Order**

In order analogies, the words are related by sequence or in a reciprocal (or opposite) circumstance.

Example:

Alpha ; omega :: Delaware : (a. Oregon   b. Florida   c. Maine   d. Hawaii)

Choice (D) is correct. Alpha is the first letter of the Greek alphabet and omega is the last letter. Delaware was the first state admitted to the union, and Hawaii was the last state admitted.

# Verbal Analogies Practice Test

1.  carat : weight :: fathom :
    a. capacity
    b. perspective
    c. mass
    d. depth

2.  mollify : enrage :: quell :
    a. exonerate
    b. bifurcate
    c. incite
    d. denounce

3.  Electron :_____:: satellite : planet
    a. proton
    b. nucleus
    c. atom
    d. neutron

4.  Habitat : location :: _____: role
    a. capacity
    b. competition
    c. niche
    d. predation

5.  26 : even :: _____: prime
    a. 8
    b. 11
    c. 15
    d. 20

6.  Cytology : cells :: _____ : fungi
    a. mycology
    b. ornithology
    c. oncology
    d. phrenology

7.  Darwin : evolution :: Mendel :
    a. blood groups
    b. popular culture
    c. relative dating
    d. genetics

8.      Sacramento : California :: _____: Florida
        a. Orlando
        b. Tallahassee
        c. Miami
        d. Jacksonville

9.      appease : placate :: obviate :
        a. disregard
        b. clarify
        c. decide
        d. preclude

10.     Cortez : Mexico :: Cartier :
        a. North America
        b. Canada
        c. East Indies
        d. Florida

11.     chicken : brood :: cats :
        a. clowder
        b. herd
        c. swarm
        d. army

12.     _____: Missouri :: Granite : New Hampshire
        a. Tar Heel
        b. Sunshine
        c. Show Me
        d. Buckeye

13.     latitude : longitude :: parallels :
        a. lines
        b. equator
        c. degrees
        d. meridians

14.     *Gulliver's Travels* : Jonathan Swift :: *Frankenstein* : _____
        a. John Keats
        b. George Eliot
        c. Mary Shelley
        d. Alexander Pope

15.     newton : force  :: _____: power
        a. joule
        b. tesla
        c. watt
        d. hertz

16.     0° latitude : equator  :: 23.5° south latitude : _____
                a. prime meridian
                b. tropic of Capricorn
                c. middle latitude
                d. tropic of Cancer

17.     clarinet : _____ :: cello : string
                a. brass
                b. woodwind
                c. percussion
                d. horn

18.     hatching : parallel lines :: stippling : _____
                a. squares
                b. dots
                c. perpendicular lines
                d. curves

19.     capacity : liter :: mass : _____
                a. meter
                b. kilometer
                c. gram
                d. pound

20.     inaugurate: President  ::  coronate : _____
                a. pope
                b. cardinal
                c. bishop
                d. monarch

21.     positive : negative ::_____ : flat
                a. sharp
                b. tone
                c. bass
                d. treble

22.     Poseidon : sea  :: _____: war
                a.  Hades
                b. Ares
                c. Apollo
                d. Pan

23.     Hindi : India  :: _____ : Brazil
                a. Spanish
                b. English
                c. Portuguese
                d. French

24. Michelangelo : painter  ::  Frank Lloyd Wright : _____
        a. writer
        b. sculptor
        c. playwright
        d. architect

25. Judaism : temple :: Islam : _____
        a. church
        b. synagogue
        c. mosque
        d. mecca

# Verbal Analogies Practice Test Answer Key

1. D
2. C
3. B
4. C
5. B
6. A
7. D
8. B
9. D
10. B
11. A
12. C
13. D
14. C
15. C
16. B
17. B
18. B
19. C
20. D
21. A
22. B
23. C
24. D
25. C

# Chapter 2: Arithmetic Reasoning

The Arithmetic Reasoning tests your ability to use fundamental math concepts to solve word problems. During the test, you will have 29 minutes to answer 25 problems. The most important step in solving any word problem is to read the entire problem before beginning to solve. You shouldn't skip over words or assume you know what the question is from the first sentence. The following are the general steps used to solve word problems:

## Solving Word Problems

Any of the math concepts discussed here can be turned into a word problem, and you'll likely see word problems in various forms throughout the test. (In fact, you may have noticed that several examples in the ratio and proportion sections were word problems.)

The most important step in solving any word problem is to read the entire problem before beginning to solve it. One of the most common mistakes on word problems is providing an answer to a question that was not asked. Also, remember that not all of the information given in a problem is always needed to solve it.

When working multiple-choice word problems like those on the AFOQT, it's important to check your answer. Many of the incorrect choices will be answers that test-takers arrive at by making common mistakes. So even if an answer you calculated is a given as an answer choice, that doesn't necessarily mean you've worked the problem correctly—you have to check your work to make sure.

## General Steps for Word Problem Solving

Step 1:  Read the entire problem and determine what the question is asking.

Step 2:  List all of the given data and define the variables.

Step 3:  Determine the formula(s) needed or set up equations from the information in the problem.

Step 4:  Solve.

Step 5:  Check your answer. (Is the amount too large or small? Are the answers in the correct unit of measure?)

## Key Words

Word problems contain keywords that can help you determine what math processes may be required in order to solve them.

Addition: added, combined, increased by, in all, total, perimeter, sum, and more than

Subtraction: how much more, less than, fewer than, exceeds, difference, and decreased

Multiplication: of, times, area, and product

Division: distribute, share, average, per, out of, percent, and quotient

Equals: is, was, are, amounts to, and were

**Basic Word Problems**

A word problem in algebra is just an equation or a set of equations described using words. Your task when solving these problems is to turn the "story" of the problem into mathematical equations.

Examples

1)    A store owner bought a case of 48 backpacks for $476.00. He sold 17 of the backpacks in his store for $18 each, and the rest were sold to a school for $15 each. What was the salesman's profit?

Answer:
Start by listing all the data and defining the variable:
total number of backpacks = 48
cost of backpacks = $476.00
backpacks sold in store at a price of $18 = 17
backpacks sold to school at a price of $15 = 48 − 17 = 31
total profit = $x$

Now set up an equation:
$$total\ profit\ =\ income\ -\ cost$$
$$x = [(17 \times 18) + (31 \times 15)] - 476$$
$$x = 771 - 476 = 295$$

The store owner made a profit of **$295**.

2)    Thirty students in Mr. Joyce's room are working on projects over two days. The first day, he gave them 3/5 hour to work. On the second day, he gave them half as much time as the first day. How much time did each student have to work on the project?

Answer:
Start by listing all the data and defining your variables. Note that the number of students, while given in the problem, is not needed to find the answer:

time on 1st day = $\frac{3}{5}$ hr. = 36 min.

time on 2nd day = $\frac{1}{2}$ (36) = 18 min.

total time = $x$

Now set up the equation and solve:
$$total\ time\ =\ time\ on\ 1st\ day\ +\ time\ on\ 2nd\ day$$
$$x = 36 + 18 = 54$$

The students had **54 minutes** to work on the projects.

**Distance Word Problems**

Distance word problems involve something traveling at a constant or average speed. Whenever you read a problem that involves *how fast, how far,* or *for how long*, you should think of the distance equation, $d\ =\ rt$, where $d$ stands for distance, $r$ for rate (speed), and $t$ for time.

These problems can be solved by setting up a grid with $d$, $r$, and $t$ along the top and each moving object on the left. When setting up the grid, make sure the units are consistent. For example, if the distance is in meters and the time is in seconds, the rate should be meters per second.

## Examples
1)     Will drove from his home to the airport at an average speed of 30 mph. He then boarded a helicopter and flew to the hospital with an average speed of 60 mph. The entire distance was 150 miles, and the trip took 3 hours. Find the distance from the airport to the hospital.

Answer:
The first step is to set up a table and fill in a value for each variable:

|  | $d$ | $r$ | $t$ |
|---|---|---|---|
| driving | $d$ | 30 | $t$ |
| flying | $150 - d$ | 60 | $3 - t$ |

You can now set up equations for driving and flying. The first row gives the equation $d = 30t$, and the second row gives the equation $150 - d = 60(3 - t)$.

Next, you can solve this system of equations. Start by substituting for $d$ in the second equation:

$d = 30t$
$150 - d = 60(30 - t) \rightarrow 150 - 30t = 60(30 - t)$
Now solve for $t$:
$150 - 30t = 180 - 60t$
$-30 = -30t$
$1 = t$

Although you've solved for $t$, you're not done yet. Notice that the problem asks for distance. So, you need to solve for $d$. It does not ask for time, but the time is needed to solve the problem.

Driving: $30t = 30$ miles
Flying: $150 - d = 120$ miles
The distance from the airport to the hospital is **120 miles**.

2)     Two riders on horseback start at the same time from opposite ends of a field that is 45 miles long. One horse is moving at 14 mph and the second horse is moving at 16 mph. How long after they begin will they meet?

Answer:
First, set up the table. The variable for time will be the same for each because they will have been on the road for the same amount of time when they meet:

|  | $d$ | $r$ | $t$ |
|---|---|---|---|
| Cyclist #1 | $d$ | 14 | $t$ |
| Cyclist #2 | $45 - d$ | 16 | $t$ |

Nest set up two equations:

Horse #1: $d = 14t$
Horse #2: $45 - d = 16t$
Now substitute and solve:
$d = 14t$
$45 - d = 16t \rightarrow 45 - 14t = 16t$
$45 = 30t$
$t = 1.5$

They will meet **1.5 hr.** after they begin.

## Work Problems

**Work problems** involve situations where several people or machines are doing work at different rates. Your task is usually to figure out how long it will take these people or machines to complete a task while working together. The trick to doing work problems is to figure out how much of the project each person or machine completes in the same unit of time. For example, you might calculate how much of a wall a person can paint in 1 hour, or how many boxes an assembly line can pack in 1 minute.

Once you know that, you can set up an equation to solve for the total time. This equation usually has a form similar to the equation for distance, but here *work = rate × time*.

<u>Examples</u>
1)      Hayden can clean an entire house in 12 hours while his sister Jo takes 8 hours. How long would it take for Hayden and Jo to clean 2 houses together?

Answer:
Start by figuring out how much of a house each sibling can clean on his or her own. Hayden can clean the house in 12 hours, so he can clean $\frac{1}{12}$ of the house in an hour. Using the same logic, Jo can clean $\frac{1}{8}$ of a house in an hour.

By adding these values together, you get the fraction of the house they can clean together in an hour:

$$\frac{1}{12} + \frac{1}{8} = \frac{5}{24}$$

They can do $\frac{5}{24}$ of the job per hour.

Now set up variables and an equation to solve:

t = time spent cleaning (in hours)
h = number of houses cleaned = 2

*work = rate × time*

$$h = \frac{5}{24}t \rightarrow$$

$$2 = \frac{5}{24}t \rightarrow$$

$$t = \frac{48}{5} = 9\frac{3}{5}\,\textbf{hr.}$$

2)    Farmer Dan needs to water his corn field. One hose can water a field 1.25 times faster than a second pipe. When both hoses are running, they water the field in 5 hours. How long would it take to water the field if only the slower hose is used?

Answer:
In this problem, you don't know the exact time, but you can still find the hourly rate as a variable:

The second hose completes the job in *f* hours, so it waters $\frac{1}{f}$ field per hour. The faster hose waters the field in 1.25*f*, so it waters the field in $\frac{1}{1.25f}$ hours. Together, they take 5 hours to water the field, so they water $\frac{1}{5}$ of the field per hour.

Now you can set up the equations and solve:

$$\frac{1}{f} + \frac{1}{1.25f} = \frac{1}{5} \rightarrow$$

$$1.25f\left(\frac{1}{f} + \frac{1}{1.25f}\right) = 1.25f\left(\frac{1}{5}\right) \rightarrow$$

$$1.25 + 1 = 0.25f$$

$$2.25 = 0.25f$$

$$f = 9$$

The slow hose takes **9 hours** to water the field. The fast hose takes 1.25(9) = 11.25 hours.

3)    Cynthia takes 2 hours to pluck 500 apples, and Stephan takes 3 hours to pluck 450 apples. How long will they take, working together, to pluck 1000 apples?

Answer:
Calculate how many apples each person can pluck per hour:

Cynthia: $\frac{500\text{ apples}}{2\text{ hr.}} = \frac{250\text{ apples}}{\text{hr.}}$

Stephan: $\frac{450\text{ apples}}{3\text{ hr.}} = \frac{150\text{ apples}}{\text{hr.}}$

Together: $\frac{(250 + 150)\text{apples}}{\text{hr}} = \frac{400\text{ apples}}{\text{hr.}}$

Now set up an equation to find the time it takes to pick 1000 apples:

$$total\ time = \frac{1\text{ hr.}}{400\text{ apples}} \times 1000\text{ apples} = \frac{1000}{400}\text{ hr.} = \textbf{2.5 hr.}$$

# Arithmetic Reasoning Practice Test

1. Allison collects 300 plastic bottles in week one, 420 plastic bottles in week two, and 180 plastic bottles in the last week for recycling. Plastic bottles can be traded for reusable tote bags. If 25 plastic bottles earn her one tote bag, how many tote bags can Allison collect?
A. 36
B. 50
C. 20
D. 25

2. Grendel is 10 years older than Freddie, who is 16. How old is Grendel?
A. 26
B. 30
C. 36
D. 25

3. Josh and Jeff got summer jobs at the local burger joint. They were each supposed to work 15 hours per week for two months. During that time, Jeff went on a family vacation for one week and Josh took his shifts. How many hours in total did Josh work during these eight weeks?
A. 120 hours
B. 135 hours
C. 150 hours
D. 185 hours

4. A shirt originally priced at $40 is on sale for $30. What percent has the shirt been discounted?
A. 25%
B. 33%
C. 70%
D. 75%

5. If Lobelia purchases an item that costs $30 or less, she will pay with cash. If Lobelia purchases an item that costs between $30 and $70, she will pay with a check. If Lobelia purchases an item that costs $70 or greater, she will use a credit card. If Lobelia recently made a payment for a certain item through check, which of the following statements could be true?
A. The item cost $80.
B. If the item had cost $20 more, she would have paid with cash.
C. The item cost at least $70.
D. The item cost more than $25.

6. Which of the options given best represents the following sentence? Carmen (C) had three apples and ate one.
A. $C = 3 - 1$
B. $3 - 2 = C$
C. $C = 3 \times 2$
D. $3C - 2$

7. If there are 8 pints in a gallon, how many pints are in 3.5 gallons of ice cream?
A.  27.725
B.  25
C.  26.125
D.  28

8. A 650 square foot apartment in Boston costs $1800 per month to rent. What is the monthly rent per square foot?
A)  $13
B)  $0.36
C)  $2.77
D)  $3.66

9. A radio station plays songs that last an average of 3.5 minutes and has commercial breaks that last 2 minutes. If the station is required to play 1 commercial break for every 4 songs, how many songs can the station play in an hour?
A)  15
B)  11
C)  16
D)  17

10. Students in a particular math class received an average score of 84% on a recent test. If there are 20 boys and 30 girls in the class, and the boys' average score was 82%, what was the girls' average score?
A)  83%
B)  88%
C)  85%
D)  86%

11. 1/10 of a company's employees are in their 20s, 2/5 are in their 30s, 1/3 are in their 40s and the remaining 5 employees are 50 or older. How many employees work at the company?
A)  5
B)  30
C)  60
D)  24

12. A chemical experiment requires that a solute be diluted with 4 parts (by mass) water for every 1 part (by mass) solute. If the desired mass for the solution is 90 grams, how much solute should be used?
A)  15 grams
B)  72 grams
C)  22.5 grams
D)  18 grams

13. Lisa rides her bike at 10 miles per hour for 28 minutes, 15 miles per hour for 49 minutes, and 12 miles per hour for 15 minutes. How far did she travel in total?
A)  11.95 miles
B)  18.91 miles
C)  19.92 miles
D)  20.21 miles

14. A plane makes a trip of 246 miles. For some amount of time, the plane's speed is 115 miles per hour. For the remainder of the trip, the plane's speed is 250 miles per hour. If the total trip time is 72 minutes, how long did the plane fly at 115 miles per hour?
A)      18 minutes
B)      23 minutes
C)      24 minutes
D)      34 minutes

15. A runner completes a 12 mile race in 1 hour and 30 minutes. If her pace for the first part of the race was 7 minutes per mile, and her pace for the second part of the race was 8 minutes per mile, for how many miles did she sustain her pace of 7 minutes per mile?
A)      4 miles
B)      5.5 miles
C)      6 miles
D)      7 miles

16. A swimmer is swimming 25 meter sprints. If he swims 4 sprints in 3 minutes, 6 more sprints in 5 minutes, and then 4 final sprints in 2 minutes, what was his average speed during his sprints?
A)      35 meters per minute
B)      1.4 meters per minute
C)      350 meters per minute
D)      17.9 meters per minute

17. A cheetah in the wild can accelerate from 0 miles per hour to 60 miles per hour in 2.8 seconds. Then, it can sustain a speed of 60 miles per hour for up to 60 seconds before it has to rest. How much total distance can the cheetah travel from when it starts to accelerate to the moment it has to stop?
A)      3,684 miles
B)      2.4 miles
C)      1.046 miles
D)      1.023 miles

18. 2 warehouse workers can pack 5 boxes in 6 minutes. If 1 worker can pack 6 boxes by himself in 15 minutes, how many boxes can the other worker pack by himself in the same amount of time?
A)      6.5 boxes
B)      6 boxes
C)      12.5 boxes
D)      7.5 boxes

19. Nick needs to purchase a study guide for a test. The study guide costs $80.00, and the sales tax is 8.25%. Nick has $100. How much change will Nick receive back?
A.  $6.20
B.  $7.45
C.  $13.40
D.  $19.85

20. John and Jake are working at a car wash. It takes John 1 hour to wash 3 cars; Jake can wash 3 cars in 45 minutes. If they work together, how many cars can they wash in 1 hour?
A)    6 cars
B)    7 cars
C)    9 cars
D)    12 cars

21. Ed is going to fill his swimming pool with a garden hose. His neighbor, a volunteer firefighter, wants to use a fire hose attached to the hydrant in the front yard to make the job go faster. The fire hose sprays 13.5 times as much water per minute as the garden hose. If the garden hose and the fire hose together can fill the pool in 107 minutes, how long would it have taken to fill the pool with the garden hose alone?
A)    7 hours,37.9 min
B)    7 hours,55.6 min
C)    1 day,4.5 min
D)    1 day,1 hour,51.5 min

22. Dr. Green has asked you to give Anna 20 mg of morphine. The morphine is stored as 4 mg per 5-mL dose. How many milliliters does Anna need?
A.  15 mL
B.  20 mL
C.  25 mL
D.  30 mL

23. Suppose Mark can mow the entire lawn in 47 minutes, and Mark's dad can mow the entire lawn in 53 minutes. If Mark and his dad work together (each with their own lawnmowers), how long will it take them to mow the entire lawn?
A)    15.6 minutes
B)    24.9 minutes
C)    26.5 minutes
D)    50 minutes

24. Rafael and Marco are repainting their garage. If Rafael can paint 1/6 of the garage in 20 minutes, and Marco can paint 1/5 of the garage in 30 minutes, how long will it take them to paint the entire garage if they work together?
    A)    1 hr,6.7 min
    B)    2 hr,43.6 min
    C)    0 hr,54 min
    D)    6 hr,12 min25

25. During a 5-day convention, the number of visitors tripled each day. If the convention started on a Tuesday with 345 visitors, what was the attendance on that Friday?
A.  9,315
B.  8,035
C.  10,725
D.  6,105

# Arithmetic Reasoning Practice Test Answer Key

1. A
2. A
3. B
4. A
5. D
6. A
7. D
8. C
9. A
10. C
11. B
12. D
13. C
14. C
15. C
16. A
17. D
18. A
19. C
20. B
21. D
22. C
23. B
24. A
25. A

# Chapter 3: Word Knowledge

The military considers clear and concise communication so important that it is taught and graded at all levels of leadership training. If you are planning a military career, you will be tested on your verbal skills as you move through the ranks.

The good news is that most individuals have been exposed to all of the vocabulary words used on the subtest by the time they have reached the tenth grade. This does not mean that you are going to recognize every single word. It *does* mean, however, that you won't be expected to know advanced Latin or graduate science terminology.

This section of the test gives you 25 questions to answer in 5 minutes. This may seem like a disproportionate amount of time – it comes out to about 12 seconds per question – but don't worry! We're going to arm you with all of the knowledge you'll need to work quickly and efficiently through this section.

As an extra challenge to this section, the questions are formatted, so the word has to be matched without context. You will typically be given a single word in all capital letters, and then you must choose from the answer choices that word matches or has the same meaning. For example:

> Garner most nearly means:
> a) Create.
> b) Propose.
> c) Demonstrate.
> d) Gather.

The correct answer is: d) Gather

You will note that as we work through this section, not all questions will be formatted this way and that is for a reason. Words can be tricky and there is no shortcut to learning to understand them, or even refreshing what you might have learned years ago. The biggest mistake one can make is thinking they will just memorize a bunch of vocabulary words. This is a wasted effort. First of all, it is very unlikely you will retain that information long enough from rote memorization. Secondly, it would take endless hours to memorize enough of them. Finally, you would still be missing the key elements that allow you to figure out the meaning of a word. Without knowing its definition OR knowing what it certainly does not mean allows you to eliminate wrong answer choices.

## VOCABULARY BASIC TRAINING
The first step in getting ready for this section of the AFOQT consists of reviewing the basic techniques used to determine the meanings of words you are not familiar with. The good news is that you have been using various degrees of these techniques since you began to speak. Sharpening these skills will help you with the paragraph comprehension subtest.
Following each section you will find a practice drill. Use your scores on these to determine if you need to study a particular subject matter further. At the end of each section, you will find a Practice Drill to test your Knowledge.

The questions found on the practice drills are not given in the two formats found on the Word Knowledge subtest; rather they are designed to reinforce the skills needed to score well on the Word Knowledge subtest.

## Context Clues

Although you won't get any context to reference words on the AFOQT, for training purposes we will start with words in context, so you can start to see how to break down a word into its meaning. Your ability to observe sentences closely is extremely useful when it comes to understanding new vocabulary words.

## Types of Context

There are two different types of context that can help you understand the meaning of unfamiliar words: **sentence context** and **situational context**. Regardless of which context is present, these types of questions are not testing your knowledge of the vocabulary; they are testing your ability to comprehend the meaning of a word through its usage.

**Situational context** is the basis of the Paragraph Comprehension subtest and will be discussed in chapter two.

**Sentence context** occurs in the sentence containing the vocabulary word. To figure out words using sentence context clues, you should first determine the most important words in the sentence.

For Example: I had a hard time reading her <u>illegible</u> handwriting.
  a) Neat.
  b) Unsafe.
  c) Sloppy.
  d) Educated.

Already, you know that this sentence is discussing something that is hard to read. Look at the word that **illegible** is describing: **handwriting**. Based on context clues, you can tell that illegible means that her handwriting is hard to read.

Next, look at the choices. Choice **a) Neat** is obviously wrong because neat handwriting would not be difficult to read. Choice **b) Unsafe** and **d) Educated** don't make sense. Therefore, choice **c) Sloppy** is the best answer choice.

## Types of Clues

There are four types of clues that can help you understand the context, which in turn helps you define the word. They are **restatement**, **positive/negative**, **contrast**, and **specific detail**.

**Restatement** clues occur when the definition of the word is clearly stated in the sentence.

For Example: The dog was <u>dauntless</u> in the face of danger, braving the fire to save the girl.
  a) Difficult.
  b) Fearless.
  c) Imaginative.
  d) Pleasant.

Demonstrating **bravery** in the face of danger would be **fearless**, choice **b)**. In this case, the context clues tell you exactly what the word means.

**Positive/negative** clues can tell you whether a word has a positive or negative meaning.

> For Example: The magazine gave a great review of the fashion show, stating the clothing was **sublime**.
> > a) Horrible.
> > b) Exotic.
> > c) Bland
> > d) Gorgeous.

The sentence tells us that the author liked the clothing enough to write a **great** review, so you know that the best answer choice is going to be a positive word. Therefore, you can immediately rule out choices **a)** and **c)** because they are negative words. **Exotic** is a neutral word; alone, it doesn't inspire a **great** review. The most positive word is gorgeous, which makes choice **d) Gorgeous** the best answer.

The following sentence uses both restatement and positive/negative clues:

"Janet suddenly found herself <u>destitute</u>, so poor she could barely afford to eat."

The second part of the sentence clearly indicates that destitute is a negative word; it also restates the meaning: very poor.

**Contrast clues** include the opposite meaning of a word. Words like **but, on the other hand,** and **however** are tip-offs that a sentence contains a contrast clue.

> For Example: Beth did not spend any time preparing for the test, but Tyron kept a <u>rigorous</u> study schedule.
> > a) Strict.
> > b) Loose.
> > c) Boring.
> > d) Strange.

In this case, the word **but** tells us that Tyron studied in a different way than Beth. If Beth did not study very hard, then Tyron did study hard for the test. The best answer here, therefore, is choice **a) Strict**.

**Specific detail** clues give a precise detail that can help you understand the meaning of the word.

> For Example: The box was heavier than he expected and it began to become <u>cumbersome</u>.
> > a) Impossible.
> > b) Burdensome.
> > c) Obligated.
> > d) Easier.

Start by looking at the specific details of the sentence. Choice **d)** can be eliminated right away because it is doubtful it would become **easier** to carry something that is **heavier**.

There are also no clues in the sentence to indicate he was **obligated** to carry the box, so choice **c)** can also be disregarded. The sentence specifics, however, do tell you that the package was cumbersome because it was heavy to carry; something heavy to carry is a burden, which is **burdensome, choice b)**.

It is important to remember that more than one of these clues can be present in the same sentence. The more there are, the easier it will be to determine the meaning of the word, so look for them.

## Denotation and Connotation

As you know, many English words have more than one meaning. For example, the word **quack** has two distinct definitions: the sound a duck makes; and a person who publicly pretends to have a skill, knowledge, education, or qualification that they do not possess.

The **denotations** of a word are the dictionary definitions.

The **connotations** of a word are the implied meaning(s) or emotion that the word makes you think.

> For Example:

> "Sure," Pam said excitedly, "I'd just love to join your club; it sounds so exciting!"

> Now, read this sentence:

> "Sure," Pam said sarcastically, "I'd just love to join your club; it sounds so exciting!"

Even though the two sentences only differ by one word, they have completely different meanings. The difference, of course, lies in the words "excitedly" and "sarcastically."

Look back to the underlined word – **reinforce** - in the second paragraph of page 13. Can you think of several words that could be used and the sentence have the same meaning?

## ROOTS, PREFIXES, and SUFFIXES

You just got done with what could be called a "warm up" exercise, and now we will get into the tougher material you need to know specifically for the AFOQT. Although you are not expected to know every word in the English language, you are expected to have the ability to use deductive reasoning to find the choice that is the best match for the word in question. This is why we are going to explain how to break a word into its parts of meaning:

**prefix – root – suffix**

One trick in dividing a word into its parts is first to divide the word into its **syllables**. To show how syllables can help you find roots and affixes, we'll use the word **descendant,** which means one who comes from an ancestor. Start by dividing the word into its individual syllables; this word has three: **de-scend-ant**. The next step is to look at the beginning and end of the word, and then determine if these syllables are prefixes, suffixes, or possible roots. You can then use the meanings of each part to guide you in defining the word. When you divide words into their specific parts, they do not always add up to an exact definition, but you will see a relationship between their parts.

*Note*: This trick won't always work in every situation, because not all prefixes, roots, and suffixes have only one syllable. For example, take the word **monosyllabic** (which ironically means "one syllable"). There are five syllables in that word, but only three parts. The prefix is "mono," meaning "one." The root "syllab" refers to "syllable," while the suffix "ic" means "pertaining to." Therefore, we have one very long word which means "pertaining to one syllable."

The more familiar you become with these fundamental word parts, the easier it will be to define unfamiliar words. Although the words found on the Word Knowledge subtest are considered vocabulary words learned by the tenth grade level of high school, some are still less likely to be found in an individual's everyday vocabulary. The root and affixes list in this chapter uses more common words as examples to help you learn them more easily. Don't forget that you use word roots and affixes every day, without even realizing it. Don't feel intimidated by the long list of roots and affixes (prefixes and suffixes) at the end of this chapter. You already know and use them every time you communicate with some else, verbally and in writing. If you take the time to read through the list just once a day for two weeks, you will be able to retain most of them and understand a high number of initially unfamiliar words.

## Roots
Roots are the building blocks of all words. Every word is either a root itself or has a root. Just as a plant cannot grow without roots, neither can vocabulary because a word must have a root to give it meaning.

> For Example: The test instructions were **unclear.**

The root is what is left when you strip away all the prefixes and suffixes from a word. In this case, take away the prefix "un-", and you have the root **clear**.

Roots are not always recognizable words because they come from Latin or Greek words, such as **nat**, a Latin root meaning **born**. The word native, which means a person born of a referenced placed, comes from this root, so does the word prenatal, meaning before birth. Yet, if you used the prefix **nat** instead of born, just on its own, no one would know what you were talking about.

Words can also have more than one root. For example, the word **omnipotent** means all powerful. Omnipotent is a combination of the roots **omni-**, meaning all or every, and **-potent**, meaning power or strength. In this case, **omni** cannot be used on its own as a single word, but **potent** can. Again, it is important to keep in mind that roots do not always match the exact definitions of words. They can have several different spellings, but breaking a word into its parts is still one of the best ways to determine its meaning.

## Prefixes and Suffixes
Prefixes are syllables added to the beginning of a word and suffixes are syllables added to the end of the word. Both carry assigned meanings. The common name for prefixes and suffixes is **affixes**. Affixes do not have to be attached directly to a root and a word can often have more than one prefix and/or suffix. Prefixes and suffixes can be attached to a word to change completely the word's meaning or to enhance the word's original meaning. Although they don't mean much to us on their own, when attached to other words affixes can make a world of difference.

We can use the word **prefix** as an example:

> **Fix** means to place something securely.
> **Pre** means before.
> **Prefix** means to place something before or in front.

An example of a suffix:

> **Femin** is a root. It means female, woman.
> **-ism** means act, practice or process.
> **Feminism** is the defining and establishing of equal political, economic, and social rights for women.

Unlike prefixes, **suffixes** can be used to change a word's part of speech.

> For example, take a look at these sentences:
> Randy raced to the finish line.
> Shana's costume was very racy.

> In the first sentence, raced is a verb. In the second sentence, racy is an adjective. By changing the suffix from **-ed** to **-y**, the word race changes from a verb into an adjective, which has an entirely different meaning.

Although you cannot determine the meaning of a word by a prefix or suffix alone, you *can* use your knowledge of what root words mean to eliminate answer choices. Indicate if the word is positive or negative and you will get a partial meaning of the word.

## SYNONYMS and ANTONYMS

**Synonyms** are groups of words that mean the same, or almost the same, thing as each other. The word synonym comes from the Greek roots **syn-,** meaning same, and **-nym,** meaning name. **Hard, difficult, challenging,** and **arduous** are synonyms of one another.

**Antonyms** are sets of words that have opposite, or nearly opposite, meanings of one another. The word antonym comes from the Greek roots **ant-,** meaning opposing, and **−nym** (name). **Hard** and **easy** are antonyms.

**Synonyms do not always have exactly the same meanings, and antonyms are not always exact opposites.** For example, scalding is an adjective that means burning. Boiling water can be described as scalding or as hot. **Hot** and **scalding** are considered synonyms, even though the two words do not mean exactly the same thing; something that is scalding is considered to be extremely hot.

In the same manner, antonyms are not always exact opposites. **Cold** and **freezing** are both antonyms of scalding. Although freezing is closer to being an exact opposite of scalding, cold is still considered an antonym. Antonyms can often be recognized by their prefixes and suffixes.

Here are rules that apply to prefixes and suffixes of antonyms:

- **Many antonyms can be created simply by adding prefixes.** Certain prefixes, such as *a-*, *de-*, *non-*, and *un-*, can be added to words to turn them into antonyms. **Atypical** is an antonym of **typical,** and **nonjudgmental** is an antonym of **judgmental.**

- **Some prefixes and suffixes are antonyms of one another.** The prefixes **ex-** (out of) and **in-/il-/im-/ir-** (into) are antonyms, and are demonstrated in the antonym pair **exhale/inhale.** Other prefix pairs that indicate antonyms include **pre-/post-, sub-/super-,** and **over-/under-.** The suffixes **-less**, meaning without, and **-ful,** meaning full of, often indicate that words are antonyms as well. For example: **meaningless** and **meaningful** are antonyms.

## REVIEW

Remember that roots are the basic unit of meaning in words. When you read a word that is unfamiliar to you, divide the word into syllables and look for the root by removing any prefixes and suffixes.

You have also learned that prefixes and suffixes are known collectively as **affixes**. Although affixes are not words by themselves, they are added to roots or words to change the meaning of roots or change a word's part of speech. **Prefixes** that change or enhance the meanings of words, and are found at the beginning of words. **Suffixes** change or enhance the meanings of words and/or change parts of speech and are found at the end of words.

You have also learned that **synonyms** are words that have the same or almost the same meaning, while **antonyms** are words that have opposite or nearly opposite meanings. Synonyms and antonyms of a word will always share the same part of speech. That is, a synonym or antonym of a verb has to be a verb; a synonym or antonym of an adjective has to be an adjective; and so forth. We also learned that not all words have synonyms or antonyms, and that synonyms do not always have exactly the same meaning, just as antonyms do not have to be exact opposites.

### Tips
Use words that you are very familiar with as examples when you study word roots. The more familiar the word is to you, the easier it will be for you to remember the meaning of the root word. Use words that create a vivid picture in your imagination.

Be sure to look at all parts of the word to determine meaning.

Remember the power of elimination on an exam. Use your knowledge of word roots to eliminate incorrect answers. The more you narrow down your choices, the better your chances of choosing the correct answer. You have to do so quickly of course, but even eliminating one wrong answer before guessing greatly increases your chances.
Roots do not always match the exact definitions of words. Another important thing to keep in mind is that sometimes one root will have several different spellings.

Affixes do not have to be attached directly to a root. A word can often have more than one affix, even more than one prefix or suffix. For instance, the word **unremarkably** has two prefixes (un- and re-) and two suffixes (-able and -ly).

| Root or Affix | Meaning | Examples |
| --- | --- | --- |
| a, ac, ad, af, ag, al, an, ap, as, at | to, toward, near, in addition to, by | aside, accompany, adjust, aggression, allot, annihilate, allocate, associate, attend, affixed |
| a-, an- | not, without | apolitical, atheist, anterior, anonymous, apathy, |
| ab, abs | away from, off | Absent, above, abrupt, |
| -able, -ible | Adjective: worth, ability | solvable, edible |
| acer, acid, acri | bitter, sour, sharp | acerbic, acidity, acrid, |
| act, ag | do, act, drive | activate, react, agent, active, agitate |
| acu | sharp | acute, acupuncture, accurate |
| -acy, -cy | Noun: state or quality | fancy, infancy, adequacy, intimacy, supremacy, privacy |
| -ade | act, product, sweet drink | blockade, aide, pink lemonade |
| aer, aero | air, atmosphere, aviation | aerial, aerosol, aerodrome |
| ag, agi, ig, act | do, move, go | agent, agenda, navigation, agitate, ambiguous, active |
| -age | Noun: activity, or result of action | courageous, adage, shrinkage, engage |
| agri, agro | pertaining to fields or soil | agriculture, agronomics, |
| -al | Noun: action, result of action | deferral, disavowal, disposal, festival |
| -al, -ial, -ical | Adjective: quality, relation | biannual, territorial, categorical |
| alb, albo | white, without pigment | albino, albeit |
| ali, allo, alter | other | alias, alibi, alloy, alter, alter ego, alternative |
| alt | high, deep | altitude |
| am, ami, amor | love, like, liking | amorous, amid, amicable, enamored |
| ambi | both | ambidextrous, ambient |
| ambul | to walk | ambulatory, amble, ambulance |
| -an | Noun: person | librarian, guardian, historian, magician |
| ana, ano | up, back, again, anew | anode, anagram |

| -ance, -ence | Noun: action, state, quality or process | indulgence, independence, extravagance, enhance |
|---|---|---|
| -ancy, -ency | Noun: state, quality or capacity | emergency, agency, truancy, latency |
| andr, andro | male, characteristics of men | androcentric, androgyny |
| ang | angular | angle, dangle, triangle |
| anim | mind, life, spirit, anger | animal, animation, animosity |
| ann, annu, enni | yearly | annual, annuity, anniversary, perennial, biannual, |
| -ant, -ent | Noun: an agent, something that performs the action | disinfectant, dependent, fragrant, agent, |
| -ant, -ent, -ient | Adjective: kind of agent, indication | important, independent, inconvenient |
| ante | before | anterior, antedate, antecedent |
| anthrop | man | philanthropy, misanthropy, philanthropy |
| anti, ant | against, opposite | antitrust, antigen, antithesis, antibody, antifreeze, anteroom |
| anti, antico | old | antique |
| apo, ap, aph | away from, detached, formed | apology, apocalypse, apogee |
| aqu | water | aqueous, aquatic |
| -ar, -ary | Adjective: resembling, related to | spectacular, contrary |
| arch | chief, first, rule | archangel, architect, archaic, monarchy, matriarchy, patriarchy |
| -ard, -art | Noun: characterized | braggart, drunkard, wizard |
| aster, astr | star | aster, asterisk, astronaut, astronomy, astray |
| -ate | Noun: state, office, function | electorate, delegate, emancipate |
| -ate | Verb: cause to be | graduate, ameliorate, amputate, colligate |
| -ate | Adjective: kind of state | inviolate |
| -ation | Noun: action, resulting state | aggravating, alternate, specialization |
| auc, aug, aut | to originate, to increase | augment, authored, augment, auction |

| | | |
|---|---|---|
| aud, audi, aur, aus | to hear, listen | audible, auditory, aura, auditorium, audiovisual, audition |
| aug, auc | increase | augment, auction, |
| aut, auto | self | auto, automatic, automobile, autoimmune, |
| bar | weight, pressure | barometer, barometric pressure |
| be | on, around, over, about, excessively, make, cause, name, affect | belittle, berate, become, believe, |
| belli | war | belligerent, rebellious |
| bene | good, well, gentle | beneficiary, benefactor, benevolent, benefit |
| bi, bine | two | bicentennial, biannual, bipod, bipolar |
| bibl, bibli, biblio | book | bibliography, bibliotheca, bible |
| bio, bi | life | bio-dome, biology, biological |
| brev | short | breviate, brevity, brief |
| cad, cap, cas, ceiv, cept, capt, cid, cip | to take, to seize, to hold | captivate, captive, capsize, cast, deceive, capture, reciprocate, deception |
| cad, cas | to fall | cadence, cascade, cast |
| -cade | procession | motorcade |
| calor | heat | caloric, calories |
| capit, capt | head | decapitate, captain, capital |
| carn | flesh | carnivore, carnivorous, carnal, carnage |
| cat, cata, cath | down, with | catalog, categorical, catheter |
| caus, caut | burn, heat | cauterize, caustic, cautious |
| cause, cuse, cus | cause, motive | because, cautious, accuse |
| ceas, ced, cede, ceed, cess | to go, to yield, move, go, surrender | succeed, proceed, precede, recede, succession, secede |
| cent | hundred | centennial, century, centipede |
| centr, centri | center | eccentricity, centrifugal, concentric, eccentric |

| chrom | color | chromatic, chromosome, chromatography |
|---|---|---|
| chron | time | chronological, chronology, chronicle |
| cide, cis, cise | to kill, to cut, cut down | incision, euthanize, homicide, concise |
| circum | around | circumvent, circumcise, circumference |
| cit | call, start | cited, incite, citation |
| civ | citizen | civilian, civil |
| clam, claim | cry out | clamor, reclaim, reclamation |
| clin | lean, bend | incline, decline |
| clud, clus claus | to close, shut | clause, include, enclose |
| co, cog, col, coll, con, com, cor | with, together | collaborate, convene, commitment, compress, contemporary, converge, correct, combine, conjoin, converse |
| cogn, gnos | to know | recognize, cognizant, incognito, prognosis, cognitive |
| com, con | fully | complete, confirm, condense, condescend, conscious, confess |
| contr, contra, counter | against, opposite | counteract, contradict, contrary, counterintuitive, contraband |
| cord, cor, cardi | heart | encourage, cordial, cardiac, myocardialenfarction |
| corp | body | corpse, corporal, corporation, corps |
| cort | correct | escort, cortege |
| cosm | universe, world | cosmonaut, cosmopolitan, microcosm, macrocosm |
| cour, cur, curr, curs | run, course | course, occur, curry, cursory, curse |
| crat, cracy | rule | aristocrat, aristocracy, democracy, democrat |
| cre, cresc, cret, crease | grow | create, crescent, accretion, increase |
| crea | create | creature, creation, crease |
| cred | believe | credit, incredible, accredited, credible, credence |

| | | |
|---|---|---|
| cresc, cret, crease, cru | rise, grow | increase, crescendo, accrue |
| crit | separate, choose | critic, critical |
| cur, curs | run | current, currier, occurs, precursor, cursive, concurrent, concur, incur |
| cura | care | curator, curative, manicure |
| cycl, cyclo | wheel, circle, circular | cyclops, unicycle, bicycle, cyclone, cyclic |
| de- | from, down, away, to do the opposite, reverse, against | decrease, descent, deflate, deplete, deceptive |
| dec, deca | ten, ten times | decathlon, decimal, decagon |
| dec, dign | suitable | decent, decadent |
| dei, div | God | divine, deity, divinity, deify |
| dem, demo | people, populace, population | epidemic, demographics, democracy |
| dent, dont | tooth | dentist, periodontal, dental |
| derm | skin, covering | hypodermic, dermatology, epidermis, taxidermy, subdermal |
| di-, dy- | two, twice, double | divide, dividend, |
| dia | through, across, between | diameter, dialect, diagonal, diatribe |
| dic, dict, dit | say, speak | dictation, dictionary, dictate, dictator, Dictaphone |
| dis, dif | not, opposite of, reverse, separate, deprive of, away | dismiss, differ, disallow, disperse, dissuade, difference, distance, differed |
| dit | give | credit, audit |
| doc, doct | teach, prove | docile, document, doctor, indoctrinate |
| domin | master, that which is under control | dominance, dominate, domineer |
| don | give | donate, condone |
| dorm | sleep | dormant, dormitory |
| dox | thought, opinion, praise | orthodox, heterodox, paradox, doxology |
| -drome | run, step | syndrome, aerodrome |

| duc, duct | to lead, pull | produce, abduct, product, transducer, aqueduct, induct, deduct, reduce, induce |
|---|---|---|
| dura | hard, lasting | durable, duration, endure |
| dynam | power | dynamo, dynamic, dynamite, hydrodynamics |
| dys- | bad, abnormal, difficult, impaired, unfavorable | dysfunctional, dyslexia |
| e- | not, missing, out, fully, away, computer network related | emit, embed, email, erase, either |
| ec- | out of, outside | eclectic, echo, eclipse, ecstasy |
| eco- | household, environment, relating to ecology or economy | ecology, economics, ecospheres |
| ecto- | outside, external | ectoplasm, ectomorph |
| -ed | Verb: past tense | introduced, closed, dressed, faded |
| -ed | Adjective: having the quality or characteristics of | winged, gained, tried, tiered |
| -en | Verb: to cause to become | sharpen, lengthened, moistened |
| -en | Adjective: material | golden, molten, silken |
| en-, em- | put into, make, provide with, surround with | enable, entangle, embolden, endeavor |
| -ence, -ency | Noun: action or process, quality or state | emergency, reference, dependence |
| end- | inside, within | endoskeleton, endorse, endoscope |
| epi- | upon, close to, over, after, altered | epilogue, epicenter, epic |
| equi- | equal | equidistant, equation, equator, equinox, |
| -er, -ier | Adjective: comparative | better, sooner, brighter, happier, hotter |
| -er, -or | Noun: person or thing that does something | flyer, collector, concentrator, reporter, player, fryer |
| -er, -or | Verb: action | ponder, clamor, dishonor |
| erg | work, effect | energy, erg, ergometer, allergy |
| -ery | collective qualities, art, practice, trade, collection, state, condition | robbery, snobbery, cavalierly, gallery, slavery |

| -es, -ies | Noun: plural of most nouns ending in -ch, -s, -sh, -o and -z and some in -f and -y | heroes, ladies, passes, ladies, classes |
|---|---|---|
| | | |
| -es, -ies | Verb: third person singular present indicative of verbs | blesses, fizzes, busses, flies |
| -ess | female | actress, goddess |
| | | |
| -est, -iest | Adjective or Adverb: superlative | easiest, latest, fastest |
| | | |
| ev-, et- | time, age | medieval, eternal |
| | | |
| ex- | out of, away from, lacking, former | exit, exist, external |
| | | |
| exter-, extra-, extro- | outside of, beyond | external, extraterrestrial, extrapolate, Extrovert, |
| | | |
| fa, fess | speak | confess, fabulous, confession, fakeness, famous |
| | | |
| fac, fact, fec, fect, fic, fas, fea | do, make | difficult, fashion, feasible, feature, factory, effect, amplification, faction, fasting |
| | | |
| fall, fals | deceive | fallacy, falsify, false |
| | | |
| femto | quadrillionth | femtosecond |
| | | |
| fer | bear, carry | fertile, defer, infer, ferry, refer, transfer |
| | | |
| fic, feign, fain, fit, feat | shape, make, fashion | fiction, faint, feign |
| | | |
| fid | belief, faith | confide, diffident, fidelity |
| | | |
| fid, fide, feder | faith, trust | confidante, confident, infidelity, infidel, federal, confederacy, fidelity |
| | | |
| fig | shape, form | effigy, figment, figurine |
| | | |
| fila, fili | thread | filet, filibuster, fillament |
| | | |
| fin | end, ended, finished | final, finite, finish, confine, fine, refine, define, finale |
| | | |
| fix | repair, attach | fix, fixation, fixture, affix, prefix, suffix |
| | | |
| flex, flect | bend | flex, reflex, flexible, flexor, inflexibility, reflect, deflect, circumflex |
| | | |
| flict | strike | inflict, affliction, afflicted |

| flu, fluc, fluv, flux | flow | influence, influx, reflux, flush, fluently, fluctuate, flue, fluid |
|---|---|---|
| -fold | Adverb: in a manner of, marked by | fourfold |
| for, fore | before | forecast, fortune, foresee |
| forc, fort | strength, strong | Inforce, fort, fortune, fortifiable, fortify, forte, fortitude |
| form | shape, resemble | form, format, conform, formulate, perform, formal, formula |
| fract, frag, frai | break | fracture, infraction, fragile, fraction, refract, frail |
| fuge | flee | subterfuge, centrifuge |
| -ful | Noun: an amount or quantity that fills | mouthful, full, plentiful |
| -ful | Adjective: having, giving, marked by | fanciful |
| fuse | pour | confuse, infuse, transfuse |
| -fy | make, form into | falsify, emulsify |
| gam | marriage | bigamy, polygamy, monogamy |
| gastr, gastro | stomach | gastric, gastronomic, gastritis, gastropod |
| gen | kind | generous |
| gen | birth, race, produce | genesis, eugenics, genealogy, generate, genetic, antigen, pathogen |
| geo | earth | geography, geocentric, geology |
| germ | vital part | germination, germ, germane |
| gest | carry, bear | congest, gestation, ingest |
| giga | billion | gigabyte, gigaflop |
| gin | careful | gingerly |
| gloss, glot | tongue | glossary, polyglot, epiglottis |
| glu, glo | lump, bond, glue | glue, conglomerate |

| gor | to gather, to bring together | category, categorize |
|---|---|---|
| grad, gress, gree | to gather, to bring together, step, go | grade, degree, progress, gradual, graduate, egress |
| graph, gram, graf | write, written, draw | graph, graphic, autograph, photography, graphite, telegram, polygraph, grammar, biography, lithograph, graphic |
| grat<br>grat | pleasing | congratulate, gratuity, grateful, ingrate |
| grav | heavy, weighty | grave, gravitate, gravity |
| greg | herd | gregarious, congregation, segregate |
| hale, heal | make whole, sound | inhale, exhale, heal, healthy, healthiness |
| helio | sun | heliograph, heliotrope, heliocentric |
| hema, hemo | blood | hemophilia, hemostat, hemoglobin, hemorrhage |
| her, here, hes | stick | adhere, cohere, cohesion, inherent, hereditary, hesitate |
| hetero | other, different | heterodox, heterogeneous, heterosexual, heterodyne |
| hex, ses, sex | six | hexagon, hexameter, sestet, sextuplets |
| homo | same | homogenous, homosexual, homonym, homophone |
| hum, human | earth, ground, man | humus, inhumane, exhume, human |
| hydr, hydra, hydro | water | hydrophobia, dehydrated, hydrate, hydraulic, hydraulics, hydrogen, hydrophilic |
| hyper | over, above | hyperbolic, hyperventilate, hyperactive, hypertensive, hypersensitive, hyperkinetic |
| hypn | sleep | hypnosis, hypnotherapy, hypnotic |
| -ia | Noun: names, diseases | Phobia, hydrophobia |
| -ian, an | Noun: related to, one that is | pedestrian, human |
| -iatry | Noun: art of healing | psychiatry |
| -ic | Adjective: quality, relation | generic, cleric |
| -ic, ics | Noun: related to the arts and sciences | arithmetic, macro-economics, micro-economics |

| -ice | Noun: act | malice, suffice |
|------|-----------|-----------------|
| -ify | Verb: cause | specify, identify |
| | | |
| ignis | fire | ignition, ignite |
| -ile | Adjective: having the qualities of | projectile, file |
| in, im | into, on, near, towards | into, import, inner |
| in, im, il, ir | not | impregnable, innocent, illegible, inaction, inviolate, innocuous, impossible, intractable, imposter |
| infra | beneath | infrastructure, infrared light |
| -ing | Noun: material made for, activity, result of an activity | clothing |
| -ing | Verb: present participle | locating, deciphering |
| -ing | Adjective: activity | cohering |
| inter | between, among | international, internal, intermittent, intercept, interject, intermission, interact |
| intra | within, during, between layers, underneath | intranet |
| intro | into, within, inward | interoffice, introvert, introspection, introduce |
| -ion | Noun: condition or action | action, faction, interaction |
| -ish | Adjective: having the character of | finnish, newish |
| -ism | Noun: doctrine, belief, action or conduct | Catholicism, Judaism |
| -ist | Noun: person or member | gastroenterologist, gynecologist |
| -ite | Noun: state or quality | graphite, lite |
| -ity, ty | Noun: state or quality | nativity, nudity, quality, lucidity |
| -ive | Noun: condition | native, naive |
| -ive, -ative, -itive | Adjective: having the quality of | festive, cooperative, sensitive |
| -ize | Verb: cause | fantasize, euthanize, summarize |

| jac, ject | throw | reject, adjacent, eject, trajectory, interject, dejected, inject, |
|---|---|---|
| join, junct | join | juncture, adjoining, enjoin, conjunction, injunction |
| judice | judge | prejudice |
| jug, junct, just | to join | junction, conjugal, adjust |
| juven | young | juvenile, rejuvenate |
| labor | work | laborious, belabor |
| lau, lav, lot, lut | wash | dilute, launder, lavatory, ablution |
| lect, leg, lig | choose, gather, select, read | legible, eligible, collect |
| leg | law | legal, legitimate, legally |
| -less | Adjective: without, missing | motionless, relentless, countless |
| levi | light | levitate, alleviate |
| lex, leag, leg | law | lexicon, legally, illegally, legitimate |
| liber, liver | free | liberty, deliverance, libertarian |
| lide | strike | collide |
| liter | letters | obliterate, literary, literature, alliteration |
| loc, loco | place, area | local, location, locality, allocate, locomotion |
| log, logo, ology | word, study, say, speech, reason, study | catalog, logo, ecology, log |
| loqu, locut | talk, speak | colloquial, eloquent, circumlocution |
| luc, lum, lun, lus, lust | light | translucent, luster, illuminate, illustrate, lunar, luminary |
| lude | play | prelude, elude, conclude |
| -ly | Adverb: in the manner of | fluently, frequently |
| macr-, macer | lean | emaciated, meager |

| magn | great | magnify, magnum, magnitude, magician, magnate, magnificent |
|------|-------|----------------------------------------------------------------|
| main | strength, foremost | mainstream, domain, remain |
| mal | bad, badly | malformation, maladjusted, dismal, malicious, malcontent |
| man, manu | hand, make, do | manual, manufacture, manpower, maneuver, emancipate, management |
| mand | command | mandatory, reprimand, mandate |
| mania | madness | mania, maniac, pyromaniac |
| mar, mari, mer | sea, pool | marine, marsh, maritime, mermaid |
| matri | mother | matrimony, maternal, matriarchate, matron |
| medi | half, middle, between, halfway | meditate, mediate, medieval, Mediterranean, mediocre |
| mega | great, million | megabyte, megaphone, megalopolis |
| mem | recall, remember | memorize, memorable, memoir, commemoration, memento |
| ment | mind | mental, mentality, mention, mentor |
| -ment | Noun: condition or result | document, cement, payment |
| meso | middle | mesopotamia, mesosphere |
| meta | beyond, change | metabolic, metabolism, metadata |
| meter | measure | thermometer, meter, barometer |
| metr | admeasure, apportion | metrics, symmetric, plyometric |
| micro | small, millionth | micrometer, microscope, microwave |
| migra | wander | migration, emigrant, immigrate |
| mill, kilo | thousand | millennium, kilometer, kilogram |
| milli | thousandth | millisecond, millipede, millimeter |
| min | little, small | minute, minor, mini |

| | | |
|---|---|---|
| mis | bad, wrong | misbehave, misinterpret, mistake |
| mit, miss | send | emit, submit, admit, commit, transmit, omit, dismiss, mission, misnomer |
| mob, mov, mot | move | motion, removable, motivate, motor |
| mon | warn, remind | monument, monitor, premonition |
| mono | one | monopoly, mononucleosis, monologue, mononucleosis |
| mor, mort | mortal, death | mortal, immortal, morbid, mortician |
| morph | shape, form | amorphous, metamorphosis, polymorphic |
| multi | many, much | multifaceted, multiple, multitude, multipurpose |
| nano | billionth | nanosecond, nanometer |
| nasc, nat, gnant, nai | to be born | native, pregnant, nascent |
| nat, nasc | to be from, to spring forth | prenatal, native, innate |
| neo | new | neolithic, neoliberal, neonate |
| -ness | state, condition, quality | kindness, sweetness, politeness |
| neur | nerve | neurological, neurosis, neurotic |
| nom | law, order | autonomy, astronomy, economy |
| nom, nym | name | misnomer, synonym |
| nomen, nomin | name | nominate, nomenclature |
| non | nine | nonagon |
| non | not | nonsense, nonabrasive, nonbeliever |
| nov | new | renovate, innovative, novel |
| nox, noc | night | equinox, nocturne, nocturnal |
| numer | number | numerous, enumerate, innumerable |

| | | |
|---|---|---|
| nunci, nunc, nounc | speak, declare | pronounce, annunciate, announcement |
| ob, oc, of, op | toward, in the way, against | obtained, opposition, occur, offer |
| oct | eight | octagon, octopus, octogenarian |
| oligo | few, little | oligarchy, oligodactyly |
| omni | all, every | omniscient, omnipresent, omnivorous |
| onym | name | antonym, synonym, pseudonym, anonymous |
| oper | work | operate, cooperate, operation |
| -or | Noun: condition or activity | stupor, honor, humorous |
| ortho | straight, correct | orthodox, orthopedic, orthodontist |
| -ory | Noun: place for, serves for | territory, directory |
| -ous, -eous, -ose, -ious | Adjective: having the quality of, relating to | wondrous, courageous, verbose, infectious |
| over | excessive, above | overwork, overachieving |
| pac | peace | pacifist, pacify |
| pair, pare | arrange, assemble, two | impair, compare |
| paleo | old | paleontology, Paleolithic |
| pan | all | pansexual, panacea, pandemonium |
| para | beside | paradox, paraphrase |
| pat, pass, path | feel, suffer | patient, passive, pathology |
| pater, patr | father | paternity, patriarch, patriot, paternal, patronize |
| path, pathy | feeling, suffering | pathos, empathetic, apathy |
| ped, pod | foot | bipedal, pedestrian, tripod |
| pedo | child | pediatrics |
| pel, puls | drive, urge | compel, repel, propel, impulse, compulsory, repulsive |
| pend, pens, pond | hang, weigh | pendant, pendulum, suspend, pensive |
| per | through, intensive | persecute, permit, persuade |

| | | |
|---|---|---|
| peri | around | perimeter, perioral |
| phage | eat | phagocyte, bacteriophage |
| phan, phas, phen, fan, phant, fant | show, make visible | phantom, fantasy, phase |
| phe | speak | blaspheme, philosopher |
| phil | love | philosopher, philanthropy, bibliophile |
| phlegma | inflammation | phlegmatic, phlegm |
| phobia, phobos | fear | phobia, claustrophobia, agoraphobia |
| phon | sound | telephone, phonics, microphone, symphony |
| phot, photo | light | photograph, photosynthesis |
| pict | paint, show | picture, depict |
| plac, plais | please | placid, complacent |
| pli, ply | fold | reply, pliable |
| plore | cry out, wail | implore, exploration, deplorable |
| plu, plur, plus | more | plural, plus |
| pneuma, pneumon | breath | pneumonia |
| pod | foot, feet | podiatry |
| poli | city | metropolis, police, politics |
| poly | many | polytheist, polygon |
| pon, pos, pound | place, put | component, opponent, expose, impose, deposit, position, impound |
| pop | people | population, popular |
| port | carry | portable, transport, export, import, transportation |
| portion | part, share | portion, proportion |
| post | after, behind | postpone, postcard |

| pot | power | potential, potent |
|---|---|---|
| pre, pur | before | precede, precipitous |
| prehendere | seize, grasp | apprehend, comprehend |
| prin, prim, prime | first | primary, primal, primeval, principal |
| pro | for, forward | propel, proponent |
| proto | first | protagonist, prototype, protocol |
| psych | mind, soul | psyche, psychiatry, psychological |
| punct | point, dot | punctual, puncture, punctuation |
| pute | think | computer, disputed |
| quat, quad | four | quadrangle, quadriceps |
| quint, penta | five | quintet, quintuplets, pentagon |
| quip | ship | equip, equipment |
| quir, quis, quest, quer | seek, ask | enquire, exquisite, quest, query |
| re | back, again | return, retract, redo, regain |
| reg, recti | straighten | regular, rectify, correct |
| retro | backwards | retrospect, retroactive |
| ri, ridi, risi | laughter | deride, ridiculous, derisive |
| rog, roga | ask | interrogation, derogatory |
| rupt | break | rupture, interrupt, disrupt |
| sacr, sanc, secr | sacred | sacral, secret, sanction |
| salv, salu | safe, healthy | salute, salvage, salvation |
| sanct | holy | sanctuary, sanctify, sanction, sanctimonious, |
| sat, satis | enough | satisfy, satisfied |
| sci, scio, scientia | know | science, scientific, conscience |
| scope | see, watch | periscope, microscope, telescope, endoscope |

| scrib, script | write | script, scribble, scribe, description, inscription, prescription |
| --- | --- | --- |
| se | apart, move away from | secede |
| sect, sec | cut | dissect, section, intersection |
| sed, sess, sid | sit | sediment, session, beside, bedside |
| semi | half, partial | semiannual, semicircle, semiformal |
| sen, scen | old, grow old | senior, senile, senator, evanescent |
| sent, sens | feel, think | sentiment, consent, resent, dissent, sentimental, sensitive, sensory, |
| sept | seven | septet, septennial |
| sequ, secu, sue | follow | sequence, consequence, sequel, subsequent, prosecute, sequential |
| serv | save, serve, keep | deserve, service, servitude, preserve, conserve, observant, reservation, deserve, conservation |
| -ship | Noun: status, condition | friendship |
| sign, signi | sign, mark, seal | design, signal, signature, significant |
| simil, simul | like, resembling | similar, similarity |
| sist, sta, stit | stand, withstand, make up | insist, persist, circumstance, assist, status, stamina, consists, stable, stationary, substitute |
| soci | to join, companions | societal, society, social |
| sol, solus | alone | solo, soliloquy, solitaire, solitude, insolate |
| solv, solu, solut | loosen, explain | solution, solvent, solve, absolute, insolvent |
| somn | sleep | insomnia |
| soph | wise | philosophy, sophisticated |
| spec, spect, spi, spic | look, see | specimen, specific, spectator, spectacle, aspect, conspicuous, speculate, introspect, respect, prospect, retrospective, expectation |
| sper | render favorable | prosper |
| sphere | ball, sphere | sphere, stratosphere, hemisphere, spherical |

| spir | breath | spirit, respiration, inspire, aspire, expire, perspire, respiration, conspire |
|---|---|---|
| | | |
| stand, stant, stab, stat, stan, sti, sta, stead | stand | stature, statue, stable, homestead |
| | | |
| -ster | person | gangster, monster, hipster |
| | | |
| strain, strict, string, stige | bind, pull, draw tight | constrict, strict, restricted constricted, restrain, strained, stringent |
| | | |
| stru, struct, stroy, stry | build | structure, construct, obstruction, instruct, destroy, industry, ministry |
| | | |
| sub, suc, suf, sup, sur, sus | under, below, from, secretly, instead of | submarine, sustain, survive, suffice, surprises, support, succeed, submerge, submarine, subvert |
| | | |
| sume, sump | take, use, waste | consumption, consume, assumption, sump, presume |
| | | |
| super, supra | over, above | superimpose, superior, superscript, supernatural, super |
| | | |
| syn, sym | together, at the same time | synchronous, synthetic, symbolism, synchrony, symbolic |
| | | |
| tact, tang, tag, tig, ting | touch | tactile, contagious, intact, contact, intangible, tangible, contingent |
| | | |
| tain, ten, tent, tin | hold, keep, have | retention, retain, continue, content, tenacious |
| | | |
| tect, teg | cover | protection, protect, detect |
| | | |
| tele | distance, far, from afar | telephone, telegraph, teleport |
| | | |
| tem, tempo | time | tempo, temporary, temporal, contempt, contemporary |
| | | |
| ten, tin, tain | hold | tenacious, tenant, tenure, untenable, detention, pertinent, continent, contain, abstain, pertain, detain, content, retentive |
| | | |
| tend, tent, tens | stretch, strain | tendency, extend, intend, contend, pretend, superintendent, tenderly, extent, extension |
| | | |
| tera | trillion | terabyte, teraflop |
| | | |
| term | end, boundary, limit | exterminate, terminate, terminal |
| | | |

| terr, terra | earth | terrain, territory, extraterrestrial, terrestrial |
|---|---|---|
| test | to bear witness | testament, attest, detest, tested, testified, testify |
| the, theo | God, a god | monotheism, polytheism, atheism, theology |
| therm | heat | thermometer, theorem, thermostat, thermal, hypothermia |
| thesis, thet | place, put | hypothesis, synthesis, epithet, antithesis |
| tire | draw, pull | retire, entire |
| tom | cut | appendectomy, tonsillectomy, dichotomy, anatomy |
| tor, tors, tort | twist | torture, retort, extort, distort, contort, torsion, tortuous, torturous |
| tox | poison | toxic, intoxicate, antitoxin, toxin |
| tract, tra, trai, treat | drag, draw, pull | attract, tractor, traction, extract, retract, protract, detract, subtract, contract, intractable |
| trans | across, beyond, change | transform, transatlantic, transgender, transmit, transportation, transducer |
| tri | three | tripod, triangle, trilateral |
| trib | pay, bestow | tribute, attribute, retribution, tributary, contribute |
| tribute | give | contribute, distribute, tribulation |
| turbo | disturb | turbulent, turbo, turbid, turmoil |
| typ | print | type, prototype, typical, typography, typify, atypical |
| ultima | last | ultimate, penultimate |
| umber, umbraticum | shadow | umbra, penumbra, (take) umbrage, slumber |
| un | not, against, opposite | untrue, uneasy, unsure |
| uni | one | unite, uniform, unilateral, unique, unicorn |
| -ure | Noun: act, condition, process, function | measure, exposure, sure, closure |
| vac | empty | evacuate, vacation, vacuum, vacate, vacuole |

| vade | go | invade, evade, evader |
|---|---|---|
| vale, vali, valu | strength, worth | value, valiant, equivalent, valor |
| veh, vect | to carry | vehement, vector, convection |
| ven, vent | come | convene, intervene, venue, convenient, invent, circumvent, convent, venture, event, prevent |
| ver, veri | true | very, verdict, verify |
| verb, verv | word | verify, veracity, verbalize, verbs |
| vert, vers | turn, change | convert, revert, advertise, versatile, diversion, invert, versatility |
| vi | way | vibrate, vibrant, viable, vital |
| vic, vicis | change, substitute | vicarious, vicious, vicissitude |
| vict, vinc | conquer | victory, eviction, convict, convince, invincibility |
| vid, vis | see | revise, vista, visual, revisit, video, videography, visceral |
| viv, vita, vivi | alive, life | revive, survive, vivid, vivacious, vitality, revitalize, vitamins |
| voc, voke | call | provocation, vocation, vocational, evoke, invoke, vocal, voice |
| vol | will | malevolent, volunteer, volition, benevolent |
| volcan | fire | volcano, vulcanize |
| volv, volt, vol | turn about, roll | revolt, revolving, voluminous, convolution, revolution, evolution |
| vor | eat greedily | voracious, carnivorous, herbivorous, omnivorous, devour |
| -ward | Adverb: in a direction or manner | onward, homeward, forward |
| -wise | Adverb: in the manner of, with regard to | clockwise, counterclockwise, wise, wisdom, |
| with | against | without, withstanding, withholding |
| -y | Noun: state, condition, result of an activity | victory, society, agency, clemency |
| -y | Adjective: marked by, having | hungry, angry, smelly, hilly |

| | | |
|---|---|---|
| zo | animal | zoological, zoology, zoo, zoophyte |

# Word Knowledge Practice Test

1. They investigated the <u>alleged</u> human rights violations.
    a. Proven
    b. False
    c. Unproven
    d. Horrific

2. Cede most nearly means:
    a. Consign
    b. Surrender
    c. Keep
    d. Abandon

3. Afflict most closely means:
    a. Attack
    b. Perturb
    c. Assist
    d. Agonize

4. Conspicuous most nearly means:
    a. Bold
    b. Unremarkable
    c. Quiet
    d. Dull

5. <u>Insurgents</u> were responsible for a number of attacks, including suicide bombings.
    a. Anarchists
    b. Communists
    c. Rebels
    d. Patriots

6. Austere most nearly means:
    a. Welcoming
    b. Ornate
    c. Simple
    d. Fanciful

7. Admonish most closely means:
    a. Denounce
    b. Dislike
    c. Reprimand
    d. Praise

8. Deference most nearly means:
    a. Defiance
    b. Submissiveness
    c. Hostility
    d. Sociability

9. The site had been <u>neglected</u> for years.
    a. Ignored
    b. Maintained
    c. Crumbling
    d. Growing

10. Insinuate most closely means:
    a. Infiltrate
    b. Introduce
    c. Proclaim
    d. Abbreviate

11. Explicate most nearly means:
    a. Obscure
    b. Decipher
    c. Clarify
    d. Confuse

12. Decorum most nearly means:
    a. Propriety
    b. Decoration
    c. Drunkenness
    d. Indecency

13. He was <u>chagrined</u> when he tripped and fell in the hallway.
    a. Injured
    b. Embarrassed
    c. Unharmed
    d. Angry

14. Audacious most nearly means:
    a. Frightening
    b. Engaging
    c. Daring
    d. Boring

15. The <u>intrepid</u> volunteers worked in the refugee camps.
    a. Uncaring
    b. Caring
    c. Compassionate
    d. Fearless

16. Surreptitious most nearly means:
    a. Hidden
    b. Clandestine
    c. Public
    d. Illegal

17. To take <u>precaution</u> is to:
    a) Prepare before doing something.
    b) Remember something that happened earlier.
    c) Become aware of something for the first time.
    d) Try to do something again.

18. To <u>reorder</u> a list is to:
    e) Use the same order again.
    f) Put the list in a new order.
    g) Get rid of the list.
    h) Find the list.

19. An <u>antidote</u> to a disease is:
    i) Something that is part of the disease.
    j) Something that works against the disease.
    k) Something that makes the disease worse.
    l) Something that has nothing to do with the disease.

20. Someone who is <u>multiethnic:</u>
    m) Likes only certain kinds of people.
    n) Lives in the land of his or her birth.
    o) Is from a different country.
    p) Has many different ethnicities.

21. Someone who is <u>misinformed</u> has been:
    q) Taught something new.
    r) Told the truth.
    s) Forgotten.
    t) Given incorrect information

22. <u>Awe</u> is most dissimilar to:
    a) Contempt.
    b) Reverence.
    c) Valor.
    d) Distortion.

23. <u>Intricate</u> is most similar to:
    e) Delicate.
    f) Costly.
    g) Prim.
    h) Complex.

24. <u>Skeptic</u> is most dissimilar to:
    i) Innovator.
    j) Friend.
    k) Politician.
    l) Believer.

25. <u>Hypothetical</u> is most dissimilar to:
    m) Uncritical.
    n) Actual.
    o) Specific.

# Word Knowledge Practice Test Answer Key

1. C
2. B
3. D
4. A
5. C
6. C
7. B
8. B
9. A
10. A
11. C
12. A
13. B
14. C
15. D
16. B
17. A
18. B
19. B
20. D
21. D
22. A
23. D
24. D
25. B

# Chapter 4: Mathematics Knowledge

The Math Knowledge section tests various concepts in numbers and operations, algebra, geometry, data analysis, statistics, and probability. In this test section, you will be provided with 25 questions to answer within a 22-minute time limit, which gives you a little less than a minute to solve each problem. This seems like less time than it actually is, so don't worry! Before taking the AFOQT, you want to make sure that you have a good understanding of the math areas covered. You will need to sharpen your skills, but don't worry – we'll provide you with the knowledge that you'll need to know for the test.

As also mentioned in the Arithmetic Reasoning section, the practice questions here are combined for the obvious reason that the concepts are tied together and most effectively studied as a single concept. Don't focus on how the questions are formatted slightly different, the mathematical fundamentals are identical and that's what it always comes down to. The only difference in the Arithmetic Reasoning section is to not get distracted by the excess information and to read quickly.

## Math Concepts Tested

You have a much better chance of getting a good Math Knowledge score if you know what to expect. The test covers math up to and including the first semester of Algebra II as well as fundamental geometry. You will not be given any formulas, such as those required for geometry calculations, so you need to make sure that you have studied them, so they are fresh in your mind.

Here is a breakdown of areas covered:

### Numbers and Operations
Absolute values, inequalities, probabilities, exponents, and radicals.

### Algebra and Functions
Basic equation solving, simultaneous equations, binomials & polynomials, and inequalities.

### Geometry and Measurement
Angle relationships, area and perimeter of geometric shapes, and volume.

Math skills that you won't need:
- Working with bulky numbers or endless calculations.
- Working with imaginary numbers or the square roots of negative numbers.
- Trigonometry or Calculus.

***Important Note:* You are not allowed to use a calculator for any section of the AFOQT.**
**The Most Common Mistakes**

Here is a list of the four most commonly- made mistakes concerning mathematics, starting with the most common.

1. Answer is the wrong sign (positive/negative).

2. Order of Operations not following when solving.

3. Misplaced decimal.

4. Solution is not what the question asked for.

These are the basics that individuals tend to overlook when they only have a minute or less to do their calculations. This is why it is so important that you pay attention right from the start of the problem. You may be thinking, "But, those are just common sense." Exactly! Remember, even simple mistakes still result in an incorrect answer.

## Strategies

**Review the Basics**: First and foremost, practice your basic skills such as sign changes, order of operations, simplifying fractions, and equation manipulation. These are the skills you will use the most on almost every problem on the Math Knowledge and the Arithmetic tests sections. Remember when it comes down to it, there are still only four math operations used to solve any math problem. Adding, subtracting, multiplying and dividing; the only thing that changes is the order they are used to solve the problem.

Although accuracy counts more than speed; **Don't Waste Time** stuck on a question! Remember, you only have 22 minutes to answer 25 questions for this section test. This is why your knowledge of the basics is so important. If you have to stop and think about what 9 * 6 equals, or use your fingers to add 13 + 8, then you need to spend time on these fundamentals before going on to the concepts. There are minute tests at the end of this chapter. If you can complete those tests in the time specified, the time required for you to calculate the more complex problems during the test will decrease greatly.

**Make an Educated Guess**: If necessary, eliminate at least one answer choice as most probably incorrect and guess which one is most likely correct from the remaining choices.

## Math Formulas, Facts, and Terms that You Need to Know

The next few pages will cover the various math subjects (starting with the basics, but in no particular order) along with worked examples. Use this guide to determine the areas in which you need more review and work those areas first. You should take your time at first and let your brain recall the math necessary to solve the problems, using the examples given to remember these skills.

## Order of Operations

**PEMDAS** – **P**arentheses/**E**xponents/**M**ultiply/**D**ivide/**A**dd/**S**ubtract

Perform the operations within parentheses first, and then any exponents. After those steps, perform all multiplication and division. (These are done from left to right, as they appear in the problem) Finally, do all required addition and subtraction, also from left to right as they appear in the problem.

**Example**: Solve $(-(2)^2 - (4 + 7))$
$(-4 - 11) = \mathbf{-15}$.

**Example**: Solve $((5)^2 \div 5 + 4 * 2)$
$25 \div 5 + 4 * 2$

$5 + 8 = \mathbf{13}$

## Positive & Negative Number Rules

(+) + (-) = Subtract the two numbers. The solution gets the sign of the larger number.

(-) + (-) = Negative number.

(-) * (-) = Positive number.

(-) * (+) = Negative number.

(-) / (-) = Positive number.

(-) / (+) = Negative number.

## Greatest Common Factor (GCF)

The greatest factor that divides two numbers.

**Example**: The GCF of 24 and 18 is 6. 6 is the largest number, or greatest factor, that can divide both 24 and 18.

## Geometric Sequence

Each term is equal to the previous term multiplied by *x*.

**Example**: 2, 4, 8, 16.

***x* = 2**.

## Fractions

Adding and subtracting fractions requires a common denominator.

Find a common denominator for:

$$\frac{2}{3} - \frac{1}{5}$$

$$\frac{2}{3} - \frac{1}{5} = \frac{2}{3}\left(\frac{5}{5}\right) - \frac{1}{5}\left(\frac{3}{3}\right) = \frac{10}{15} - \frac{3}{15} = \frac{7}{15}$$

To add mixed fractions, work first the whole numbers, and then the fractions.

$$2\frac{1}{4} + 1\frac{3}{4} = 3\frac{4}{4} = 4$$

To subtract mixed fractions, convert to single fractions by multiplying the whole number by the denominator and adding the numerator. Then work as above.

$$2\frac{1}{4} - 1\frac{3}{4} = \frac{9}{4} - \frac{7}{4} = \frac{2}{4} = \frac{1}{2}$$

To multiply fractions, convert any mixed fractions into single fractions and multiply across; reduce to lowest terms if needed.

$$2\frac{1}{4} * 1\frac{3}{4} = \frac{9}{4} * \frac{7}{4} = \frac{63}{16} = 3\frac{15}{16}$$

To divide fractions, convert any mixed fractions into single fractions, flip the second fraction, and then multiply across.

$$2\frac{1}{4} \div 1\frac{3}{4} = \frac{9}{4} \div \frac{7}{4} = \frac{9}{4} * \frac{4}{7} = \frac{36}{28} = 1\frac{8}{28} = 1\frac{2}{7}$$

## Probabilities

A probability is found by dividing the number of desired outcomes by the number of possible outcomes. (The piece divided by the whole.)

**Example**: What is the probability of picking a blue marble if 3 of the 15 marbles are blue?

3/15 = 1/5. The probability is **1 in 5** that a blue marble is picked.

## Prime Factorization

Expand to prime number factors.

**Example**: 104 = 2 * 2 * 2 * 13

## Absolute Value

The absolute value of a number is its distance from zero, not its value.

So in $|x| = a$, "$x$" will equal "$-a$" as well as "$a$."

Likewise, $| \, 3 \, | = 3$, and $| \, {-3} \, | = 3$.

Equations with absolute values will have two answers. Solve each absolute value possibility separately. All solutions must be checked into the original equation.

**Example:** Solve for $x$:
$|2x - 3| = x + 1$.

Equation One: $2x - 3 = -(x + 1)$.
$\qquad 2x - 3 = -x - 1$.
$\qquad 3x = 2$.
$\qquad$ **$x = 2/3$**.

Equation Two: $2x - 3 = x + 1$.
$\qquad$ **$x = 4$**.

## Mean, Median, Mode

**Mean** is a math term for "average." Total all terms and divide by the number of terms.

Find the mean of 24, 27, and 18.
$24 + 27 + 18 = 69 \div 3 = $ **23**.

**Median** is the middle number of a given set, found after the numbers have all been put in numerical order. In the case of a set of even numbers, the middle two numbers are averaged. What is the median of 24, 27, and 18?

18, **24**, 27.

What is the median of 24, 27, 18, and 19?

18, 19, 24, 27 (19 + 24 = 43. 43/2 = **21.5**).

**Mode** is the number that occurs most frequently within a given set.

What is the mode of 2, 5, 4, 4, 3, 2, 8, 9, 2, 7, 2, and 2?

The mode would be **2** because it appears the most within the set.

## Exponent Rules

| Rule | Example |
|---|---|
| $x^0 = 1$ | $5^0 = 1$ |
| $x^1 = x$ | $5^1 = 5$ |
| $x^a \cdot x^b = x^{a+b}$ | $5^2 * 5^3 = 5^5$ |
| $(xy)^a = x^a y^a$ | $(5 * 6)^2 = 5^2 * 6^2 = 25 * 36$ |
| $(x^a)^b = x^{ab}$ | $(5^2)^3 = 5^6$ |
| $(x/y)^a = x^a/y^a$ | $(10/5)^2 = 10^2/5^2 = 100/25$ |
| $x^a/y^b = x^{a-b}$ | $5^4/5^3 = 5^1 = 5$ (remember $x \neq 0$) |
| $x^{1/a} = \sqrt[a]{x}$ | $25^{1/2} = \sqrt[2]{25} = 5$ |
| $x^{-a} = \dfrac{1}{x^a}$ | $5^{-2} = \dfrac{1}{5^2} = \dfrac{1}{25}$ (remember $x \neq 0$) |
| $(- x)^a$ = positive number if "a" is even; negative number if "a" is odd. | |

## Roots

Root of a Product:  $\sqrt[n]{a \cdot b} = \sqrt[n]{a} \cdot \sqrt[n]{b}$

Root of a Quotient:  $\sqrt[n]{\dfrac{a}{b}} = \dfrac{\sqrt[n]{a}}{\sqrt[n]{b}}$

Fractional Exponent:  $\sqrt[n]{a^m} = a^{m/n}$

## Literal Equations

Equations with more than one variable. Solve in terms of one variable first.
**Example**: Solve for $y$: $4x + 3y = 3x + 2y$.

Step 1 – Combine like terms: $3y - 2y = 4x - 2x$.

Step 2 – Solve for $y$: $\boldsymbol{y = 2x}$.

## Midpoint

To determine the midpoint between two points, simply add the two $x$ coordinates together and divide by 2 (midpoint $x$). Then add the $y$ coordinates together and divide by 2 (midpoint $y$).

$$\left(\frac{x_1 + x_2}{2}, \frac{y_1 + y}{2}\right)$$

## Inequalities

Inequalities are solved like linear and algebraic equations, except the sign must be reversed when dividing by a negative number.

**Example**: $-7x + 2 < 6 - 5x$.

Step 1 – Combine like terms: $-2x < 4$.

Step 2 – Solve for x. (Reverse the sign): $\boldsymbol{x > \textbf{-2.}}$

Solving compound inequalities will give you two answers.

**Example**: $-4 \leq 2x - 2 \leq 6$.

Step 1 – Add 2 to each term to isolate $x$: $-2 \leq 2x \leq 8$.

Step 2: Divide by 2: $-1 \leq x \leq 4$.

Solution set is **[-1, 4]**.

## Algebraic Equations

When simplifying or solving algebraic equations, you need to be able to utilize all math rules: exponents, roots, negatives, order of operations, etc.

1. Add & Subtract: Only the coefficients of like terms.

**Example**: $5xy + 7y + 2yz + 11xy - 5yz = 16xy + 7y - 3yz$.

2. Multiplication: First the coefficients then the variables.

**Example**: Monomial * Monomial.

$(3x^4y^2z)(2y^4z^5) = 6x^4y^6z^6$.

(A variable with no exponent has an implied exponent of 1.)

**Example**: Monomial * Polynomial.

$(2y^2)(y^3 + 2xy^2z + 4z) = 2y^5 + 4xy^4z + 8y^2z$.

**Example**: Binomial * Binomial.

$(5x + 2)(3x + 3)$.

First: $5x * 3x = 15x^2$.

Outer: $5x * 3 = 15x$.

Inner: $2 * 3x = 6x$.

Last: $2 * 3 = 6$.

Combine like terms: $15x^2 + 21x + 6$.

**Example**: Binomial * Polynomial.

$(x + 3)(2x^2 - 5x - 2)$.

First term: $x(2x^2 - 5x - 2) = 2x^3 - 5x^2 - 2x$.

Second term: $3(2x^2 - 5x - 2) = 6x^2 - 15x - 6$.

Added Together: $2x^3 + x^2 - 17x - 6$.

## Distributive Property

When a variable is placed outside of a parenthetical set, it is *distributed* to all of the variables within that set.

$5(2y - 3x) = 10y - 15x$ [Can also be written as $(2y - 3x)5$].

$2x(3y + 1) + 6x = 6xy + 2x + 6x = 6xy + 8x$.

## Fundamental Counting Principle

(The number of possibilities of an event happening) * (the number of possibilities of another event happening) = the total number of possibilities.

**Example**: If you take a multiple choice test with 5 questions, with 4 answer choices for each question, how many test result possibilities are there?

**Solution**: Question 1 has 4 choices; question 2 has 4 choices; etc.

4 * 4 * 4 * 4 * 4 (one for each question) = **1024 possible test results**.

## Linear Systems

There are two different methods can be used to solve multiple equation linear systems:

**Substitution Method**: This solves for one variable in one equation and substitutes it into the other equation. **Example**: Solve: $3y - 4 + x = 0$ and $5x + 6y = 11$.

1. Step 1: Solve for one variable:
   $3y - 4 + x = 0$.
   $3y + x = 4$.
   $x = 4 - 3y$.

2. Step 2: Substitute into the second equation and solve:
   $5(4 - 3y) + 6y = 11$.
   $20 - 15y + 6y = 11$.
   $20 - 9y = 11$.
   $-9y = -9$.
   $y = 1$.

3. Step 3: Substitute into the first equation:
   $3(1) - 4 + x = 0$.
   $-1 + x = 0$.
   $x = 1$.

   Solution: $x = 1, y = 1$.

**Addition Method**: Manipulate one of the equations so that when it is added to the other, one variable is eliminated. **Example**: Solve: $2x + 4y = 8$ and $4x + 2y = 10$.

Step 1: Manipulate one equation to eliminate a variable when added together:     $-2(2x + 4y = 8)$.

$$-4x - 8y = -16.$$
$$(-4x - 8y = -16) + (4x + 2y = 10).$$
$$-6y = -6.$$
$$y = 1.$$

1. Step 2: Plug into an equation to solve for the other variable:
   $$2x + 4(1) = 8.$$
   $$2x + 4 = 8.$$
   $$2x = 4.$$
   $$x = 2.$$

   Solution: $x = 2$, $y = 1$.

## Quadratics

**Factoring**: Converting $ax^2 + bx + c$ to factored form. Find two numbers that are factors of $c$ and whose sum is $b$. **Example**: Factor: $2x^2 + 12x + 18 = 0$.

1. Step 1: If possible, factor out a common monomial: $2(x^2 - 6x + 9)$.

2. Step 2: Find two numbers that are factors of 9 and which equal -6 when added:
   $2(x\ \ )(x\ \ )$.
   $\ \ \ \ -3\ \ , -3$

3. Step 3: Fill in the binomials. Be sure to check your answer signs.
   $2(x - 3)(x - 3)$.

4. Step 4: To solve, set each to equal 0.
   $x - 3 = 0$. So, $x = 3$.

### Difference of squares:

$$a^2 - b^2 = (a + b)(a - b).$$

$$a^2 + 2ab + b^2 = (a + b)(a + b).$$

$$a^2 - 2ab + b^2 = (a - b)(a - b).$$

## Geometry

- **Acute Angle**: Measures less than 90°.

- **Acute Triangle**: Each angle measures less than 90°.

- **Obtuse Angle**: Measures greater than 90°.

- **Obtuse Triangle**: One angle measures greater than 90°.

- **Adjacent Angles**: Share a side and a vertex.

- **Complementary Angles**: Adjacent angles that sum to 90°.

- **Supplementary Angles**: Adjacent angles that sum to 180°.

- **Vertical Angles**: Angles that are opposite of each other. They are always congruent (equal in measure).

- **Equilateral Triangle**: All angles are equal.

- **Isosceles Triangle**: Two sides and two angles are equal.

- **Scalene**: No equal angles.

- **Parallel Lines**: Lines that will never intersect. Y **ll** X means line Y is parallel to line X.

- **Perpendicular Lines**: Lines that intersect or cross to form 90° angles.

- **Transversal Line**: A line that crosses parallel lines.

- **Bisector**: Any line that cuts a line segment, angle, or polygon exactly in half.

- **Polygon**: Any enclosed plane shape with three or more connecting sides (ex. a triangle).

- **Regular Polygon**: Has all equal sides and equal angles (ex. square).

- **Arc**: A portion of a circle's edge.

- **Chord**: A line segment that connects two different points on a circle.

- **Tangent**: Something that touches a circle at only one point without crossing through it.

- **Sum of Angles**: The sum of angles of a polygon can be calculated using $(n-1)180°$, when $n$ = the number of sides.

## Regular Polygons

Polygon Angle Principle: $S$ = The sum of interior angles of a polygon with $n$-sides.

$S = (n - 2)180$.

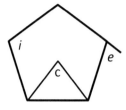

The measure of each central angle (c) is $360°/n$.
The measure of each interior angle ($i$) is $(n - 2)180°/n$.
The measure of each exterior angle ($e$) is $360°/n$.

To compare areas of similar polygons: $A_1/A_2 = (side_1/side_2)^2$.

## Triangles

The angles in a triangle add up to $180°$.

Area of a triangle = ½ * $b$ * $h$, or $\frac{1}{2}bh$.

Pythagoras' Theorem: $a^2 + b^2 = c^2$.

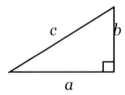

## Trapezoids

Four-sided polygon, in which the bases (and only the bases) are parallel.
Isosceles Trapezoid – base angles are congruent.

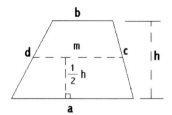

**Area and Perimeter of a Trapezoid**

$$m = \frac{1}{2}(a + b)$$

$$Area = \frac{1}{2}h * (a + b) = m * h$$

$$Perimeter = a + b + c + d = 2m + c + d$$

If $m$ is the median then: $m \parallel \overline{AB}$ and $m \parallel \overline{CD}$

## Rhombus

Four-sided polygon, in which all four sides are congruent and opposite sides are parallel.

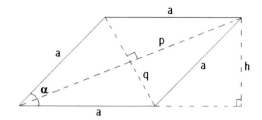

### Area and Perimeter of a Rhombus

$$Perimeter = 4a$$

$$Area = a^2 \sin\alpha = a * h = \frac{1}{2}pq$$

$$4a^2 = p^2 + q^2$$

## Rectangle

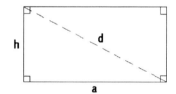

### Area and Perimeter of a Rectangle

$$d = \sqrt{a^2 + h^2}$$

$$a = \sqrt{d^2 - h^2}$$

$$h = \sqrt{d^2 - a^2}$$

$$Perimeter = 2a + 2h$$

$$Area = a \cdot h$$

## Square

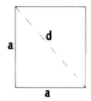

### Area and Perimeter of a Square

$$d = a\sqrt{2}$$

$$Perimeter = 4a = 2d\sqrt{2}$$

$$Area = a^2 = \frac{1}{2}d^2$$

## Circle

### Area and Perimeter of a Circle

$$d = 2r$$

$$Perimeter = 2\pi r = \pi d$$

$$Area = \pi r^2$$

# Cube

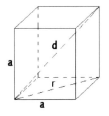

## Area and Volume of a Cube

$$r = a\sqrt{2}$$

$$d = a\sqrt{3}$$

$$Area = 6a^2$$

$$Volume = a^3$$

# Cuboid

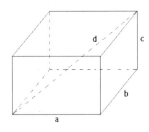

## Area and Volume of a Cuboid

$$d = \sqrt{a^2 + b^2 + c^2}$$

$$A = 2(ab + ac + bc)$$

$$V = abc$$

# Cylinder

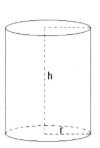

## Area and Volume of a Cylinder

$$d = 2r$$

$$A_{surface} = 2\pi rh$$

$$A_{base} = 2\pi r^2$$

$$Area = A_{surface} + A_{base}$$

$$= 2\pi r\,(h + r)$$

$$Volume = \pi r^2 h$$

# Mathematics Knowledge Practice Test

**1.** Which of these are parallel lines?
      A. x=2, y=3
      B. y=-1, x=4
      C. x=1, x=6
      D. x=9, y=100

**2.** Which of these are complementary angles?
      A. 63° and 29°
      B. 56° and 38°
      C. 33° and 57°
      D. 46° and 49°

**3.** The triangle whose one angle is greater than 90 degrees is called?
      A. Equilateral Triangle
      B. Isosceles Triangle
      C. Scalene Triangle
      D. Obtuse Triangle

**4.** a×(b+c) = ...
      A. ab+bc
      B. cb+ac
      C. ab+ac
      D. abc

**5.** Which of the following options is true for Equilateral Triangle?
      A. Three Congruent Angles
      B. Three Congruent Sides
      C. Two Congruent Angles
      D. Two Congruent Sides

**6.** If $\frac{20-x}{4} = 3y$. What will be x in terms of y?
      A. 20-12y
      B. 20+12y
      C. 12-20y
      D. 12+20y

**7.** If 38 is divided by m, then the remainder is 2, and the quotient is 12. What will be the value of "m" then?
      A. 2
      B. 3
      C. 5
      D. 4

**8.** If y = 7x, x = 3z. What will be the value of y if z = 2?
      A. 40
      B. 44
      C. 48
      D. 42

**9.** What is $\frac{4}{9}$ of $\frac{1}{2}$ of $\frac{6}{4}$?
      A)   $\frac{1}{3}$
      B)   $\frac{64}{3}$
      C)   $\frac{12}{18}$
      D)   $\frac{2}{9}$

**10.** Which one of the following options shows the correct answer of y with respect to its equation?
      A. If 2(y-1)+6=0, then y= 2
      B. If 3(y-3)=3, then y=4
      C. If 2(y+2)=6, then y=-1
      D. If 6y-18 = 6, then y=5

**11.** A = $x^2+3x-4$, B = $2x^2-2x+3$. What will be the value of "B-A"?
      A. $x^2-5x+7$
      B. $3x^2-x-1$
      C. $x^2-3x+7$
      D. $x^2-5x-7$

**12.** Pythagorean Theorem applies to which one of the following triangles?
      A. Equilateral Triangle
      B. Acute Triangle
      C. Obtuse Triangle
      D. Right-Angled Triangle

**13.** x=3 is the solution of which one of the following equations?
      A. 6(x+3)-12 = 0
      B. 8(x-2)-4 = 0
      C. 7(x-6)+21 = 0
      D. 3(x+4)-9 = 0

**14.** There are two parallel lines x and y. One line s is passing through both these parallel lines such that <smx = 60°. What will be the value of angle x?

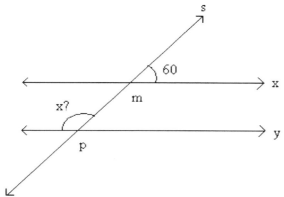

    A. 120°
    B. 60°
    C. 80°
    D. 150°

**15.** What will be the product of 3p³-2p²+p and -2p?
    A. -6p⁴+4p³-2p²
    B. 6p⁴-4p³+2p²
    C. -6p³+4p²-2p
    D. 6p⁴+4p³-2p²

**16.** We have two numbers x and y such that x+y=15, x-y=3. What will be the numbers?
    A. x=8, y=5
    B. x=10, y=7
    C. x=8, y=7
    D. x=9, y=6

**17.** What is the volume of a box whose width is 5 inches?
    A. 25 cubic inches
    B. 75 cubic inches
    C. 100 cubic inches
    D. 125 cubic inches

**18.** $\frac{|2k+4|}{8} = 2$ Which of the following values of 'k' satisfies this equation?
    A. (12, 2)
    B. (4, 5)
    C. (3, 6)
    D. (-10, 6)

19. Find all possible values of x given the following equations: 16-x≤7x and 2x-40<6
   - A)  $2<x\leq23$
   - B)  $3\leq x<23$
   - C)  $2\leq x<23$
   - D)  $2\leq x>-10$

20. What is the result when we multiply these given fractions?

$$\frac{4}{5} * \frac{14}{25} * \frac{125}{7} * \frac{4}{2}$$

   - A. 16
   - B. $\frac{24}{25}$
   - C. 32
   - D. 18

21. What is the result when we multiply these given fractions?

$$\frac{2}{9} * \frac{3}{25} * \frac{125}{6} * \frac{3}{10}$$

   - A. $\frac{6}{30}$
   - B. $\frac{1}{6}$
   - C. 6
   - D. $\frac{11}{30}$

22. What is the result when we add these given fractions?

$$\frac{1}{5} + \frac{4}{25} = \underline{\hspace{2cm}}$$

   - A. $\frac{8}{25}$
   - B. $\frac{5}{29}$
   - C. $\frac{9}{25}$
   - D. $\frac{5}{20}$

23. If 3x + 2 > 5, which of the following options is correct?
   - A. x <1
   - B. x >-1
   - C. x >1
   - D. x <3

24. What is the median of the following list of numbers: 4, 5, 7, 9, 10, and 12?
    A. 6
    B. 7.5
    C. 7.8
    D. 8

25. If 4x-12 < 12, which of the following options is correct?
    A. x <5
    B. x >5
    C. x >15
    D. x >21

# Math Knowledge Practice Test Answer Key

1. C
2. C
3. D
4. C
5. A
6. A
7. B
8. D
9. A
10. B
11. A
12. D
13. C
14. A
15. A
16. D
17. D
18. D
19. C
20. A
21. B
22. C
23. C
24. D
25. A

# Chapter 5: Instrument Comprehension

The Instrument Comprehension section will test your ability to understand basic aviation instrumentation by providing two dials, a compass and artificial horizon. Then it requiers you to identify an image of an aircraft that correlates to what is shown on the dials. It might seem difficult since you may not have any previous flight experience, but once you understand the dials, most find this section to be relatively easy and straightforward.

Let's review the dials first, and then we'll explain how the questions are formatted and how you need to use the dials to answer the questions. In each question, you will be presented two dials that look just like this:

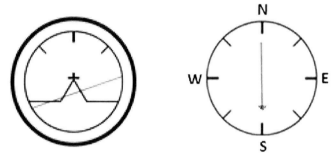

The dial on the left is your artificial horizon. This dial can be confusing the first time you see it. In the artificial horizon pictured above, the dial indicates that the aircraft is in a slight climb and banking right. What makes this confusing to people, is that it is the "horizon" that moves in the dial. The easiest way to explain it is to imagine it is the view from the aircraft. Here's how it works: the line with a triangle in the middle with the "plus sign" is intended to be the wings and nose of the aircraft. Now, think of that in relation to the diagonal line cutting across the dial, sloping to downward to the left. That sloping line is the horizon. As the aircraft climbs upward, the horizon will dip below level, just like it would be viewed from the cockpit. Then, as the aircraft banks right, visualize in your mind the wings of the aircraft turning in relation to the horizon. After you try a few, it becomes easier and easier to immediately visualize.

The dial on the right likely needs no explanation. It is a simple compass indicating the direction of travel of the aircraft. We will come back to this feature later, as it is a great way to quickly and easily eliminate wrong answers.

Now that you've been introduced to both dials let's review the artificial horizon some more by going over some examples.

In this example, the horizon is flat and level at the center point. That means there is no climb or dive, and the aircraft's wings are flat and level as represented by the image of the plane.

In the above artificial horizon, the aircraft is in a dive. As you can see, the horizon has moved above the fuselage silhouette (the line with the triangle representing the aircraft). Try to imagine you are looking through the windshield of a plane as it starts to dive. As the nose tips down, the horizon will move upward in your field of vision. That's exactly what the artificial horizon represents.

Similar to an aircraft diving, is if it is climbing. Again, imagine sitting in the cockpit as the plane climbs. In your field of vision, the horizon would go down, down, down as the nose turns up. Again, that's exactly what the artificial horizon is doing in the dial.

Banking is where most people get confused. Most people who experience frustration with this are typically visualizing the angle of the horizon as the angle of the wings. This happens because the dial is from the perspective of the pilot in the aircraft. However, on the AFOQT exam, the images you are shown are from outside the aircraft and could be viewed from the front, back, or sides. There in lies the challenge, to imagine the perspective of the pilot and translate that into the image you are shown. As you can see in the above example, the horizon is sloping down to the right, but the wings of the plane are turning leftward as it banks left. Again, visualize sitting in the aircraft as it banks and how the horizon would appear in relation to the windshield.

Here is a final example that throws you one last curveball. In this example, the aircraft appears to be coming towards you. If the aircraft is coming towards you, the artificial horizon will appear to tilt the same way as the wings because your perspective is mirrored to the direction of travel. If you get confused, remember first to think about what direction the aircraft is banking (to it's own right or it's own left), then correlate that to the image of the aircraft.

Now, let's put it all together in an example of an actual test question. The questions will appear on the exam much like the one below:

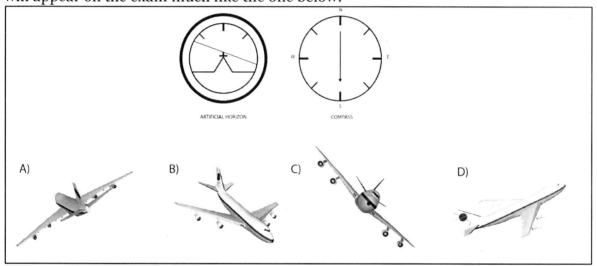

As we mentioned earlier, we are coming back to the compass. This is the easiest way to eliminate wrong answer choices, and sometimes immediately find the correct answer. You always want to reference the artificial horizon just to double check (sometimes options on the test are very similar), but it is fastest and easiest to start with the compass. In this example, we see the aircraft is heading South. On the exam, the direction of travel is simply that "South" is coming towards you, "North" is flying away, "East" is to the right, and "West" is to the left. Almost too easy, right? In this example, the compass indicates "South" and looking at the choices, there is only one aircraft heading directly towards you, which is choice C. To double check, the artificial horizon dial indicates that the aircraft is neither diving nor climbing but is banking relatively hard to the left. Choice C confirms that, as that aircraft is shown to be neither climbing nor diving and is indeed banking hard to the left. The answer is C.

Now that you've got a decent grasp on the fundamentals and have seen how the parts of the puzzle fit together, it's time to get some practice in. Keep in mind that on the actual test, you will have 6 minutes to answer 20 questions. That's about 20 seconds per question which might seem fast, but once you have some practice under your belt, you'll be able to recognize the correct answer in just a few seconds. You will have ample time to double check all the answer choices before moving on to the next question. **Always look at all of the answer choices before selecting your answer!**

# Instrument Comprehension Practice Test

1.

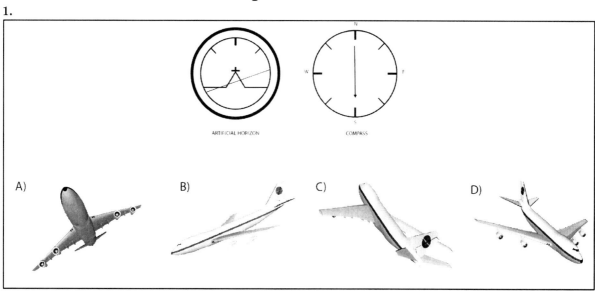

2.

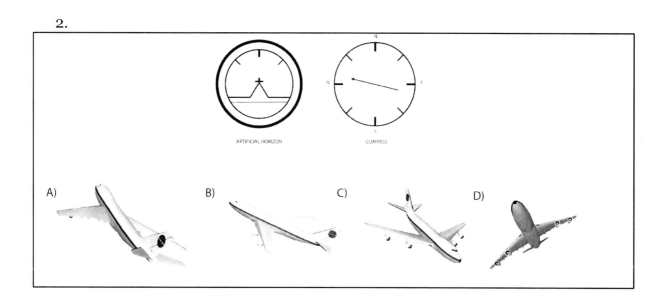

3.

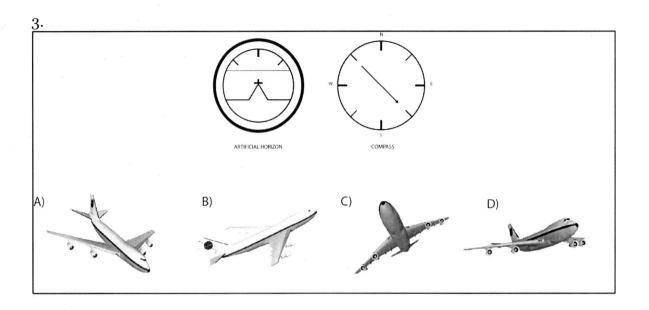

4.

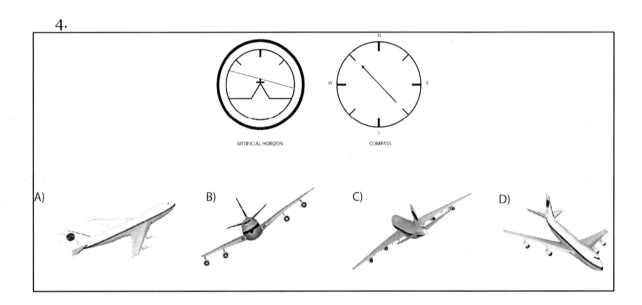

**5.**

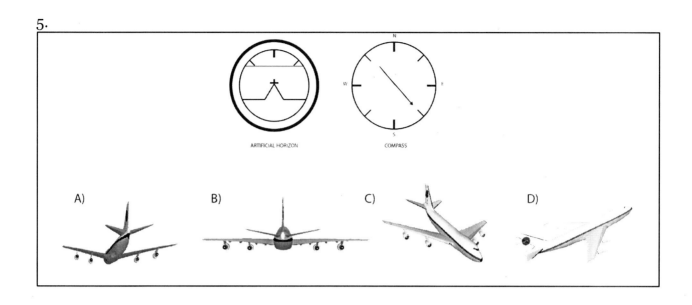

**6.**

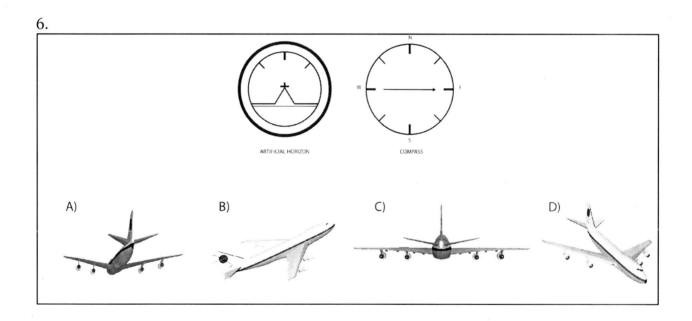

7.

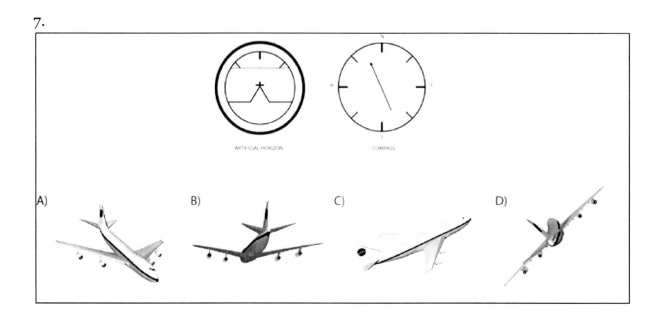

8.

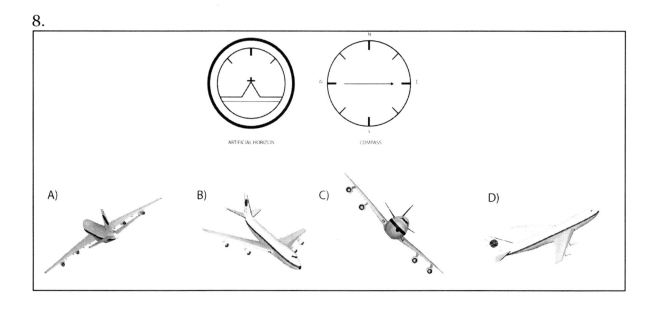

9.

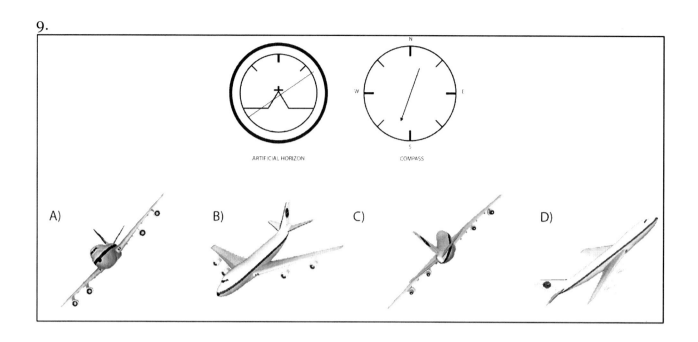

10.

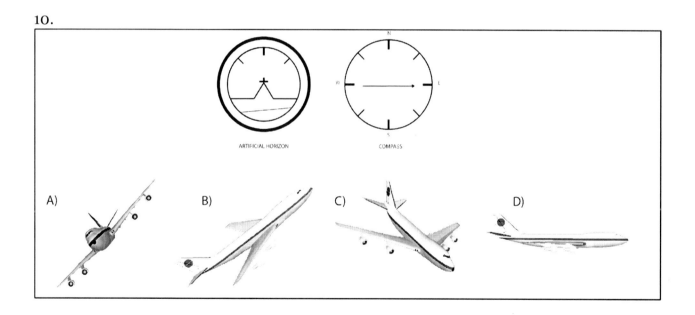

**11.**

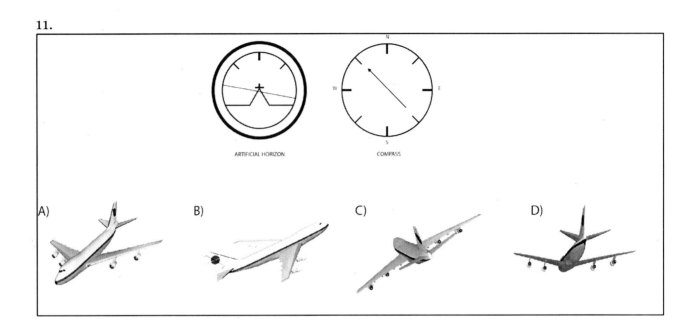

**12.**

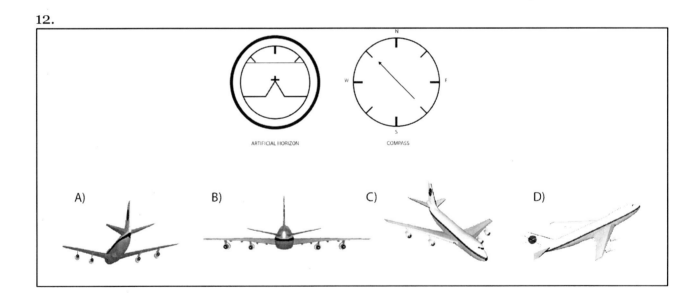

13.

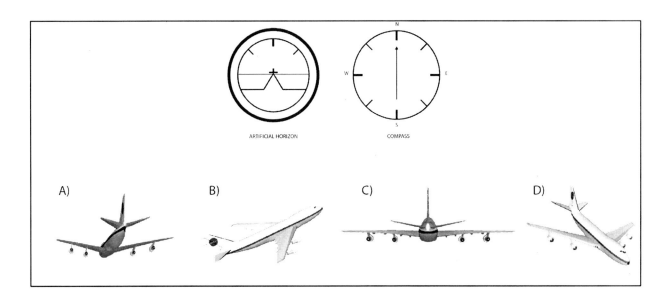

14.

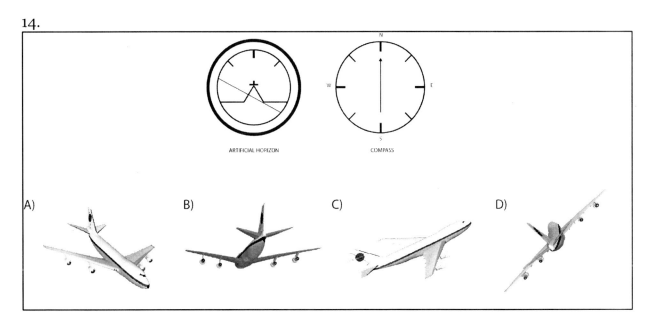

**15.**

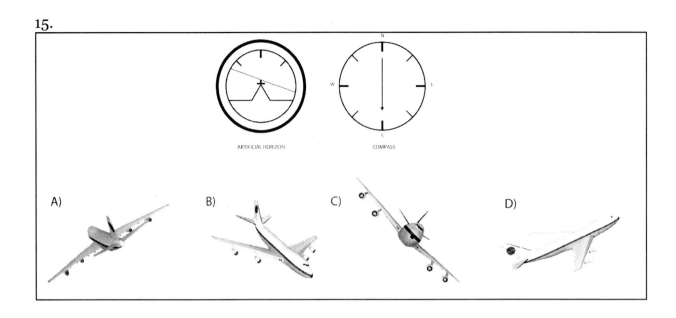

**16.**

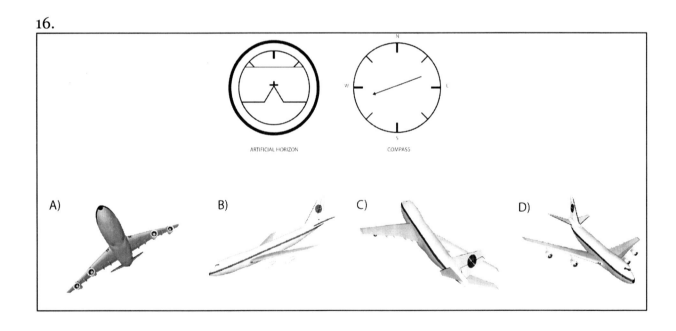

17.

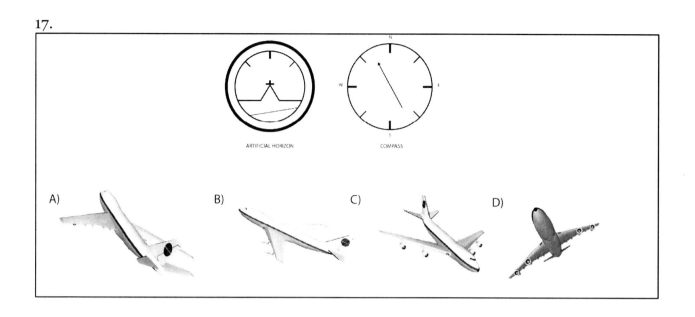

18.

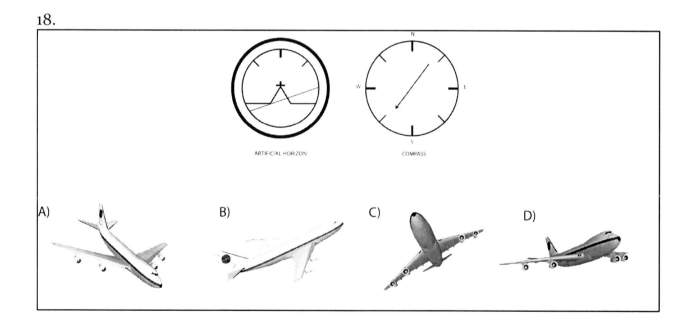

19.

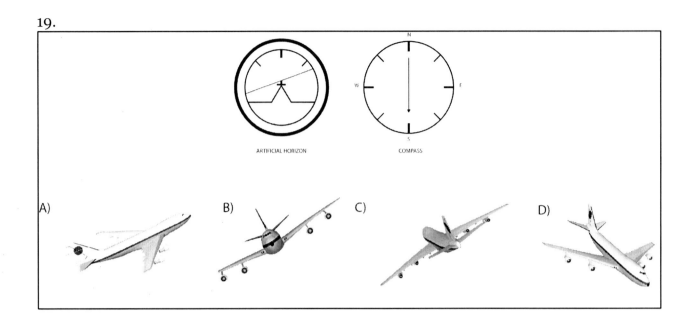

20.

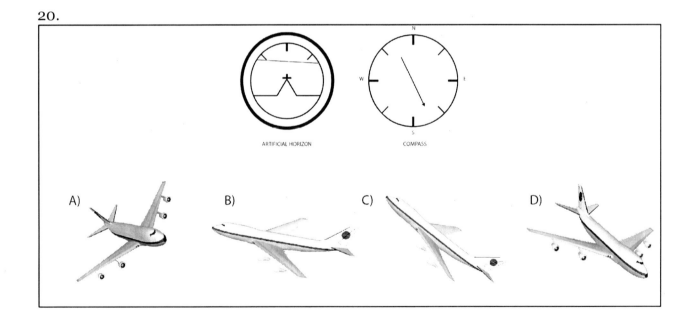

# Instrument Comprehension Practice Test Answer Key

1. A
2. B
3. A
4. C
5. C
6. B
7. B
8. D
9. A
10. B
11. C
12. A
13. C
14. D
15. C
16. B
17. A
18. C
19. B
20. D

# Chapter 6: Block Counting

The Block Counting section is relatively straightforward, but can be challenging for some people. You will be shown a shape with different stacked blocks. Some of the blocks will have a number on them, and your objective is to determine how many other blocks touch the block indicated. The challenge is that you must visualize in three-dimensionally how these blocks move through the entire structure. Most mistakes come from counting a block twice on accident.

Let's look at an example. In the below image, you can see five numbered blocks. If you were asked to count how many blocks touch block #3, what would your answer be?

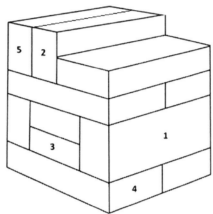

The correct answer is 5, however, some people will have landed on six. Why is this? People who have difficulty visualizing 3D images might have counted block #4 twice because they will count blocks on one side of the shape that run past the block in the question, then count blocks from the other side of the shape they can see. The block below is the same as the one in the example, but with the blocks on one side shaded.

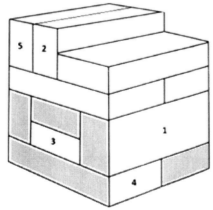

The mistake is counting the "other side" of block 4 as shown below with the hash marks. You have to keep in mind which blocks you have already counted and try to visualize the shapes moving past each other and how they connect.

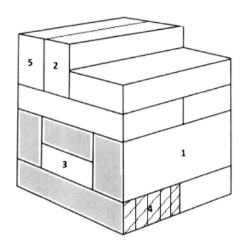

While this section is straightforward, it can be challenging. To make it even more so, keep in mind, you have only 3 minutes to complete 20 questions. That is a mere 9 seconds per question! Practice now and see how you do. If you struggle with this section, don't forget that accuracy is just as important as speed. It does no good to answer 20 questions incorrectly when you could have only answered 10, but gotten them all correct.

If you struggle with this section, the only way to get better is to practice, practice, practice. Use the example questions and make your own numbers for individual blocks and practice counting around them to sharpen your skills, and then go back and work on speed on the practice test.

# Block Counting Practice Test

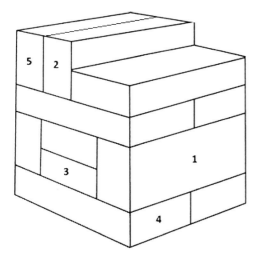

1. Block 1 is touched by _____ other blocks?
   a. 2
   b. 4
   c. 6
   d. 7
   e. 8

2. Block 2 is touched by _____ other blocks?
   a. 2
   b. 3
   c. 4
   d. 5
   e. 6

3. Block 4 is touched by _____ other blocks?
   a. 3
   b. 5
   c. 6
   d. 4
   e. 2

4. Block 5 is touched by _____ other blocks?
   a. 2
   b. 3
   c. 4
   d. 5
   e. 6

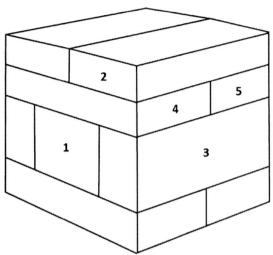

5. Block 1 is touched by _____ other blocks?
    a. 2
    b. 4
    c. 6
    d. 7
    e. 8

6. Block 2 is touched by _____ other blocks?
    a. 2
    b. 3
    c. 4
    d. 5
    e. 6

7. Block 4 is touched by _____ other blocks?
    a. 3
    b. 5
    c. 6
    d. 4
    e. 2

8. Block 3 is touched by _____ other blocks?
    a. 2
    b. 3
    c. 4
    d. 5
    e. 6

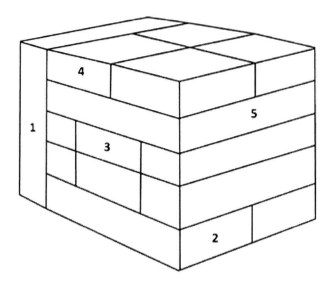

9. Block 1 is touched by _____ other blocks?
   a. 2
   b. 4
   c. 6
   d. 7
   e. 8

10. Block 2 is touched by _____ other blocks?
    a. 2
    b. 3
    c. 4
    d. 6
    e. 5

11. Block 3 is touched by _____ other blocks?
    a. 6
    b. 5
    c. 3
    d. 4
    e. 2

12. Block 5 is touched by _____ other blocks?
    a. 7
    b. 6
    c. 4
    d. 5
    e. 8

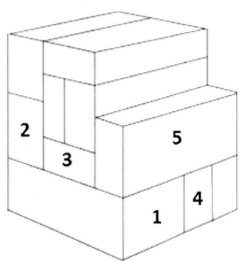

13. Block 1 is touched by _____ other blocks?
      a.  2
      b.  4
      c.  6
      d.  7
      e.  8

14. Block 2 is touched by _____ other blocks?
      a.  2
      b.  3
      c.  4
      d.  6
      e.  5

15. Block 3  is touched by _____ other blocks?
      a.  7
      b.  5
      c.  3
      d.  4
      e.  6

16. Block 5 is touched by _____ other blocks?
      a.  7
      b.  6
      c.  4
      d.  5
      e.  8

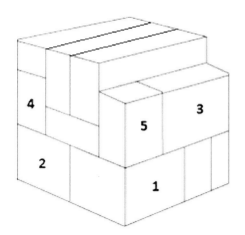

17. Block 1 is touched by _____ other blocks?
    a. 5
    b. 4
    c. 6
    d. 7
    e. 8

18. Block 2 is touched by _____ other blocks?
    a. 2
    b. 5
    c. 4
    d. 6
    e. 7

19. Block 3 is touched by _____ other blocks?
    a. 6
    b. 5
    c. 3
    d. 4
    e. 2

20. Block 5 is touched by _____ other blocks?
    a. 7
    b. 6
    c. 4
    d. 5
    e. 8

# Block Counting Practice Test Answer Key

1. C
2. C
3. D
4. B
5. C
6. B
7. C
8. D
9. D
10. E
11. A
12. E
13. B
14. D
15. A
16. D
17. A
18. B
19. A
20. C

# Chapter 7: Table Reading

In the Table Reading section, the objective is simple enough. For each question, you are given an X & Y coordinate. Find that intersection on the table and identify the number located there. Of all the sections on the AFOQT where time is a factor, none compares to Table Reading. You will only have 7 minutes to complete 40 questions, an absurdly short amount of time at only 10.5 seconds per question.

The general concept is easy enough, any 6th grader could understand how to read a simple chart. So how do you prepare for this section to overcome the obstacle of time? Practice is, of course, important, but using a systematic approach is imperative. Have you ever tried counting backward from 100 to 0 while someone is yelling random numbers in your ear? The Table Reading section is similar to that. You will see so many numbers, it becomes extraordinarily easy to forget what the coordinates were you needed and have to go back and reference the question again. By doing that, you would have already wasted 5-10 seconds minimum, which is one more question you now do not have time to answer.

Your goal is to not worry about time at all until the last 30 seconds. As you practice, force yourself to focus ONLY on the question at hand. Do not think about how much time has gone by, how many questions you have left, if you made a mistake on the last question, etc. The real test of this section is to see if, as an officer in the US Air Force, you possess the capability to stay calm under pressure, maintain your bearing, and stay focused.

As mentioned, don't worry about time until the last 30 seconds or so. When that time hits, go ahead and mark an answer for all remaining questions. There is no "wrong answer penalty" on the AFOQT, so you should never, ever leave a question blank on any section of this exam.

Let's get started on practice, so you can get a feel for this section. Do not overwhelm yourself with this section. It is not possible to substantially speed up your time any more than after the first 10-15 practice questions you try. It is simply a function of time and it takes more than 10.5 seconds to read the question, scroll through the table, find the answer, and mark your answer choice. Rushing is counter-productive. Your goal with this practice round is just to familiarize yourself with the format, and then move on. Do NOT take this practice test untimed! You want to know approximately how many questions you can answer in 7 minutes normally so that you can better track your progress on test day and not lose track of time.

For purposes of this practice test, you will be presented 10 questions per page with the same graph for reference. The chart on the left lists the X and Y coordinates you will need to find. The right chart provides answer choices A through E. Get a timer ready and give it a try. Your goal should be to have 100% correct of questions you are able to attempt before you have to start filling in before time runs out.

# Table Reading Practice Test Questions

## X - Value

| Y \ X | -16 | -15 | -14 | -13 | -12 | -11 | -10 | -9 | -8 | -7 | -6 | -5 | -4 | -3 | -2 | -1 | 0 | 1 | 2 | 3 | 4 | 5 | 6 | 7 | 8 | 9 | 10 | 11 | 12 | 13 | 14 | 15 | 16 |
|---|---|---|---|---|---|---|---|---|---|---|---|---|---|---|---|---|---|---|---|---|---|---|---|---|---|---|---|---|---|---|---|---|---|
| 16 | 7 | 3 | 5 | 2 | 8 | 10 | 9 | 9 | 10 | 11 | 12 | 12 | 13 | 14 | 15 | 15 | 16 | 17 | 18 | 19 | 19 | 20 | 21 | 22 | 22 | 23 | 24 | 25 | 26 | 26 | 27 | 28 | 29 |
| 15 | 30 | 29 | 29 | 28 | 27 | 26 | 25 | 25 | 24 | 23 | 22 | 21 | 21 | 20 | 19 | 18 | 17 | 17 | 16 | 15 | 14 | 13 | 13 | 12 | 11 | 10 | 9 | 9 | 8 | 9 | 3 | 5 | 6 |
| 14 | 7 | 23 | 4 | 5 | 11 | 7 | 23 | 39 | 30 | 29 | 7 | 23 | 39 | 29 | 26 | 15 | 45 | 7 | 23 | 9 | 36 | 30 | 29 | 7 | 24 | 3 | 9 | 36 | 7 | 23 | 11 | 21 | 24 |
| 13 | 8 | 14 | 18 | 47 | 4 | 8 | 14 | 20 | 7 | 23 | 8 | 14 | 20 | 31 | 28 | 7 | 24 | 8 | 14 | 23 | 10 | 7 | 23 | 55 | 34 | 6 | 23 | 10 | 8 | 14 | 20 | 55 | 34 |
| 12 | 3 | 9 | 19 | 46 | 19 | 3 | 9 | 15 | 8 | 14 | 3 | 9 | 15 | 32 | 30 | 55 | 34 | 3 | 9 | 29 | 16 | 8 | 14 | 9 | 42 | 2 | 29 | 16 | 3 | 9 | 15 | 9 | 42 |
| 11 | 6 | 23 | 11 | 98 | 21 | 6 | 23 | 28 | 3 | 9 | 6 | 23 | 41 | 34 | 31 | 9 | 42 | 6 | 23 | 14 | 44 | 3 | 9 | 6 | 19 | 1 | 14 | 44 | 6 | 23 | 86 | 6 | 19 |
| 10 | 2 | 29 | 17 | 58 | 11 | 16 | 7 | 18 | 6 | 23 | 10 | 17 | 18 | 13 | 18 | 6 | 19 | 8 | 19 | 66 | 20 | 6 | 23 | 11 | 21 | 29 | 26 | 15 | 3 | 9 | 19 | 5 | 24 |
| 9 | 1 | 14 | 15 | 54 | 3 | 14 | 12 | 13 | 2 | 29 | 16 | 16 | 17 | 18 | 19 | 20 | 20 | 21 | 22 | 23 | 24 | 2 | 29 | 26 | 27 | 31 | 28 | 7 | 6 | 23 | 32 | 32 | 33 |
| 8 | 9 | 11 | 11 | 44 | 3 | 9 | 36 | 5 | 1 | 14 | 44 | 48 | 22 | 43 | 29 | 44 | 48 | 22 | 43 | 7 | 23 | 1 | 14 | 11 | 21 | 32 | 30 | 55 | 2 | 29 | 7 | 23 | 29 |
| 7 | 10 | 9 | 54 | 24 | 6 | 23 | 10 | 11 | 9 | 11 | 46 | 50 | 34 | 44 | 23 | 46 | 50 | 34 | 44 | 8 | 14 | 9 | 11 | 38 | 40 | 34 | 31 | 9 | 1 | 14 | 8 | 14 | 14 |
| 6 | 21 | 5 | 81 | 4 | 2 | 29 | 16 | 17 | 10 | 9 | 48 | 51 | 91 | 44 | 14 | 48 | 51 | 91 | 44 | 3 | 9 | 10 | 9 | 22 | 22 | 22 | 7 | 24 | 9 | 11 | 3 | 9 | 11 |
| 5 | 23 | 13 | 24 | 45 | 1 | 14 | 44 | 15 | 29 | 26 | 15 | 45 | 2 | 3 | 9 | 44 | 55 | 17 | 6 | 4 | 23 | 13 | 13 | 12 | 11 | 15 | 55 | 34 | 10 | 9 | 6 | 23 | 24 |
| 4 | 25 | 33 | 35 | 36 | 38 | 40 | 11 | 11 | 31 | 28 | 7 | 24 | 41 | 6 | 23 | 23 | 26 | 28 | 31 | 33 | 18 | 7 | 33 | 23 | 26 | 28 | 9 | 42 | 36 | 38 | 41 | 55 | 34 |
| 3 | 27 | 19 | 20 | 21 | 22 | 22 | 9 | 54 | 32 | 30 | 55 | 34 | 13 | 2 | 29 | 16 | 7 | 18 | 64 | 22 | 22 | 12 | 34 | 16 | 7 | 18 | 6 | 19 | 10 | 17 | 18 | 9 | 42 |
| 2 | 29 | 14 | 13 | 13 | 12 | 11 | 5 | 81 | 34 | 31 | 23 | 11 | 11 | 1 | 14 | 7 | 24 | 44 | 48 | 22 | 43 | 13 | 36 | 14 | 12 | 13 | 2 | 29 | 16 | 16 | 17 | 6 | 19 |
| 1 | 31 | 28 | 7 | 24 | 30 | 29 | 13 | 24 | 3 | 22 | 29 | 17 | 5 | 9 | 11 | 55 | 34 | 46 | 50 | 34 | 44 | 15 | 37 | 13 | 2 | 29 | 16 | 16 | 17 | 20 | 9 | 54 | 12 |
| 0 | 32 | 30 | 55 | 34 | 7 | 23 | 21 | 23 | 26 | 28 | 3 | 9 | 36 | 38 | 41 | 9 | 42 | 48 | 51 | 91 | 44 | 17 | 39 | 23 | 9 | 81 | 16 | 15 | 14 | 13 | 5 | 81 | 81 |
| -1 | 34 | 31 | 9 | 42 | 8 | 14 | 11 | 16 | 7 | 18 | 6 | 23 | 10 | 17 | 18 | 6 | 19 | 38 | 40 | 7 | 23 | 19 | 40 | 21 | 22 | 22 | 24 | 24 | 9 | 11 | 13 | 24 | 24 |
| -2 | 7 | 33 | 25 | 38 | 3 | 9 | 3 | 14 | 12 | 13 | 2 | 29 | 16 | 16 | 17 | 20 | 21 | 22 | 22 | 8 | 14 | 36 | 22 | 13 | 12 | 11 | 34 | 34 | 10 | 9 | 7 | 24 | 24 |
| -3 | 12 | 34 | 41 | 18 | 6 | 23 | 7 | 33 | 7 | 23 | 9 | 81 | 16 | 15 | 14 | 13 | 13 | 12 | 11 | 3 | 9 | 13 | 12 | 34 | 31 | 9 | 42 | 64 | 86 | 15 | 55 | 34 | 5 |
| -4 | 13 | 36 | 52 | 39 | 2 | 29 | 12 | 34 | 8 | 14 | 23 | 24 | 28 | 31 | 33 | 3 | 9 | 36 | 26 | 6 | 23 | 9 | 36 | 3 | 33 | 3 | 9 | 36 | 63 | 89 | 9 | 42 | 42 |
| -5 | 15 | 37 | 14 | 22 | 1 | 14 | 13 | 36 | 3 | 9 | 29 | 7 | 18 | 64 | 22 | 6 | 23 | 10 | 7 | 6 | 8 | 48 | 22 | 43 | 18 | 6 | 23 | 10 | 3 | 11 | 6 | 19 | 22 |
| -6 | 17 | 39 | 21 | 40 | 9 | 11 | 15 | 37 | 6 | 23 | 14 | 22 | 26 | 30 | 7 | 2 | 29 | 16 | 24 | 6 | 46 | 50 | 34 | 44 | 8 | 2 | 29 | 16 | 35 | 36 | 30 | 29 | 31 |
| -7 | 19 | 40 | 15 | 40 | 10 | 9 | 17 | 39 | 3 | 9 | 11 | 7 | 33 | 41 | 12 | 1 | 14 | 44 | 34 | 23 | 48 | 51 | 91 | 44 | 16 | 1 | 14 | 44 | 20 | 21 | 7 | 23 | 33 |
| -8 | 36 | 22 | 4 | 41 | 7 | 33 | 19 | 40 | 26 | 10 | 9 | 12 | 34 | 41 | 13 | 36 | 33 | 35 | 36 | 38 | 40 | 20 | 3 | 9 | 36 | 23 | 26 | 28 | 3 | 9 | 36 | 38 | 41 |
| -9 | 38 | 44 | 55 | 41 | 12 | 34 | 36 | 22 | 7 | 18 | 64 | 13 | 36 | 23 | 15 | 37 | 19 | 20 | 21 | 22 | 22 | 13 | 6 | 23 | 10 | 16 | 7 | 18 | 6 | 23 | 10 | 17 | 18 |
| -10 | 40 | 36 | 7 | 42 | 13 | 36 | 5 | 81 | 3 | 9 | 36 | 15 | 37 | 29 | 17 | 39 | 14 | 13 | 13 | 12 | 11 | 3 | 2 | 29 | 16 | 14 | 12 | 13 | 2 | 29 | 16 | 16 | 17 |
| -11 | 42 | 47 | 18 | 42 | 15 | 37 | 13 | 24 | 3 | 23 | 10 | 17 | 39 | 14 | 19 | 40 | 3 | 3 | 9 | 36 | 54 | 6 | 1 | 14 | 44 | 3 | 9 | 36 | 23 | 26 | 28 | 29 | 5 |
| -12 | 44 | 48 | 22 | 43 | 17 | 39 | 22 | 1 | 2 | 29 | 16 | 19 | 40 | 11 | 36 | 22 | 24 | 6 | 23 | 10 | 81 | 2 | 21 | 23 | 26 | 28 | 31 | 33 | 7 | 24 | 1 | 14 | 48 |
| -13 | 46 | 50 | 34 | 44 | 19 | 40 | 23 | 26 | 1 | 14 | 44 | 36 | 22 | 41 | 54 | 55 | 34 | 2 | 29 | 16 | 24 | 3 | 11 | 16 | 7 | 18 | 64 | 22 | 55 | 34 | 9 | 11 | 25 |
| -14 | 48 | 51 | 91 | 44 | 36 | 22 | 16 | 7 | 18 | 6 | 23 | 10 | 17 | 18 | 81 | 9 | 42 | 1 | 14 | 44 | 28 | 3 | 9 | 36 | 38 | 41 | 43 | 46 | 9 | 42 | 10 | 9 | 1 |
| -15 | 50 | 53 | 15 | 16 | 22 | 3 | 14 | 12 | 13 | 2 | 29 | 16 | 16 | 17 | 24 | 6 | 19 | 11 | 16 | 7 | 18 | 6 | 23 | 10 | 17 | 18 | 18 | 18 | 6 | 19 | 16 | 6 | 22 |
| -16 | 51 | 27 | 5 | 45 | 54 | 15 | 3 | 54 | 10 | 11 | 24 | 20 | 4 | 89 | 6 | 55 | 4 | 2 | 14 | 12 | 13 | 2 | 29 | 16 | 16 | 17 | 18 | 19 | 5 | 20 | 20 | 4 | 33 |

Y - Value

|  | X | Y |
|---|---|---|
| 1 | -16 | 3 |
| 2 | -4 | 15 |
| 3 | 14 | 10 |
| 4 | -15 | 1 |
| 5 | 15 | -12 |
| 6 | 6 | -5 |
| 7 | -10 | 4 |
| 8 | 6 | -9 |
| 9 | -5 | -16 |
| 10 | -14 | -6 |

| A | B | C | D | E |
|---|---|---|---|---|
| 7 | 17 | 27 | 86 | 5 |
| 21 | 81 | 97 | 77 | 70 |
| 23 | 81 | 73 | 46 | 19 |
| 74 | 40 | 81 | 62 | 28 |
| 39 | 14 | 25 | 44 | 13 |
| 77 | 12 | 8 | 22 | 18 |
| 90 | 11 | 13 | 41 | 58 |
| 6 | 82 | 61 | 82 | 12 |
| 75 | 5 | 20 | 71 | 45 |
| 66 | 7 | 94 | 21 | 55 |

## X - Value

| Y | -16 | -15 | -14 | -13 | -12 | -11 | -10 | -9 | -8 | -7 | -6 | -5 | -4 | -3 | -2 | -1 | 0 | 1 | 2 | 3 | 4 | 5 | 6 | 7 | 8 | 9 | 10 | 11 | 12 | 13 | 14 | 15 | 16 |
|---|---|---|---|---|---|---|---|---|---|---|---|---|---|---|---|---|---|---|---|---|---|---|---|---|---|---|---|---|---|---|---|---|---|
| 16 | 7 | 3 | 5 | 2 | 8 | 10 | 9 | 9 | 10 | 11 | 12 | 12 | 13 | 14 | 15 | 15 | 16 | 17 | 18 | 19 | 19 | 20 | 21 | 22 | 22 | 23 | 24 | 25 | 26 | 26 | 27 | 28 | 29 |
| 15 | 30 | 29 | 29 | 28 | 27 | 26 | 25 | 25 | 24 | 23 | 22 | 21 | 21 | 20 | 19 | 18 | 17 | 17 | 16 | 15 | 14 | 13 | 13 | 12 | 11 | 10 | 9 | 9 | 8 | 9 | 3 | 5 | 6 |
| 14 | 7 | 23 | 4 | 5 | 11 | 7 | 23 | 39 | 30 | 29 | 7 | 23 | 39 | 29 | 26 | 15 | 45 | 7 | 23 | 9 | 36 | 30 | 29 | 7 | 24 | 3 | 9 | 36 | 7 | 23 | 11 | 21 | 24 |
| 13 | 8 | 14 | 18 | 47 | 4 | 8 | 14 | 20 | 7 | 23 | 8 | 14 | 20 | 31 | 28 | 7 | 24 | 8 | 14 | 23 | 10 | 7 | 23 | 55 | 34 | 6 | 23 | 10 | 8 | 14 | 20 | 55 | 34 |
| 12 | 3 | 9 | 19 | 46 | 19 | 3 | 9 | 15 | 8 | 14 | 3 | 9 | 15 | 32 | 30 | 55 | 34 | 3 | 9 | 29 | 16 | 8 | 14 | 9 | 42 | 2 | 29 | 16 | 3 | 9 | 15 | 9 | 42 |
| 11 | 6 | 23 | 11 | 98 | 21 | 6 | 23 | 28 | 3 | 9 | 6 | 23 | 41 | 34 | 31 | 9 | 42 | 6 | 23 | 14 | 44 | 3 | 9 | 6 | 19 | 1 | 14 | 44 | 6 | 23 | 86 | 6 | 19 |
| 10 | 2 | 29 | 17 | 58 | 11 | 16 | 7 | 18 | 6 | 23 | 10 | 17 | 18 | 13 | 18 | 6 | 19 | 8 | 19 | 66 | 20 | 6 | 23 | 11 | 21 | 29 | 26 | 15 | 3 | 9 | 19 | 5 | 24 |
| 9 | 1 | 14 | 15 | 54 | 3 | 14 | 12 | 13 | 2 | 29 | 16 | 16 | 17 | 18 | 19 | 20 | 20 | 21 | 22 | 23 | 24 | 2 | 29 | 26 | 27 | 31 | 28 | 7 | 6 | 23 | 32 | 32 | 33 |
| 8 | 9 | 11 | 11 | 44 | 3 | 9 | 36 | 5 | 1 | 14 | 44 | 48 | 22 | 43 | 29 | 44 | 48 | 22 | 43 | 7 | 23 | 1 | 14 | 11 | 21 | 32 | 30 | 55 | 2 | 29 | 7 | 23 | 29 |
| 7 | 10 | 9 | 54 | 24 | 6 | 23 | 10 | 11 | 9 | 11 | 46 | 50 | 34 | 44 | 23 | 46 | 50 | 34 | 44 | 8 | 14 | 9 | 11 | 38 | 40 | 34 | 31 | 9 | 1 | 14 | 8 | 14 | 14 |
| 6 | 21 | 5 | 81 | 4 | 2 | 29 | 16 | 17 | 10 | 9 | 48 | 51 | 91 | 44 | 14 | 48 | 51 | 91 | 44 | 3 | 9 | 10 | 9 | 22 | 22 | 22 | 7 | 24 | 9 | 11 | 3 | 9 | 11 |
| 5 | 23 | 13 | 24 | 45 | 1 | 14 | 44 | 15 | 29 | 26 | 15 | 45 | 2 | 3 | 9 | 44 | 55 | 17 | 6 | 4 | 23 | 13 | 13 | 12 | 11 | 15 | 55 | 34 | 10 | 9 | 6 | 23 | 24 |
| 4 | 25 | 33 | 35 | 36 | 38 | 40 | 11 | 11 | 31 | 28 | 7 | 24 | 41 | 6 | 23 | 23 | 26 | 28 | 31 | 33 | 18 | 7 | 33 | 23 | 26 | 28 | 9 | 42 | 36 | 38 | 41 | 55 | 34 |
| 3 | 27 | 19 | 20 | 21 | 22 | 22 | 9 | 54 | 32 | 30 | 55 | 34 | 13 | 2 | 29 | 16 | 7 | 18 | 64 | 22 | 22 | 12 | 34 | 16 | 7 | 18 | 6 | 19 | 10 | 17 | 18 | 9 | 42 |
| 2 | 29 | 14 | 13 | 13 | 12 | 11 | 5 | 81 | 34 | 31 | 23 | 11 | 11 | 1 | 14 | 7 | 24 | 44 | 48 | 22 | 43 | 13 | 36 | 14 | 12 | 13 | 2 | 29 | 16 | 16 | 17 | 6 | 19 |
| 1 | 31 | 28 | 7 | 24 | 30 | 29 | 13 | 24 | 3 | 22 | 29 | 17 | 5 | 9 | 11 | 55 | 34 | 46 | 50 | 34 | 44 | 15 | 37 | 13 | 2 | 29 | 16 | 16 | 17 | 20 | 9 | 54 | 12 |
| 0 | 32 | 30 | 55 | 34 | 7 | 23 | 21 | 23 | 26 | 28 | 3 | 9 | 36 | 38 | 41 | 9 | 42 | 48 | 51 | 91 | 44 | 17 | 39 | 23 | 9 | 81 | 16 | 15 | 14 | 13 | 5 | 81 | 81 |
| -1 | 34 | 31 | 9 | 42 | 8 | 14 | 11 | 16 | 7 | 18 | 6 | 23 | 10 | 17 | 18 | 6 | 19 | 38 | 40 | 7 | 23 | 19 | 40 | 21 | 22 | 22 | 24 | 24 | 9 | 11 | 13 | 24 | 24 |
| -2 | 7 | 33 | 25 | 38 | 3 | 9 | 3 | 14 | 12 | 13 | 2 | 29 | 16 | 16 | 17 | 20 | 21 | 22 | 22 | 8 | 14 | 36 | 22 | 13 | 12 | 11 | 34 | 34 | 10 | 9 | 7 | 24 | 24 |
| -3 | 12 | 34 | 41 | 18 | 6 | 23 | 7 | 33 | 7 | 23 | 9 | 81 | 16 | 15 | 14 | 13 | 13 | 12 | 11 | 3 | 9 | 13 | 12 | 34 | 31 | 9 | 42 | 64 | 86 | 15 | 55 | 34 | 5 |
| -4 | 13 | 36 | 52 | 39 | 2 | 29 | 12 | 34 | 8 | 14 | 23 | 24 | 28 | 31 | 33 | 3 | 9 | 36 | 26 | 6 | 23 | 9 | 36 | 3 | 33 | 3 | 9 | 36 | 63 | 89 | 9 | 42 | 42 |
| -5 | 15 | 37 | 14 | 22 | 1 | 14 | 13 | 36 | 3 | 9 | 29 | 7 | 18 | 64 | 22 | 6 | 23 | 10 | 7 | 6 | 8 | 48 | 22 | 43 | 18 | 6 | 23 | 10 | 3 | 11 | 6 | 19 | 22 |
| -6 | 17 | 39 | 21 | 40 | 9 | 11 | 15 | 37 | 6 | 23 | 14 | 22 | 26 | 30 | 7 | 2 | 29 | 16 | 24 | 6 | 46 | 50 | 34 | 44 | 8 | 2 | 29 | 16 | 35 | 36 | 30 | 29 | 31 |
| -7 | 19 | 40 | 15 | 40 | 10 | 9 | 17 | 39 | 3 | 9 | 11 | 7 | 33 | 41 | 12 | 1 | 14 | 44 | 34 | 23 | 48 | 51 | 91 | 44 | 16 | 1 | 14 | 44 | 20 | 21 | 7 | 23 | 33 |
| -8 | 36 | 22 | 4 | 41 | 7 | 33 | 19 | 40 | 26 | 10 | 9 | 12 | 34 | 41 | 13 | 36 | 33 | 35 | 36 | 38 | 40 | 20 | 3 | 9 | 36 | 23 | 26 | 28 | 3 | 9 | 36 | 38 | 41 |
| -9 | 38 | 44 | 55 | 41 | 12 | 34 | 36 | 22 | 7 | 18 | 64 | 13 | 36 | 23 | 15 | 37 | 19 | 20 | 21 | 22 | 22 | 13 | 6 | 23 | 10 | 16 | 7 | 18 | 6 | 23 | 10 | 17 | 18 |
| -10 | 40 | 36 | 7 | 42 | 13 | 36 | 5 | 81 | 3 | 9 | 36 | 15 | 37 | 29 | 17 | 39 | 14 | 13 | 13 | 12 | 11 | 3 | 2 | 29 | 16 | 14 | 12 | 13 | 2 | 29 | 16 | 16 | 17 |
| -11 | 42 | 47 | 18 | 42 | 15 | 37 | 13 | 24 | 3 | 23 | 10 | 17 | 39 | 14 | 19 | 40 | 3 | 3 | 9 | 36 | 54 | 6 | 1 | 14 | 44 | 3 | 9 | 36 | 23 | 26 | 28 | 29 | 5 |
| -12 | 44 | 48 | 22 | 43 | 17 | 39 | 22 | 1 | 2 | 29 | 16 | 19 | 40 | 11 | 36 | 22 | 24 | 6 | 23 | 10 | 81 | 2 | 21 | 23 | 26 | 28 | 31 | 33 | 7 | 24 | 1 | 14 | 48 |
| -13 | 46 | 50 | 34 | 44 | 19 | 40 | 23 | 26 | 1 | 14 | 44 | 36 | 22 | 41 | 54 | 55 | 34 | 2 | 29 | 16 | 24 | 3 | 11 | 16 | 7 | 18 | 64 | 22 | 55 | 34 | 9 | 11 | 25 |
| -14 | 48 | 51 | 91 | 44 | 36 | 22 | 16 | 7 | 18 | 6 | 23 | 10 | 17 | 18 | 81 | 9 | 42 | 1 | 14 | 44 | 28 | 3 | 9 | 36 | 38 | 41 | 43 | 46 | 9 | 42 | 10 | 9 | 1 |
| -15 | 50 | 53 | 15 | 16 | 22 | 3 | 14 | 12 | 13 | 2 | 29 | 16 | 16 | 17 | 24 | 6 | 19 | 11 | 16 | 7 | 18 | 6 | 23 | 10 | 17 | 18 | 18 | 18 | 6 | 19 | 16 | 6 | 22 |
| -16 | 51 | 27 | 5 | 45 | 54 | 15 | 3 | 54 | 10 | 11 | 24 | 20 | 4 | 89 | 6 | 55 | 4 | 2 | 14 | 12 | 13 | 2 | 29 | 16 | 16 | 17 | 18 | 19 | 5 | 20 | 20 | 4 | 33 |

| | X | Y |
|---|---|---|
| 11 | 6 | 16 |
| 12 | -4 | 11 |
| 13 | -11 | 5 |
| 14 | 10 | -3 |
| 15 | 6 | -12 |
| 16 | 8 | 7 |
| 17 | -9 | 0 |
| 18 | -12 | -3 |
| 19 | 12 | -2 |
| 20 | 4 | -5 |

| A | B | C | D | E |
|---|---|---|---|---|
| 22 | 19 | 32 | 62 | 21 |
| 68 | 87 | 41 | 81 | 3 |
| 14 | 89 | 68 | 73 | 50 |
| 75 | 42 | 82 | 44 | 47 |
| 53 | 15 | 25 | 21 | 85 |
| 96 | 74 | 87 | 40 | 4 |
| 73 | 23 | 43 | 93 | 6 |
| 6 | 14 | 32 | 30 | 64 |
| 45 | 24 | 18 | 8 | 10 |
| 36 | 8 | 95 | 40 | 34 |

X - Value

| Y \ X | -16 | -15 | -14 | -13 | -12 | -11 | -10 | -9 | -8 | -7 | -6 | -5 | -4 | -3 | -2 | -1 | 0 | 1 | 2 | 3 | 4 | 5 | 6 | 7 | 8 | 9 | 10 | 11 | 12 | 13 | 14 | 15 | 16 |
|---|---|---|---|---|---|---|---|---|---|---|---|---|---|---|---|---|---|---|---|---|---|---|---|---|---|---|---|---|---|---|---|---|---|
| 16 | 7 | 3 | 5 | 2 | 8 | 10 | 9 | 9 | 10 | 11 | 12 | 12 | 13 | 14 | 15 | 15 | 16 | 17 | 18 | 19 | 19 | 20 | 21 | 22 | 22 | 23 | 24 | 25 | 26 | 26 | 27 | 28 | 29 |
| 15 | 30 | 29 | 29 | 28 | 27 | 26 | 25 | 25 | 24 | 23 | 22 | 21 | 21 | 20 | 19 | 18 | 17 | 17 | 16 | 15 | 14 | 13 | 13 | 12 | 11 | 10 | 9 | 9 | 8 | 9 | 3 | 5 | 6 |
| 14 | 7 | 23 | 4 | 5 | 11 | 7 | 23 | 39 | 30 | 29 | 7 | 23 | 39 | 29 | 26 | 15 | 45 | 7 | 23 | 9 | 36 | 30 | 29 | 7 | 24 | 3 | 9 | 36 | 7 | 23 | 11 | 21 | 24 |
| 13 | 8 | 14 | 18 | 47 | 4 | 8 | 14 | 20 | 7 | 23 | 8 | 14 | 20 | 31 | 28 | 7 | 24 | 8 | 14 | 23 | 10 | 7 | 23 | 55 | 34 | 6 | 23 | 10 | 8 | 14 | 20 | 55 | 34 |
| 12 | 3 | 9 | 19 | 46 | 19 | 3 | 9 | 15 | 8 | 14 | 3 | 9 | 15 | 32 | 30 | 55 | 34 | 3 | 9 | 29 | 16 | 8 | 14 | 9 | 42 | 2 | 29 | 16 | 3 | 9 | 15 | 9 | 42 |
| 11 | 6 | 23 | 11 | 98 | 21 | 6 | 23 | 28 | 3 | 9 | 6 | 23 | 41 | 34 | 31 | 9 | 42 | 6 | 23 | 14 | 44 | 3 | 9 | 6 | 19 | 1 | 14 | 44 | 6 | 23 | 86 | 6 | 19 |
| 10 | 2 | 29 | 17 | 58 | 11 | 16 | 7 | 18 | 6 | 23 | 10 | 17 | 18 | 13 | 18 | 6 | 19 | 8 | 19 | 66 | 20 | 6 | 23 | 11 | 21 | 29 | 26 | 15 | 3 | 9 | 19 | 5 | 24 |
| 9 | 1 | 14 | 15 | 54 | 3 | 14 | 12 | 13 | 2 | 29 | 16 | 16 | 17 | 18 | 19 | 20 | 20 | 21 | 22 | 23 | 24 | 2 | 29 | 26 | 27 | 31 | 28 | 7 | 6 | 23 | 32 | 32 | 33 |
| 8 | 9 | 11 | 11 | 44 | 3 | 9 | 36 | 5 | 1 | 14 | 44 | 48 | 22 | 43 | 29 | 44 | 48 | 22 | 43 | 7 | 23 | 1 | 14 | 11 | 21 | 32 | 30 | 55 | 2 | 29 | 7 | 23 | 29 |
| 7 | 10 | 9 | 54 | 24 | 6 | 23 | 10 | 11 | 9 | 11 | 46 | 50 | 34 | 44 | 23 | 46 | 50 | 34 | 44 | 8 | 14 | 9 | 11 | 38 | 40 | 34 | 31 | 9 | 1 | 14 | 8 | 14 | 14 |
| 6 | 21 | 5 | 81 | 4 | 2 | 29 | 16 | 17 | 10 | 9 | 48 | 51 | 91 | 44 | 14 | 48 | 51 | 91 | 44 | 3 | 9 | 10 | 9 | 22 | 22 | 22 | 7 | 24 | 9 | 11 | 3 | 9 | 11 |
| 5 | 23 | 13 | 24 | 45 | 1 | 14 | 44 | 15 | 29 | 26 | 15 | 45 | 2 | 3 | 9 | 44 | 55 | 17 | 6 | 4 | 23 | 13 | 13 | 12 | 11 | 15 | 55 | 34 | 10 | 9 | 6 | 23 | 24 |
| 4 | 25 | 33 | 35 | 36 | 38 | 40 | 11 | 11 | 31 | 28 | 7 | 24 | 41 | 6 | 23 | 23 | 26 | 28 | 31 | 33 | 18 | 7 | 33 | 23 | 26 | 28 | 9 | 42 | 36 | 38 | 41 | 55 | 34 |
| 3 | 27 | 19 | 20 | 21 | 22 | 22 | 9 | 54 | 32 | 30 | 55 | 34 | 13 | 2 | 29 | 16 | 7 | 18 | 64 | 22 | 22 | 12 | 34 | 16 | 7 | 18 | 6 | 19 | 10 | 17 | 18 | 9 | 42 |
| 2 | 29 | 14 | 13 | 13 | 12 | 11 | 5 | 81 | 34 | 31 | 23 | 11 | 11 | 1 | 14 | 7 | 24 | 44 | 48 | 22 | 43 | 13 | 36 | 14 | 12 | 13 | 2 | 29 | 16 | 16 | 17 | 6 | 19 |
| 1 | 31 | 28 | 7 | 24 | 30 | 29 | 13 | 24 | 3 | 22 | 29 | 17 | 5 | 9 | 11 | 55 | 34 | 46 | 50 | 34 | 44 | 15 | 37 | 13 | 2 | 29 | 16 | 16 | 17 | 20 | 9 | 54 | 12 |
| 0 | 32 | 30 | 55 | 34 | 7 | 23 | 21 | 23 | 26 | 28 | 3 | 9 | 36 | 38 | 41 | 9 | 42 | 48 | 51 | 91 | 44 | 17 | 39 | 23 | 9 | 81 | 16 | 15 | 14 | 13 | 5 | 81 | 81 |
| -1 | 34 | 31 | 9 | 42 | 8 | 14 | 11 | 16 | 7 | 18 | 6 | 23 | 10 | 17 | 18 | 6 | 19 | 38 | 40 | 7 | 23 | 19 | 40 | 21 | 22 | 22 | 24 | 24 | 9 | 11 | 13 | 24 | 24 |
| -2 | 7 | 33 | 25 | 38 | 3 | 9 | 3 | 14 | 12 | 13 | 2 | 29 | 16 | 16 | 17 | 20 | 21 | 22 | 22 | 8 | 14 | 36 | 22 | 13 | 12 | 11 | 34 | 34 | 10 | 9 | 7 | 24 | 24 |
| -3 | 12 | 34 | 41 | 18 | 6 | 23 | 7 | 33 | 7 | 23 | 9 | 81 | 16 | 15 | 14 | 13 | 13 | 12 | 11 | 3 | 9 | 13 | 12 | 34 | 31 | 9 | 42 | 64 | 86 | 15 | 55 | 34 | 5 |
| -4 | 13 | 36 | 52 | 39 | 2 | 29 | 12 | 34 | 8 | 14 | 23 | 24 | 28 | 31 | 33 | 3 | 9 | 36 | 26 | 6 | 23 | 9 | 36 | 3 | 33 | 3 | 9 | 36 | 63 | 89 | 9 | 42 | 42 |
| -5 | 15 | 37 | 14 | 22 | 1 | 14 | 13 | 36 | 3 | 9 | 29 | 7 | 18 | 64 | 22 | 6 | 23 | 10 | 7 | 6 | 8 | 48 | 22 | 43 | 18 | 6 | 23 | 10 | 3 | 11 | 6 | 19 | 22 |
| -6 | 17 | 39 | 21 | 40 | 9 | 11 | 15 | 37 | 6 | 23 | 14 | 22 | 26 | 30 | 7 | 2 | 29 | 16 | 24 | 6 | 46 | 50 | 34 | 44 | 8 | 2 | 29 | 16 | 35 | 36 | 30 | 29 | 31 |
| -7 | 19 | 40 | 15 | 40 | 10 | 9 | 17 | 39 | 3 | 9 | 11 | 7 | 33 | 41 | 12 | 1 | 14 | 44 | 34 | 23 | 48 | 51 | 91 | 44 | 16 | 1 | 14 | 44 | 20 | 21 | 7 | 23 | 33 |
| -8 | 36 | 22 | 4 | 41 | 7 | 33 | 19 | 40 | 26 | 10 | 9 | 12 | 34 | 41 | 13 | 36 | 33 | 35 | 36 | 38 | 40 | 20 | 3 | 9 | 36 | 23 | 26 | 28 | 3 | 9 | 36 | 38 | 41 |
| -9 | 38 | 44 | 55 | 41 | 12 | 34 | 36 | 22 | 7 | 18 | 64 | 13 | 36 | 23 | 15 | 37 | 19 | 20 | 21 | 22 | 22 | 13 | 6 | 23 | 10 | 16 | 7 | 18 | 6 | 23 | 10 | 17 | 18 |
| -10 | 40 | 36 | 7 | 42 | 13 | 36 | 5 | 81 | 3 | 9 | 36 | 15 | 37 | 29 | 17 | 39 | 14 | 13 | 13 | 12 | 11 | 3 | 2 | 29 | 16 | 14 | 12 | 13 | 2 | 29 | 16 | 16 | 17 |
| -11 | 42 | 47 | 18 | 42 | 15 | 37 | 13 | 24 | 3 | 23 | 10 | 17 | 39 | 14 | 19 | 40 | 3 | 3 | 9 | 36 | 54 | 6 | 1 | 14 | 44 | 3 | 9 | 36 | 23 | 26 | 28 | 29 | 5 |
| -12 | 44 | 48 | 22 | 43 | 17 | 39 | 22 | 1 | 2 | 29 | 16 | 19 | 40 | 11 | 36 | 22 | 24 | 6 | 23 | 10 | 81 | 2 | 21 | 23 | 26 | 28 | 31 | 33 | 7 | 24 | 1 | 14 | 48 |
| -13 | 46 | 50 | 34 | 44 | 19 | 40 | 23 | 26 | 1 | 14 | 44 | 36 | 22 | 41 | 54 | 55 | 34 | 2 | 29 | 16 | 24 | 3 | 11 | 16 | 7 | 18 | 64 | 22 | 55 | 34 | 9 | 11 | 25 |
| -14 | 48 | 51 | 91 | 44 | 36 | 22 | 16 | 7 | 18 | 6 | 23 | 10 | 17 | 18 | 81 | 9 | 42 | 1 | 14 | 44 | 28 | 3 | 9 | 36 | 38 | 41 | 43 | 46 | 9 | 42 | 10 | 9 | 1 |
| -15 | 50 | 53 | 15 | 16 | 22 | 3 | 14 | 12 | 13 | 2 | 29 | 16 | 16 | 17 | 24 | 6 | 19 | 11 | 16 | 7 | 18 | 6 | 23 | 10 | 17 | 18 | 18 | 18 | 6 | 19 | 16 | 6 | 22 |
| -16 | 51 | 27 | 5 | 45 | 54 | 15 | 3 | 54 | 10 | 11 | 24 | 20 | 4 | 89 | 6 | 55 | 4 | 2 | 14 | 12 | 13 | 2 | 29 | 16 | 16 | 17 | 18 | 19 | 5 | 20 | 20 | 4 | 33 |

| | X | Y |
|---|---|---|
| 21 | 15 | 1 |
| 22 | -13 | 4 |
| 23 | 12 | 15 |
| 24 | -14 | -10 |
| 25 | -5 | -13 |
| 26 | -2 | -16 |
| 27 | -4 | -4 |
| 28 | -12 | 9 |
| 29 | 5 | 1 |
| 30 | 3 | 9 |

| A | B | C | D | E |
|---|---|---|---|---|
| 76 | 95 | 54 | 16 | 39 |
| 36 | 87 | 69 | 89 | 15 |
| 23 | 72 | 62 | 8 | 40 |
| 7 | 15 | 74 | 24 | 26 |
| 30 | 36 | 76 | 27 | 48 |
| 59 | 2 | 6 | 41 | 66 |
| 29 | 50 | 45 | 28 | 59 |
| 60 | 25 | 85 | 59 | 3 |
| 2 | 15 | 14 | 83 | 79 |
| 38 | 43 | 23 | 61 | 34 |

## X - Value

| Y \ X | -16 | -15 | -14 | -13 | -12 | -11 | -10 | -9 | -8 | -7 | -6 | -5 | -4 | -3 | -2 | -1 | 0 | 1 | 2 | 3 | 4 | 5 | 6 | 7 | 8 | 9 | 10 | 11 | 12 | 13 | 14 | 15 | 16 |
|---|---|---|---|---|---|---|---|---|---|---|---|---|---|---|---|---|---|---|---|---|---|---|---|---|---|---|---|---|---|---|---|---|---|
| 16 | 7 | 3 | 5 | 2 | 8 | 10 | 9 | 9 | 10 | 11 | 12 | 12 | 13 | 14 | 15 | 15 | 16 | 17 | 18 | 19 | 19 | 20 | 21 | 22 | 22 | 23 | 24 | 25 | 26 | 26 | 27 | 28 | 29 |
| 15 | 30 | 29 | 29 | 28 | 27 | 26 | 25 | 25 | 24 | 23 | 22 | 21 | 21 | 20 | 19 | 18 | 17 | 17 | 16 | 15 | 14 | 13 | 13 | 12 | 11 | 10 | 9 | 9 | 8 | 9 | 3 | 5 | 6 |
| 14 | 7 | 23 | 4 | 5 | 11 | 7 | 23 | 39 | 30 | 29 | 7 | 23 | 39 | 29 | 26 | 15 | 45 | 7 | 23 | 9 | 36 | 30 | 29 | 7 | 24 | 3 | 9 | 36 | 7 | 23 | 11 | 21 | 24 |
| 13 | 8 | 14 | 18 | 47 | 4 | 8 | 14 | 20 | 7 | 23 | 8 | 14 | 20 | 31 | 28 | 7 | 24 | 8 | 14 | 23 | 10 | 7 | 23 | 55 | 34 | 6 | 23 | 10 | 8 | 14 | 20 | 55 | 34 |
| 12 | 3 | 9 | 19 | 46 | 19 | 3 | 9 | 15 | 8 | 14 | 3 | 9 | 15 | 32 | 30 | 55 | 34 | 3 | 9 | 29 | 16 | 8 | 14 | 9 | 42 | 2 | 29 | 16 | 3 | 9 | 15 | 9 | 42 |
| 11 | 6 | 23 | 11 | 98 | 21 | 6 | 23 | 28 | 3 | 9 | 6 | 23 | 41 | 34 | 31 | 9 | 42 | 6 | 23 | 14 | 44 | 3 | 9 | 6 | 19 | 1 | 14 | 44 | 6 | 23 | 86 | 6 | 19 |
| 10 | 2 | 29 | 17 | 58 | 11 | 16 | 7 | 18 | 6 | 23 | 10 | 17 | 18 | 13 | 18 | 6 | 19 | 8 | 19 | 66 | 20 | 6 | 23 | 11 | 21 | 29 | 26 | 15 | 3 | 9 | 19 | 5 | 24 |
| 9 | 1 | 14 | 15 | 54 | 3 | 14 | 12 | 13 | 2 | 29 | 16 | 16 | 17 | 18 | 19 | 20 | 20 | 21 | 22 | 23 | 24 | 2 | 29 | 26 | 27 | 31 | 28 | 7 | 6 | 23 | 32 | 32 | 33 |
| 8 | 9 | 11 | 11 | 44 | 3 | 9 | 36 | 5 | 1 | 14 | 44 | 48 | 22 | 43 | 29 | 44 | 48 | 22 | 43 | 7 | 23 | 1 | 14 | 11 | 21 | 32 | 30 | 55 | 2 | 29 | 7 | 23 | 29 |
| 7 | 10 | 9 | 54 | 24 | 6 | 23 | 10 | 11 | 9 | 11 | 46 | 50 | 34 | 44 | 23 | 46 | 50 | 34 | 44 | 8 | 14 | 9 | 11 | 38 | 40 | 34 | 31 | 9 | 1 | 14 | 8 | 14 | 14 |
| 6 | 21 | 5 | 81 | 4 | 2 | 29 | 16 | 17 | 10 | 9 | 48 | 51 | 91 | 44 | 14 | 48 | 51 | 91 | 44 | 3 | 9 | 10 | 9 | 22 | 22 | 22 | 7 | 24 | 9 | 11 | 3 | 9 | 11 |
| 5 | 23 | 13 | 24 | 45 | 1 | 14 | 44 | 15 | 29 | 26 | 15 | 45 | 2 | 3 | 9 | 44 | 55 | 17 | 6 | 4 | 23 | 13 | 13 | 12 | 11 | 15 | 55 | 34 | 10 | 9 | 6 | 23 | 24 |
| 4 | 25 | 33 | 35 | 36 | 38 | 40 | 11 | 11 | 31 | 28 | 7 | 24 | 41 | 6 | 23 | 23 | 26 | 28 | 31 | 33 | 18 | 7 | 33 | 23 | 26 | 28 | 9 | 42 | 36 | 38 | 41 | 55 | 34 |
| 3 | 27 | 19 | 20 | 21 | 22 | 22 | 9 | 54 | 32 | 30 | 55 | 34 | 13 | 2 | 29 | 16 | 7 | 18 | 64 | 22 | 22 | 12 | 34 | 16 | 7 | 18 | 6 | 19 | 10 | 17 | 18 | 9 | 42 |
| 2 | 29 | 14 | 13 | 13 | 12 | 11 | 5 | 81 | 34 | 31 | 23 | 11 | 11 | 1 | 14 | 7 | 24 | 44 | 48 | 22 | 43 | 13 | 36 | 14 | 12 | 13 | 2 | 29 | 16 | 16 | 17 | 6 | 19 |
| 1 | 31 | 28 | 7 | 24 | 30 | 29 | 13 | 24 | 3 | 22 | 29 | 17 | 5 | 9 | 11 | 55 | 34 | 46 | 50 | 34 | 44 | 15 | 37 | 13 | 2 | 29 | 16 | 16 | 17 | 20 | 9 | 54 | 12 |
| 0 | 32 | 30 | 55 | 34 | 7 | 23 | 21 | 23 | 26 | 28 | 3 | 9 | 36 | 38 | 41 | 9 | 42 | 48 | 51 | 91 | 44 | 17 | 39 | 23 | 9 | 81 | 16 | 15 | 14 | 13 | 5 | 81 | 81 |
| -1 | 34 | 31 | 9 | 42 | 8 | 14 | 11 | 16 | 7 | 18 | 6 | 23 | 10 | 17 | 18 | 6 | 19 | 38 | 40 | 7 | 23 | 19 | 40 | 21 | 22 | 22 | 24 | 24 | 9 | 11 | 13 | 24 | 24 |
| -2 | 7 | 33 | 25 | 38 | 3 | 9 | 3 | 14 | 12 | 13 | 2 | 29 | 16 | 16 | 17 | 20 | 21 | 22 | 22 | 8 | 14 | 36 | 22 | 13 | 12 | 11 | 34 | 34 | 10 | 9 | 7 | 24 | 24 |
| -3 | 12 | 34 | 41 | 18 | 6 | 23 | 7 | 33 | 7 | 23 | 9 | 81 | 16 | 15 | 14 | 13 | 13 | 12 | 11 | 3 | 9 | 13 | 12 | 34 | 31 | 9 | 42 | 64 | 86 | 15 | 55 | 34 | 5 |
| -4 | 13 | 36 | 52 | 39 | 2 | 29 | 12 | 34 | 8 | 14 | 23 | 24 | 28 | 31 | 33 | 3 | 9 | 36 | 26 | 6 | 23 | 9 | 36 | 3 | 33 | 3 | 9 | 36 | 63 | 89 | 9 | 42 | 42 |
| -5 | 15 | 37 | 14 | 22 | 1 | 14 | 13 | 36 | 3 | 9 | 29 | 7 | 18 | 64 | 22 | 6 | 23 | 10 | 7 | 6 | 8 | 48 | 22 | 43 | 18 | 6 | 23 | 10 | 3 | 11 | 6 | 19 | 22 |
| -6 | 17 | 39 | 21 | 40 | 9 | 11 | 15 | 37 | 6 | 23 | 14 | 22 | 26 | 30 | 7 | 2 | 29 | 16 | 24 | 6 | 46 | 50 | 34 | 44 | 8 | 2 | 29 | 16 | 35 | 36 | 30 | 29 | 31 |
| -7 | 19 | 40 | 15 | 40 | 10 | 9 | 17 | 39 | 3 | 9 | 11 | 7 | 33 | 41 | 12 | 1 | 14 | 44 | 34 | 23 | 48 | 51 | 91 | 44 | 16 | 1 | 14 | 44 | 20 | 21 | 7 | 23 | 33 |
| -8 | 36 | 22 | 4 | 41 | 7 | 33 | 19 | 40 | 26 | 10 | 9 | 12 | 34 | 41 | 13 | 36 | 33 | 35 | 36 | 38 | 40 | 20 | 3 | 9 | 36 | 23 | 26 | 28 | 3 | 9 | 36 | 38 | 41 |
| -9 | 38 | 44 | 55 | 41 | 12 | 34 | 36 | 22 | 7 | 18 | 64 | 13 | 36 | 23 | 15 | 37 | 19 | 20 | 21 | 22 | 22 | 13 | 6 | 23 | 10 | 16 | 7 | 18 | 6 | 23 | 10 | 17 | 18 |
| -10 | 40 | 36 | 7 | 42 | 13 | 36 | 5 | 81 | 3 | 9 | 36 | 15 | 37 | 29 | 17 | 39 | 14 | 13 | 13 | 12 | 11 | 3 | 2 | 29 | 16 | 14 | 12 | 13 | 2 | 29 | 16 | 16 | 17 |
| -11 | 42 | 47 | 18 | 42 | 15 | 37 | 13 | 24 | 3 | 23 | 10 | 17 | 39 | 14 | 19 | 40 | 3 | 3 | 9 | 36 | 54 | 6 | 1 | 14 | 44 | 3 | 9 | 36 | 23 | 26 | 28 | 29 | 5 |
| -12 | 44 | 48 | 22 | 43 | 17 | 39 | 22 | 1 | 2 | 29 | 16 | 19 | 40 | 11 | 36 | 22 | 24 | 6 | 23 | 10 | 81 | 2 | 21 | 23 | 26 | 28 | 31 | 33 | 7 | 24 | 1 | 14 | 48 |
| -13 | 46 | 50 | 34 | 44 | 19 | 40 | 23 | 26 | 1 | 14 | 44 | 36 | 22 | 41 | 54 | 55 | 34 | 2 | 29 | 16 | 24 | 3 | 11 | 16 | 7 | 18 | 64 | 22 | 55 | 34 | 9 | 11 | 25 |
| -14 | 48 | 51 | 91 | 44 | 36 | 22 | 16 | 7 | 18 | 6 | 23 | 10 | 17 | 18 | 81 | 9 | 42 | 1 | 14 | 44 | 28 | 3 | 9 | 36 | 38 | 41 | 43 | 46 | 9 | 42 | 10 | 9 | 1 |
| -15 | 50 | 53 | 15 | 16 | 22 | 3 | 14 | 12 | 13 | 2 | 29 | 16 | 16 | 17 | 24 | 6 | 19 | 11 | 16 | 7 | 18 | 6 | 23 | 10 | 17 | 18 | 18 | 18 | 6 | 19 | 16 | 6 | 22 |
| -16 | 51 | 27 | 5 | 45 | 54 | 15 | 3 | 54 | 10 | 11 | 24 | 20 | 4 | 89 | 6 | 55 | 4 | 2 | 14 | 12 | 13 | 2 | 29 | 16 | 16 | 17 | 18 | 19 | 5 | 20 | 20 | 4 | 33 |

|  | X | Y |
|---|---|---|
| 31 | 15 | -14 |
| 32 | -4 | -9 |
| 33 | 1 | 6 |
| 34 | -6 | -9 |
| 35 | 5 | 7 |
| 36 | -7 | -5 |
| 37 | 4 | 8 |
| 38 | 14 | 10 |
| 39 | 5 | -16 |
| 40 | -11 | 16 |

| A | B | C | D | E |
|---|---|---|---|---|
| 9 | 93 | 33 | 45 | 83 |
| 51 | 1 | 36 | 41 | 43 |
| 91 | 63 | 14 | 26 | 57 |
| 71 | 37 | 91 | 50 | 64 |
| 98 | 9 | 15 | 15 | 88 |
| 67 | 11 | 25 | 9 | 28 |
| 57 | 9 | 23 | 15 | 39 |
| 19 | 85 | 92 | 12 | 43 |
| 86 | 2 | 27 | 76 | 22 |
| 45 | 12 | 88 | 29 | 10 |

**Page | 109**

# Table Reading Practice Test Answer Key

1. C
2. A
3. E
4. E
5. B
6. D
7. B
8. A
9. C
10. D
11. E
12. C
13. A
14. B
15. D
16. D
17. B
18. A
19. E
20. B
21. C
22. A
23. D
24. A
25. B
26. C
27. D
28. E
29. B
30. C
31. A
32. C
33. A
34. E
35. B
36. D
37. C
38. A
39. B
40. E

# Chapter 8: Aviation Information

While the Aviation Information (AI) subtest consists of 20 items (questions) and lasts just eight of the 210 minutes of AFOQT testing, the amount of knowledge required to obtain a good score is substantial. The AI subtest measures the applicant's knowledge of general aeronautical concepts and terminology.

There are excellent online and printed study resources, including the Federal Aviation Administration's 281-page "Airplane Flying Handbook" (in pdf format at faa.gov). Instructional videos about aeronautics, aircraft structures and instruments, airports, and other AI topics are on YouTube.

The following information and sample multiple-choice questions will help the applicant prepare for the AI portion of the AFOQT. However, it is suggested to supplement what you find here with other expert sources if you are serious about maximizing your score. Since the AI portion of the AFOQT is so critical, we have provided double the amount of practice questions – 40 in total – to help you prepare effectively.

## Types of aviation and aircraft categories

Since the early 20th century, two main types of aviation have developed: *civil* and *military*, both of which involve *fixed-wing* and *rotary-wing* aircraft. Fighter jets, bombers, airliners, and corporate jets are examples of the former while the latter group includes helicopters, gyrocopters, and tilt-rotor flying machines.

An aircraft is a machine supported aloft by lift created by air flowing across *airfoil* surfaces. The *wings* attached to an airplane's fuselage, a *propeller* rotated by gears connected to an engine drive shaft, or spinning helicopter *rotor blades*, or by *buoyancy*, as in the case of airships and hot air balloons.

In the United States, civilian aircraft are certified under the following categories: normal, utility, acrobatic, commuter, transport, manned free balloons, and special classes. Special Airworthiness Certificates are issued by the Federal Aviation Administration for the following categories: primary, restricted, multiple, limited, light-sport, experimental, special flight permit, and provisional.

Military aircraft are categorized by the mission they perform: air superiority, anti-submarine warfare, coastal and sea lane patrolling, electronic warfare, ground attack (close air support), interdiction, mid-air refueling, mine sweeping, reconnaissance, search and rescue, strategic bombing, surveillance, training, transport, and weather observation.

## Aircraft structure and components

Fixed-wing aircraft – called airplanes, or informally, planes – have a fuselage, wings, and an empennage (tail). A nose section, including the cockpit and cabin comprise the *fuselage*. The *empennage* consists of a vertical stabilizer and an attached (hinged) *rudder* that can be moved left or right by the pilot via cockpit controls (pedals), and a horizontal *stabilizer* and hinged *elevator* that is also under the pilot's control and moves up and down. Some aircraft, like the U.S. Air Force's F-16 fighter jet, have an all-moving horizontal stabilizer-elevator called a *stabilator*.

The inboard portion of airplane wings have extendible sections called *flaps*, which are located along the trailing (aft) edge. They are used to increase the wing's surface area and deflect the airflow downward, thereby augmenting lift at reduced speeds. With flaps extended, planes can take off and land at a lower velocity, which requires less runway.

Some airplanes have leading-edge *slats*, which are also extended to maintain lift at relatively low airspeeds. Like flaps, slats help an airplane takeoff and land at a lower velocity, allowing for operations on shorter runways. The Air Force's C-17 strategic airlifter is an example of a military plane with slats and flaps.

On top of the wings of many turbine-powered aircraft are *spoilers*, hinged panels that move upward after landing and destroy the residual lift in order to put the plane's full weight on the landing gear and maximize tire friction on the runway, thereby enhancing deceleration.

High-performance airplanes often have one or more *air brakes* – also called *speed brakes* – to help decelerate the aircraft, and in flight, increase the rate of descent. For example, the USAF's F-15 fighter jet has a large airbrake on the top fuselage that extends after landing. Air brakes are not spoilers because they are not designed to destroy lift.

The main structural member inside each wing of an airplane is the *spar*, which runs the length of the wing. Larger wings usually have more than one spar to provide extra support. Shaped *ribs* are attached perpendicularly to the spar or spars in order to provide the wing with more structure and greater strength. A *skin* of aircraft aluminum (in most cases) is attached to the framework of spar(s) and ribs.

Airplanes that fly substantially below the speed of sound typically have wings that are *perpendicular* to the aircraft's longitudinal (nose-to-tail) axis. The wings of most jet planes are *swept* back to delay the drag associated with air compressibility at high subsonic speeds. Swept wings increase the performance of high performance airplanes.

Some military aircraft have a *delta wing* (shaped like a triangle) while others have *variable-geometry wings*. In the case of the latter, the pilot swings the wings forward to a position that is roughly perpendicular to the fuselage for takeoff. This is also done when landing, flight at low airspeeds, and back when flying at high subsonic, transonic, and supersonic velocities. The Air Force's B-1B Lancer bomber is a variable-geometry airplane.

Toward the outer trailing edge of each wing is a hinged flight control surface called an *aileron* that moves up and down. Ailerons operate in a direction opposite to each other and control the plane's rolling motion around the longitudinal axis. Ailerons are used to perform banking turns.

A *trim tab* on the rear of the rudder, elevator, and one aileron (usually) act to change the aerodynamic load on the surface and reduce the need for constant pilot pressure on the control column (or joystick) and left and right pedal. Each trim tab is controlled by the pilot via a switch or wheel in the cockpit.

Regarding a source of thrust, most aircraft are powered by one or more *piston* or *turbine* engines. In terms of propulsion type, the latter group consists of *turboprop*, *turbojet*, and *turbofan*. Fighter aircraft have one turbojet engine or a pair of them, each equipped with an *afterburner*, which provides an increase in thrust above non-afterburner full throttle (called military power).

The pilot controls engine operation (start, ground idle, checks, throttle movement, reverse thrust, shutdown) via switches and levers in the cockpit. The number of engine controls corresponds to the number of engines. In single- and multi-engine planes with adjustable-pitch propellers, blade angle is also controlled from the cockpit via levers.

*Reverse thrust* is a feature of turboprop and many jet-powered aircraft, including airliners, aerial tankers, and transport planes. Reverse thrust is used after landing to shorten the ground roll, the runway distance required by the decelerating airplane. Turboprop reverse thrust involves the rotation of propeller blades (three to six, typically) to a blade angle that causes air to be forced forward (away from the plane), not backward over the wings and tail surfaces, as happens when the aircraft taxis and during takeoff, climb, cruise, descent, and landing.

Reverse thrust on jet aircraft is achieved by temporarily directing the engine exhaust forward. After landing, the pilot moves the reverse thrust levers on the cockpit throttle quadrant, which causes two rounded metallic sections on the back end of each engine – called buckets, or clamshell doors – to pneumatically move and come together. When deployed, they stop the engine exhaust from going aft and direct the hot airflow forward at an angle.

Another type of reverse thrust on some jet aircraft involves pivoting doors located roughly half way along the engine. After landing, the pilot moves the reverse thrust levers, which causes the doors (four on each engine) to open. As with the buckets/clamshell doors, the result is exhaust deflected forward, which increases aircraft deceleration greatly.

Most aircraft land on wheels – called *landing gear* – and many types of planes have retractable wheels. Wheel retraction results in less drag when the aircraft is airborne. Fixed- and rotary-wing aircraft equipped with *skis* are able to land and maneuver on surfaces covered with snow and/or ice.

Airplanes that takeoff and land on water have *floats* attached to supports that are connected to the fuselage, or a *boat-like hull* on the bottom of the fuselage. *Amphibious* aircraft can take off and land on both land and water due to retractable wheels.

Rotary-wing aircraft (the U.S. Air Force has two fleets of them) have a *fuselage, tail,* and *fin* (in most cases), and *landing gear* (e.g., skids, wheels, inflatable floats). The most common type of rotary-wing aircraft is the helicopter.

## Aerodynamic forces

There are four main aerodynamic forces that act on an aircraft when it is airborne: weight, lift, thrust, and drag.

The aircraft and everything in it – pilots, passengers, fuel, cargo, etc. – have mass (weight). Because of the earth's gravitational pull, the combined mass of the aircraft and its contents acts downward. From a physics perspective, the total weight force is deemed to act through the aircraft's *center of gravity.*

Aerodynamic loads associated with flight maneuvers and air turbulence affect the aircraft's weight. Whenever an aircraft flies a curved flight path at a certain altitude, the load factor (force of gravity, or "G") exerted on the airfoils (e.g., wings, rotor blades) is greater than the aircraft's total weight.

When a pilot turns an aircraft by banking (rolling) left or right, the amount of "G" increases. Banking further in order to turn more tightly causes the machine's effective weight ("G" loading) to increase more. An airplane banked 30 degrees weighs an additional 16 percent, but at 60 degrees of bank – a very steep turn – it weighs twice as much as it does in straight and level flight in smooth air.

Gusts produced by turbulent air can quickly impose aerodynamic forces that also increase the aircraft's "G" (weight) force.

*Lift* is the force that counteracts an aircraft's weight and causes the machine to rise into the air and stay aloft. Lift is produced by airfoils that move through the air at a speed sufficient to create a pressure differential between the two surfaces and a resulting upward force. Lift acts perpendicular to the direction of flight through the airfoil's *center of pressure* or *center of lift.*

*Thrust* is an aircraft's forward force, which is created by one or more engines (the largest plane in the world, the Antonov An-225 Mriya, has six huge turbofan jet engines). In propeller-driven airplanes and rotary-wing aircraft, the power output of the engine(s) is transformed into rotary motion via one or more transmissions (gear boxes). Generally, thrust acts parallel to the aircraft's longitudinal axis.

*Drag* opposes thrust; it is a rearward-acting force caused by airflow passing over the aircraft's structure and becoming disrupted. Drag acts parallel to the *relative wind* and is a function of aircraft shape and size, its velocity and angle (inclination) in relation to airflow, and the air's mass, viscosity, and compressibility.

An aircraft's *total drag* is the sum of its *profile drag, induced drag*, and *parasite drag*. When total drag is the lowest, the aircraft experiences its maximum endurance (in straight and level flight), best rate of climb, and for helicopters, minimum rate-of-descent speed for autorotation.

*Profile drag* is the sum of *form drag* and *skin friction*. Form drag varies with air pressure around the aircraft and its cross-sectional shape. Skin friction is a function of the roughness of the outer surface of an aircraft (due to surface imperfections, protruding rivet heads, etc.).

*Induced drag* is a product of lift; stationary aircraft generate no such drag. However, as lift is created during acceleration along the runway or strip (in the case of airplanes) or increased rotor rpm and angle of attack (in the case of helicopters), the resulting pressure differential between the airfoil surfaces creates an air vortex at the wing's or rotor blade's tip. The vortex moves parallel to the aircraft's longitudinal axis and expands in diameter with distance from the airfoil. The effect of each vortex is a retarding aerodynamic force called induced drag.

Parts of an aircraft that do not contribute to the production of lift create *parasite drag* when the machine is moving. On airplanes, such components include the nose section and fuselage, landing gear, engine pylons and cowlings, vertical stabilizer, and rudder. On helicopters, the cockpit and cabin, landing skids or wheels, externally mounted engines (on some types), tail boom, and fin create parasite drag.

## Scientific principles of relevance to aeronautics

*Bernoulli's Principle*
In 1738, a Swiss scientist named Daniel Bernoulli published a book entitled *Hydrodynamica*. In it he explained that an increase of the inviscid flow of a fluid (i.e., the flow of an ideal, zero-viscosity liquid or gas) resulted in a decrease of static pressure exerted by the fluid. Bernoulli's famous equation is $P + \frac{1}{2}\rho v^2 = $ a constant, where $P$ = pressure (a force exerted divided by the area exerted upon); $\rho$ (the Greek letter "rho") = the fluid's density; and $v$ = the fluid's velocity.

The constant in Bernoulli's formula is derived from the scientific principle that energy cannot be created or destroyed – only its form can be changed – and a system's total energy does not increase or decrease.
*Conservation laws – conservation of energy*

Bernoulli's Principle is based on the conservation of energy. It says that in a steady flow the sum of all forms of mechanical energy – a fluid's potential energy plus its kinetic energy – along a streamline (e.g., a tube) is the same at all points. Thus, greater fluid flow rate (a higher speed) results in increased kinetic energy and dynamic pressure and reduced potential energy and static pressure.

An aircraft filled with fuel has a finite amount of energy. Through combustion in the engine, the fuel's heat energy is converted into kinetic energy. Either in the form of jet exhaust or at least one rotating propeller (many types of planes have two or more propellers). Spinning helicopter rotor blades also have kinetic energy.

If an aircraft is airborne when it runs out of fuel, it still has potential energy as a function of its height above the ground. As the pilot noses down to keep air flowing over the airfoils (wings, rotor blades) and create lift, the aircraft's potential energy is transformed into kinetic energy.

Combining Bernoulli's Principle with the fact that airfoils provide lift at varying speeds during different phases of flight (takeoff, climb, cruise, descent, landing), the lift produced at a given instant can be calculated using the following equation: **$L = \frac{1}{2}\rho v^2 A C_l$, where L = the lift force, $\frac{1}{2}\rho v^2$** was previously explained, A = the airfoil's area (length multiplied by width), and $C_l$ is the coefficient of lift of the airfoil.

Pilots need to remember that the lifting force on their aircraft is proportional to the density ($\rho$) of air through which they fly (higher altitude = less dense air), the aircraft's speed, and airfoil angle of attack (AOA).

*Conservation of mass*
In the scientific field of fluid dynamics, it has been established that a fluid's mass cannot be created or destroyed within a flow of interest (e.g., airflow in sub-zero temperature conditions). Conservation of mass is mathematically expressed as the mass continuity equation.

*Conservation of momentum*
Momentum, an object's mass times its velocity, cannot be created or destroyed. However, it can be changed through an applied force. Because it involves magnitude and direction, momentum is a vector quantity. It is conserved in all three directions (longitudinally, laterally, and in terms of yaw) simultaneously.

*Venturi Effect*
To understand how a machine with airfoils can take to the air and remain airborne, we need to examine a phenomenon called the Venturi Effect. In the late 18th century, an Italian physicist, Giovanni Battista Venturi, conducted experiments with a pump and an unusual tube. The diameter of one end of the tube was constant, and the circumference of the tube's central portion was smaller. Downstream from the bottleneck, the tube's diameter increased. It was as though someone had squeezed the center of the tube, creating a constriction.

Venturi noticed that as fluids moved through the tube, the flow rate increased (accelerated) and the force (static pressure) against the tube's surface decreased as the diameter became smaller. The opposite phenomenon – reduced flow rate (deceleration) and greater static pressure – happened as the tube diameter downstream of the constriction widened. Venturi published his findings in 1797 and the effect that he observed, measured, and wrote about became associated with his name. It has certainly been integral to aviation since the advent of gliding centuries ago.

If a Venturi tube is cut in half longitudinally, the curvature of the tube wall will look similar to that of an airplane wing's upper surface or the top of helicopter rotor blades. A moving airfoil "slices" the air, forcing molecules to travel along one side or the other. Those moving across the curved side have to travel a greater distance to reach the trailing edge than those moving across the relatively flat side. Consequently, the air molecules moving across the curved surface accelerate, as they did in Venturi's tube, and the static pressure drops.

Because pressure flows from high to low, the static pressure differential experienced between an airfoil's two sides imposes an aerodynamic force acting from the high-pressure (flat) surface to the low-pressure (curved) side. When acting upward, the force is called lift.

*Newton's First Law of Motion*
A stationary object remains at rest and an object in motion continues to move at the same rate (speed) and in the same direction unless acted upon by a force.

*Newton's Second Law of Motion*
Acceleration results from a force being applied to an object. The heavier the body, the greater the amount of force needed to accelerate it.

*Newton's Third Law of Motion*
Sir Isaac Newton (1642–1727) was a brilliant English physicist and mathematician who formulated universal laws of motion, including his third, which said that for every action there is an equal and opposite reaction. Consequently, when an airfoil is deflected up, the airstream flowing over the airfoil reacts by moving downward. Also, when exhaust from jet engines is directed backward the resulting reactive force on the engines, engine pylons, wings, and the rest of the airplane is forward.

### Aircraft axes (pronounced "axe-eez")

Aircraft motion occurs around three axes – longitudinal, lateral, and yaw – that go through the machine's center of gravity. The longitudinal axis has been explained; an aircraft rolls around it. The lateral axis is horizontal and perpendicular to the longitudinal axis; on basic airplane images it is depicted as a straight line going through one wingtip to the other. The yaw axis is vertical; an aircraft is said to yaw (rotate) around it.

### Flight control

When lift = weight and thrust = drag, the aircraft is either stationary on the ground, or aloft in straight-and-level, unaccelerated flight. To make an aircraft accelerate requires an increase in thrust, which the pilot controls from the cockpit by moving one or more throttle controls (on piston aircraft) or power lever(s) on turbine aircraft.

During takeoff, the airplane accelerates along the runway, strip, or body of water and reaches a speed at which it is going fast enough for the wings to generate lift. To make the plane go skyward, the pilot pulls back on the control column, or joystick, which causes (via cables in lighter, smaller aircraft, or a hydraulic system in larger, heavier planes) the hinged elevator to tilt up.

The inclined elevator forces air passing over it to deflect up, resulting in a downward reaction force on the airplane's tail. Because the elevator is aft of the aircraft's center of gravity, the tail drops as the nose of the plane rises and the aircraft climbs.

To make the plane descend, the opposite happens.

To turn an airplane, the pilot moves the control wheel or joystick to the left or right (as desired) to change the machine's direction. The aileron on the wing on the plane's side to where the pilot wants to turn rises into the airstream. This forces the flow upward and reduces the lift produced by the outer portion of the wing where the aileron is located. The result is a wing that drops, rolling (banking) the aircraft.

On the opposite side of the airplane, the aileron moves down into the airstream, deflecting the airflow downward and creating more lift, which causes the wing to rise. With one wing down and the opposite wing up, the airplane rolls to the left or right.

For a coordinated banked turn, the pilot needs to move the aircraft's rudder to the side of the turn (left, right), which is accomplished by pushing on the corresponding pedal in front of him or her. As the pilot does so, the airflow passing over the moved rudder is deflected to the left or right, corresponding to the pushed pedal. The reactive force against the vertical stabilizer is opposite (right, left) and because the tail is aft of the plane's center of gravity, the nose yaws around the yaw axis in the opposite direction (left, right).

## Additional aviation terms and definitions

*Airfoil*: A wing or helicopter blade that generates more lift than drag as air flows over its upper and lower surfaces. A propeller is also an airfoil. Airfoils are carefully designed and can be made of non-metallic materials such as composites.

*Angle of attack*: The angle between the chord line of an airfoil and its direction of motion relative to the air (i.e., the relative wind). AOA is an aerodynamic angle.

*Angle of incidence*: In the context of fixed-wing airplanes, the angle of incidence is the inclination of the wing or tail surface attached to the fuselage relative to an imaginary line that is parallel to the aircraft's longitudinal axis.

*Anhedral angle*: The downward angle of an airplane's wings and tailplane from the horizontal is called the anhedral angle, or negative dihedral angle.

*Attitude*: An aircraft's position relative to its three axes and a reference such as the earth's horizon.

*Center of gravity (CG)*: An aircraft's center of mass, the theoretical point through which the entire weight of the machine is assumed to be concentrated.

*Chord*: The distance between the leading and trailing edges along the chord line is an airfoil's chord. In the case of a tapered airfoil, as viewed from above, the chord at its tip will be different than at its root. Average chord describes the average distance.

*Chord line*: An imaginary straight line from the airfoil's leading (front) edge to its trailing (aft) edge.

*Constant speed propeller*: A controllable-pitch propeller whose angle is automatically changed in flight by a governor in order to maintain a constant number of revolutions per minute (rpm) despite changing aerodynamic loads.

*Controllability*: A measure of an aircraft's response relative to flight control inputs from the pilot.

*Controllable pitch propeller*: A propeller that can be varied in terms of its blade angle by the pilot via a control in the cockpit.

*Coordinated flight*: When the pilot applies flight and power control inputs to prevent slipping or skidding during any aircraft maneuver, the flight is said to be coordinated.

*Critical angle of attack*: The angle of attack at which an airfoil stalls (loses lift) regardless of the aircraft's airspeed, attitude, or weight.

*Dihedral angle*: The upward angle of an airplane's wings and tailplane from the horizontal.

*Dihedral effect*: The amount of roll moment produced per degree of sideslip is called dihedral effect, which is crucial in terms of an aircraft's rolling stability about its longitudinal axis.

*Directional stability*: An aircraft's initial tendency about its yaw (vertical) axis. When an aircraft is disturbed yaw-wise from its equilibrium state due to a gust, for example, and returns to that state (i.e., aligned with the relative wind) because of the aerodynamic effect of the vertical stabilizer, it is said to be directionally stable.

*Downwash*: Air that is deflected perpendicular to an airfoil's motion.

*Drag coefficient*: A dimensionless quantity that represents the drag generated by an airfoil of a particular design.

*Drag curve*: A constructed image of the amount of aircraft drag at different airspeeds.

*Dynamic stability*: Describes the tendency of an aircraft after it has been disturbed from straight-and-level flight to restore the aircraft to its original condition of flying straight and level by developing corrective forces and moments.

*Equilibrium*: In the context of aviation, equilibrium is an aircraft's state when all opposing forces acting on it are balanced, resulting in unaccelerated flight at a constant altitude.

*Feathering Propeller*: A controllable-pitch propeller that can be rotated sufficiently by the pilot (via a control lever in the cockpit connected to a governor in the propeller hub) so that the blade angle is parallel to the line of flight, thereby minimizing propeller drag.

*Forward slip*: A pilot-controlled maneuver where the aircraft's longitudinal axis is inclined to its flight path.

*Glide ratio*: The ratio between altitude lost and distance traversed during non-powered flight (e.g., following an engine failure, in a sailplane).

*Glidepath*: An aircraft path's across the ground while approaching to land.

*Gross weight*: An aircraft's total weight when it is fully loaded with aircrew, fuel, oil, passengers and/or cargo (if applicable), weapons, etc.

*Gyroscopic precession*: The attribute of rotating bodies to manifest movement ninety degrees in the direction of rotation from the point where a force is applied to the spinning body.

*Heading*: The direction in which the aircraft's nose is pointed.

*Inertia*: A body's opposition to a change of motion.

*Internal combustion engine*: A mechanical device that produces power from expanding hot gasses created by burning a fuel-air mixture within the device.

*Lateral stability (rolling)*: An aircraft's initial tendency relative to its longitudinal axis after being disturbed, its designed quality to return to level flight following a disturbance such as a gust that causes one of the aircraft's wings to drop.

*Lift coefficient*: A dimensionless quantity that represents the lift generated by an airfoil of a particular design.

*Lift/drag ratio*: A number that represents an airfoil's efficiency, the ratio of the lift coefficient to the drag coefficient for a specific angle of attack.

*Lift-off*: The act of rising from the earth as a result of airfoils lifting the aircraft above the ground.

*Load factor*: The ratio of load supported by an aircraft's lift-generating airfoils (wings, main rotor blades) to the aircraft's actual weight, including the mass of its contents. Load factor is also known as G-loading ("G" means gravity).

*Longitudinal stability*: An aircraft's initial tendency relative to its lateral axis after being disturbed, its designed quality to return to its trimmed angle of attack after being disrupted due to a wind gust or other factor.

*Maneuverability*: An aircraft's ability to change directions in three axes along its flight path and withstand the associated aerodynamic forces.

*Mean camber line*: An imaginary line between the leading and trailing edges and halfway between the airfoil's upper (curved) and lower (flat) surfaces.

*Minimum drag speed (L/DMAX)*: The point on the total drag curve where total drag is minimized and lift is maximized (i.e., where the lift-to-drag ratio is greatest).

*Nacelle*: An enclosure made of metal or another durable material that covers an aircraft engine.

*Non-symmetrical airfoil (cambered)*: When one surface of an airfoil has a specific curvature that the opposite side does not, the airfoil is described as non-symmetrical, or cambered. The advantage of a non-symmetrical wing, for example, is that it produces lift at an AOA of zero degrees (as long as airflow is moving past the blade). Moreover, the lift-to-drag ratio and stall characteristics of a cambered airfoil are better than those of a symmetrical airfoil. Its disadvantages are center of the pressure movement chord-wise by as much as one-fifth the chord line distance, which causes undesirable airfoil torsion, and greater production costs.

*Normal category*: An airplane intended for non-acrobatic operation that seats a maximum of nine passengers and has a certificated takeoff weight of 12,500 pounds or less.

*Payload*: In the context of aviation, the weight of an aircraft's occupants, cargo, and baggage.

*P-factor (precession factor)*: A propeller-driven aircraft's tendency to yaw to the left when the propeller rotates clockwise (as seen by the pilot) because the descending propeller blade on the right produces more thrust than the ascending blade on the left. If the propeller rotated counter-clockwise, the yaw tendency would be to the right.

*Piston engine*: Also known as a reciprocating engine, it is a heat engine that uses one or more pistons to convert pressure created by expanding, hot gases resulting from a combusted fuel-air mixture, or steam pressure, into a rotating motion.

*Pitch*: An airplane's rotation about its lateral axis, or the angle of a propeller blade as measured from the vertical plane of rotation.

*Power lever*: The cockpit lever connected to a turbine engine's fuel control unit, which changes the amount of fuel entering the combustion chambers.

*Powerplant*: An engine and its accessories (e.g., starter-generator, tachometer drive) and the attached propeller (usually via a gearbox).

*Propeller blade angle*: The angle between the chord of an airplane propeller blade and the propeller's plane of rotation.

*Propeller lever*: The cockpit control that controls propeller speed and angle.

*Propeller slipstream*: Air accelerated behind a spinning propeller.

*Propeller*: A relatively long and narrow blade-like device that produces thrust when it rotates rapidly. In aviation, the term typically includes not only the propeller blades but also the hub and other components that make up the propeller system.

*Rate of turn*: The rate of a turn expressed in degrees per second.

*Reciprocating engine*: An engine that converts heat energy created by combusted fuel mixed with air into reciprocating piston movement, which in turn is converted into a rotary motion via a crankshaft.
*Reduction gear*: A gear or set of gears that turns a propeller at a speed slower than that of the engine.

*Relative wind*: The direction of airflow relative to an airfoil, a stream of air parallel and opposite to an aircraft's flight path.

*Ruddervator*: Two control surfaces on an aircraft's tail that form a "V". When moved together via the control wheel or joystick in the cockpit, the surfaces act as elevators. When the pilot presses his or her foot against one rudder pedal or the other, the ruddervator acts like a conventional plane's rudder.

*Sideslip*: A flight maneuver controlled by the pilot that involves the airplane's longitudinal axis remaining parallel to the original flight path, but the aircraft no longer flies forward, as in normal flight. Instead, the horizontal lift component causes the plane to move laterally toward the low wing.

*Skid*: A flight condition during a turn where the airplane's tail follows a path outside of the path of the aircraft's nose.

*Slip*: A maneuver used by pilots to increase an aircraft's rate of descent or reduce its airspeed, and to compensate for a crosswind during landing. An unintentional slip also occurs when a pilot does not fly the aircraft in a coordinated manner.

*Stability*: An aircraft's inherent tendency to return to its original flight path after a force such as a wind gust disrupts its equilibrium. Aeronautical engineers design most aircraft to be aerodynamically stable.

*Stall*: A rapid decrease in lift caused by an excessive angle of attack and airflow separating from an airfoil's upper surface. An aircraft can stall at any pitch attitude or airspeed.

*Standard-rate turn*: A rate of turn of three degrees per second.

*Subsonic*: Speed below the speed of sound, which varies with altitude.

*Supersonic*: Speed in excess of the speed of sound, which varies with altitude.

*Swept wing*: A wing planform involving the tips being further back than the wing root.

*Symmetrical airfoil*: When an airfoil has identical upper and lower surfaces, it is symmetrical and produces no lift at an AOA of zero degrees. The wings of very high performance aircraft tend to be symmetrical.

*Taxiway lights*: Blue lights installed at taxiway edges.

*Taxiway turnoff lights*: Green lights installed level with the taxiway.

*Throttle*: A mechanical device that meters the amount of fuel-air mixture fed to the engine.

*Thrust line*: An imaginary line through the center of an airplane's propeller hub and perpendicular to the propeller's plane of rotation, or through the center of each jet engine.

*Total aerodynamic force (TAF)*: Two components comprise the total aerodynamic force: lift and drag. The amount of lift and drag produced by an airfoil are primarily determined by its shape and area.

*Torque*: A propeller-driven airplane's tendency to roll in the opposite direction of the propeller's rotation. Some multi-engine airplanes have propellers that rotate in opposite directions to eliminate the torque effect.

*Trailing edge*: The aft part of an airfoil where air that was separated as it hit the wing's front edge and was forced over the upper and lower surfaces come together.

*Transonic*: At the speed of sound, which varies with altitude.

*Trim tab*: A small, hinged control surface on a larger control surface (e.g., aileron, rudder, elevator) that can be adjusted in flight to a position that balances the aerodynamic forces. In still air, a trimmed aircraft in flight requires no control inputs from the pilot to remain straight and level.

*T-tail*: The description for an airplane's tail involving the horizontal stabilizer mounted on the top of the vertical stabilizer.

*Turbulence*: The unsteady flow of a fluid (e.g., air).

*Utility category*: An airplane intended for limited-acrobatic operation that seats a maximum of nine passengers and has a certificated takeoff weight of 12,500 pounds or less.

*Vector*: A force applied in a certain direction. Depicted visually, a vector shows the force's magnitude and direction.

*Velocity*: The rate of movement (e.g., miles per hour, knots) in a certain direction.

*Vertical stability*: An aircraft's designed, inherent behavior relative to its vertical axis, its tendency to return to its former heading after being disturbed by a wind gust or other disruptive force. Also called yawing or directional stability.

*V-tail*: A design involving two slanted tail surfaces that aerodynamically behave similarly to a conventional elevator and rudder, i.e., as horizontal and vertical stabilizers.

*Wing*: An airfoil attached to a fuselage that creates a lifting force when the aircraft has reached a certain speed.

*Wing area*: A wing's total surface, including its control surfaces, and winglets, if so equipped.

*Wing in ground effect (WIG)*: When an aircraft flies at a very low altitude, one roughly equal to its wingspan, it experiences WIG. The effect increases as the airplane descends closer to the surface (runway, land, water) and supports the aircraft on a cushion of air best at an altitude of one half the wing span.

*Winglet*: A surface installed on a wingtip that is angled to the wing and improves its efficiency by smoothing the airflow across the upper wing near the tip and reducing induced drag. Winglets improve an aircraft's lift-to-drag ratio.

*Wing span*: The maximum distance between wingtips.

*Wingtip vortices*: A spinning mass of air generated at a wing's tip created by outward-flowing high pressure air from underneath the wing meeting inward-flowing low air pressure on the wing's upper surface. The intensity of a wing vortex – also referred to as wake turbulence – is dependent on an airplane's weight, speed, and configuration.

*Wing twist*: A wing design feature that improves the effectiveness of aileron control at high angles of attack during an approach to a stall.

# Aviation Information Practice Test

1. A propeller-driven airplane:
   A. Is part of the rotary class of aircraft (because the propeller spins).
   B. Has a reciprocating engine only.
   C. Is a fixed-wing aircraft.
   D. Has a reverse thrust feature in all types of military and civilian aircraft.

2. Military aircraft are categorized:
   A. As normal, utility, acrobatic, special mission, or transport.
   B. Based on the mission they perform.
   C. In accordance with Department of Defense directives since 1947.
   D. None of the above.

3. A propeller is:
   A. An airfoil.
   B. A secondary source of thrust.
   C. Part of a balanced thrust system involving only 2, 4, or 6 blades.
   D. An extendible thrust-generation device used at high altitudes.

4. The four main forces acting on an aircraft are:
   A. Deflection, exponential thrust, torque, and the total mass vector modified by the earth's Coriolis Effect.
   B. Lift, weight, thrust, and drag.
   C. Wind gusts, gravity, pressure differentials, and tangential rotation.
   D. All of the above.

5. Turbine aircraft:
   A. Have a propeller source of thrust in some cases.
   B. Never have a propeller source of thrust (only jets are turbine aircraft).
   C. Have a turbocharged engine.
   D. Utilize a ducted wind fan that spins an electrical generator.

6. The empennage consists of:
   A. A vertical stabilizer and a hinged rudder.
   B. The back half of the fuselage and the tailplane.
   C. The "T" tail and nacelle.
   D. The ruddervator and associated hydraulic system.

7. Flaps are used:
   A. To decrease Dutch roll.
   B. To eliminate wingtip vortices.
   C. During takeoff only.
   D. None of the above.

8. Hinged wing panels that move upward and destroy lift after landing are called:
   A. Air brakes.
   B. Spoilers.
   C. Winglets.
   D. Vertical stabilizers.

9. Swept back wings:
   A.   Delay the drag associated with air compressibility at approach speeds.
   B.   Delay the drag associated with air compressibility at low subsonic speeds.
   C.   Delay the drag associated with air compressibility at high subsonic speeds.
   D.   All of the above.

10. Profile drag is the sum of:
    A. Skin friction and form drag.
    B. Skin friction and induced drag.
    C. Form drag and supplementary drag.
    D. Parasite drag and vortex drag.

11. Slats are located:
    A. Along the horizontal stabilizer's leading edge.
    B. Along the leading edge of both wings and the horizontal stabilizer.
    C. Along the trailing edge of the right aileron.
    D. Along the leading edge of both wings.

12. The laws of conservation that pertain to aircraft are:
    A. The law of conservation of mass, kinetic energy, and fluid flow.
    B. The law of conservation of mass, torque, and potential energy.
    C. The law of conservation of weight, thrust, and lift.
    D. The law of conservation of mass, energy, and momentum.

13. According to 18th century Swiss scientist Daniel Bernoulli:
    A. Accelerated fluid flow results in a decrease of dynamic pressure.
    B. Accelerated fluid flow results in a decrease of static pressure.
    C. Accelerated fluid flow results in an increase of total system energy.
    D. All of the above.

14. Lift produced by an airfoil is proportional to:
    A. The rate of air compressibility and the coefficients of lift and drag.
    B. The angle of airflow deflection, the relative wind's vertical vector component, and the reduction of induced drag as the aircraft accelerates.
    C. Air density, aircraft speed, wing area, and airfoil shape.
    D. None of the above.

15. The angle of attack is:
    A. The chord line's orientation in relation to the aircraft's longitudinal axis.
    B. The acute angle between the chord line of an airfoil and the relative wind.
    C. The sum of the angle of incidence of the wings and tailplane.
    D. The aircraft's downward inclination when shooting targets on the ground.

16. Parasite drag is produced by:
    A. Extended slats and flaps.
    B. Aircraft parts that do not contribute to producing lift.
    C. Improperly set trim tabs.
    D. A difference in propeller rpm on multi-engine airplanes.

17. Thrust opposes:
    A. Drag.
    B. Rudder deflection.
    C. Gyroscopic precession.
    D. Gravity.

18. Ailerons move:
    A. In opposing directions.
    B. Downward.
    C. Up or down, depending on the rudder pedal pushed by the pilot.
    D. None of the above.

19. The main types of turbine propulsion are:
    A. Axial and centrifugal flow.
    B. Non-afterburning, after-burning, and turbocharged.
    C. Turbofan, turbojet, and turboprop.
    D. Turbocharged, turbofan, and ramjet.

20. An aircraft's three axes are:
    A. Longitudinal, gyroscopic, and lateral.
    B. Directional, pitch, and gyroscopic.
    C. Yaw, longitudinal, and lateral.
    D. Deflectional, lateral, and induced.

21. Increasing an aircraft's bank in a coordinated turn, _____ its _____ and _____:

    A. increases; angle of attack; lift.
    B. increases; weight (due to "G" loading); rate of turn.
    C. decreases; angle of attack; drag.
    D. decreases; weight (due to "G" loading); angle of attack.

22. When the pilot pulls back on the control column or joystick:
    A. The elevator moves up.
    B. The elevator moves down.
    C. The left aileron moves down.
    D. None of the above.

23. To move the rudder to the right, the pilot:
    A. Turns the control wheel to the right.
    B. Pulls back on the right power lever.
    C. Moves the right throttle lever forward while pushing the right pedal.
    D. Pushes the right pedal.

24. From a physics perspective, an aircraft's total weight force is deemed to act through the _____:
    A. Weight and balance reference datum.
    B. Center of pressure.
    C. Center of gravity.
    D. Center of momentum.

25. An air vortex at the wingtip creates:
    A. Form drag.
    B. Profile drag.
    C. Induced drag.
    D. Parasite drag.

26. Momentum is:
    A. An object's mass times its velocity squared.
    B. An object's mass times its velocity.
    C. An object's weight plus one-half of its velocity squared.
    D. An object's forward velocity times its coefficient of lift.

27. When exhaust from jet engines is directed backward, the resulting reactive force on the airplane is _____:
    A. Forward.
    B. Forward but deflected downward due to the angle of incidence.
    C. Forward but reduced because of the inclined component of the total drag vector.
    D. Determined only by using the conservation of energy equation.

28. Coordinated flight is defined as:
    A. The pilot applying control inputs that are suitable for the aircraft's density altitude.
    B. The pilot applying flight and power control inputs to prevent slipping or skidding during any aircraft maneuver.
    C. The pilot reducing back pressure on the control column or joystick while turning in the opposite direction of the horizontal component of total drag.
    D. All of the above.

29. Anhedral angle is the _____ angle of an airplane's wings and tailplane from the horizontal:
    A. Upward.
    B. Obtuse.
    C. Downward.
    D. Isoceles.

30. Minimum drag speed corresponds to:
    A. The point on the total drag curve where the thrust-to-drag ratio is least.
    B. The point on the total drag curve where the drag-to-mass ratio is least.
    C. The point on the total drag curve where the lift-to-drag ratio is greatest.
    D. The point on the total drag curve where the lift-to-weight ratio is least.

31. An airfoil stalls when:
    A. The downward component of the wingtip vortices are greater than the lift produced by increasing the angle of attack.
    B. There is a rapid decrease in lift caused by an excessive angle of attack and airflow separating from an airfoil's upper surface.
    C. The pilot has mistakenly extended the flaps while flying above the maneuvering airspeed ($V_a$).
    D. The pilot deploys the air brakes.

32. A propeller with a blade angle that can be changed by the pilot is called a _____ propeller.
    A. dynamic
    B. rotational
    C. reverse thrust
    D. controllable

33. The attribute of rotating bodies to manifest movement ninety degrees in the direction of rotation from the point where a force is applied to the spinning body is called:
    A. Rotational precession.
    B. Dynamic precession.
    C. Induced precession.
    D. Gyroscopic precession.

34. An aircraft's initial tendency relative to its longitudinal axis after being disturbed and dropping a wing to return to level flight is known as:
    A. Lateral stability.
    B. Longitudinal stability.
    C. Directional stability.
    D. None of the above.

35. An imaginary line from an airfoil's leading edge to its trailing edge that is halfway between the airfoil's upper and lower surfaces is the:
    A. Mean camber line.
    B. Chord line.
    C. Angle of incidence.
    D. Elevator inclination line.

36. When one surface of an airfoil has a specific curvature that the opposite side does not have, the airfoil is described as:
    A. Non-cambered.
    B. Deflected.
    C. Non-symmetrical.
    D. Laterally torqued.

37. The phenomenon of a propeller-driven aircraft's tendency to yaw to the left when the propeller rotates clockwise (as seen by the pilot) because the descending propeller blade on the right produces more thrust than the ascending blade on the left is known as:
    A. Asymmetric thrust.
    B. Rotational precession.
    C. P-factor (precession factor).
    D. Directional instability.

38. Airflow parallel and opposite to an aircraft's flight path is called the:
    A. Relative wind.
    B. Longitudinal wind.
    C. Dynamic wind.
    D. None of the above.

39. The speed of sound varies with:
    A. Angle of attack.
    B. Angle of inclination.
    C. Induced drag.
    D. Altitude.

40. A propeller-driven airplane tends to roll in the opposite direction of the propeller's rotation because of:
    A. The induced plane of rotation.
    B. Tangential drag.
    C. Torque.
    D. Angular momentum.

# Aviation Information Practice Test Answer Key

| | |
|---|---|
| 1. C | 21. B |
| 2. B | 22. A |
| 3. A | 23. D |
| 4. B | 24. C |
| 5. A | 25. C |
| 6. A | 26. B |
| 7. D | 27. A |
| 8. B | 28. B |
| 9. C | 29. C |
| 10. A | 30. C |
| 11. D | 31. B |
| 12. D | 32. D |
| 13. B | 33. D |
| 14. C | 34. A |
| 15. B | 35. A |
| 16. B | 36. C |
| 17. A | 37. C |
| 18. A | 38. A |
| 19. C | 39. D |
| 20. C | 40. C |

## Chapter 9: General Science

The AFOQT General Science test measures your knowledge of the life sciences (plant and animal biology, human physiology), the earth and space sciences (geology, meteorology, oceanography, astronomy), and the physical sciences (physics and chemistry). You'll be asked 20 questions with a 10-minute time limit. Don't panic! You only need to know those basics learned through about the 11th grade. Of course, you aren't going to be able to cover eleven years of schooling in one book – but this chapter will refresh your memory on those fundamental principles of science required, ensuring that you do well. This is a long chapter since there are so many different aspects that each has to be covered. For this reason, we have included 29 Practice Drills – one at the end of each section – in lieu of one practice test, to help you better prepare for such a broad section.

SCIENTIFIC REASONING
To understand science, it is important to recognize the framework of scientific reasoning and the role in plays in all of the scientific fields we will cover in this guide.

### Scientific Investigations

A theory and a hypothesis are both important aspects of science. There is a common misconception that they are one and the same, which is not true; however the two are very similar. A **hypothesis** is a proposed explanation for a phenomenon; it's usually based on observations or previous research. A **theory** is an explanation for a phenomenon that has been thoroughly tested and is accepted to be true by the scientific community.

Although science can never really "prove" something, it does provide a means to answering many questions about our natural world. Scientists use different types of investigations, each providing different types of results, based upon what they are trying to find. There are three main types of scientific investigations: descriptive, experimental, and comparative.

**Descriptive investigations** start with observations. A model is then constructed to provide a visual of what was seen: a description. Descriptive investigations do not generally require hypotheses, as they usually just attempt to find more information about a relatively unknown topic. **Experimental investigations**, on the other hand, usually involve a hypothesis. These experiments are sometimes referred to as controlled experiments because they are performed in a controlled environment. During experimental investigations, all variables are controlled except for one: the dependent variable, which is part of the hypothesis being tested. Often, there are many tests involved in this process. Lastly, **comparative investigations** involve manipulating different groups in order to compare them with each other. There is no control during comparative investigations.

**The Scientific Method**

In order to ensure that experimental and comparative investigations are thorough and accurate, scientists use the scientific method, which has five main steps:

1. Observe and ask questions: look at the natural world to observe and ask questions about patterns and anomalies you see.

2. Gather information: look at what other scientists have done to see where your questions fit in with current research.

3. Construct a hypothesis: make a proposal that explains why or how something happens.

4. Experiment and test your hypothesis: set up an experimental investigation that allows you to test your hypothesis.

5. Analyze results and draw conclusions: examine your results and see whether they disprove your hypothesis. Note that you can't actually "prove" a hypothesis; you can only provide evidence to support it.

**Systems**

A **system** is set of interacting parts that work together to form an integrated whole. Many scientific disciplines study systems: doctors, for example, study organ systems like the respiratory system, which is made up of interacting parts that allow animals to breathe. Similarly, ecologists might look at all the plants and animals that interact in a specific area, and chemists might look at a set of chemicals interacting in a beaker.

While obviously different, all these systems share some common traits. We'll use the respiratory system to look at the important characteristics of systems.

- All systems have a structure. (The respiratory system is highly organized.)
- All systems perform an action. (The respiratory system allows animals to breathe.)
- All systems have interacting parts. (The respiratory system is made up of many interacting parts, including the lungs, blood vessels, and bronchial tubes.)
- All systems have boundaries. (We can separate structures that are part of the respiratory system from those that are not.)
- Systems may receive input and produce output. (The respiratory system brings oxygen into the body and gets rid of carbon dioxide.)
- The processes in a system may be controlled by feedback. (The action of breathing is controlled in part by how much oxygen and carbon dioxide are in the body.)

Sometimes larger systems are made of smaller, independent systems called **subsystems**. For example, a body cell is made of many organelles. These organelles each perform their own tasks, which together support the system of the cell.

We will be examining some important systems within the fields of biology, physiology, chemistry, physics, geology, meteorology, astronomy, and other related scientific fields in this guide. We will begin with biology.

**General Biology**

**Biological Molecules**
There are four main classes of organic molecules (molecules that contain carbon) found in living organisms: carbohydrates, lipids, proteins, and nucleic acids. These molecules facilitate the use of energy and transfer of information that make life possible. Most of the molecules are larger polymers made out of smaller molecules called **monomers**.

**Carbohydrates**, also called sugars or saccharides, consist of only hydrogen, oxygen, and carbon atoms; they are the most abundant single class of organic substances found in nature. The simplest carbohydrates are **monosaccharides** such as glucose, which the body uses in cellular respiration. Monosaccharides can be combined to form **disaccharides**, such as lactose, and **polysaccharides** like glycogen. These molecules provide a number of important functions: they store energy for cellular processes, act as structural components in plant cells and form the backbone of nucleic acids (see below).

**Lipids**, commonly known as fats, serve two main functions: they store energy and act as a protective cushion for vital organs. Lipids also combine with other molecules to form essential compounds, such as phospholipids, which make up the membranes around cells. Lipids also combine with other molecules to create hormones like estrogen and testosterone.

**Proteins** are large molecules that perform a wide variety of functions in the human body: they act as enzymes, transport other molecules and transmit information between cells, among many other tasks. The monomers that are combined to form proteins are called **amino acids**. Proteins have a four-level structure that makes each one unique:

1. primary: the sequence of amino acids
2. secondary: local, repeating structures created by the hydrogen bonds between amino acids
3. tertiary: the overall structure (or folding) of the protein created by the many interactions that take place between the atoms of the protein
4. quaternary: the structure formed by several protein molecules joined to form a protein complex.

**Nucleic acids** are large molecules made up of monomers called **nucleotides**. The main role of nucleic acids is to encode, transmit, and express the code required to produce proteins. **DNA (deoxyribonucleic acid)** stores this genetic code, while the various types of **RNA (ribonucleic acid)** help express that code.

# Practice Drill: Biological Molecules

1. Which of the following elements is NOT found in carbohydrates?
A)      carbon
B)      hydrogen
C)      oxygen
D)      sulfur

2. Amino acids are to proteins as
A)      carbohydrates are to glucose
B)      nucleotides are to nucleic acids
C)      lipids are to energy
D)      DNA is to RNA

3. Lipids are commonly known as:
A)      fats
B)      sugars
C)      enzymes
D)      proteins

Answers: 1) **D**  2) **B**  3) **A**

## Metabolism

All cellular processes require energy. For the body to breathe, circulate blood, control body temperature, move muscles, digest food, and process information, cells need to access the energy in chemical bonds. The set of chemical reactions that allow cells to access and use this energy is called **metabolism**. There are two general types of metabolism. In **catabolism**, energy is harvested from chemical bonds; in **anabolism**, that energy is used to produce new molecules.

### Respiration

**Respiration** is the catabolic process that cells use to harvest energy from the carbohydrate glucose. Glucose molecules go through a number of transformations that result in the production of **adenine triphosphate (ATP),** the main energy source for cells. The process also produces carbon dioxide and water as waste products, as shown in the equation below:

$$C_6H_{12}O_6 + 6O_2 \rightarrow 6CO_2 + 6H_2O + energy$$

This equation describes **aerobic respiration**, which requires that oxygen atoms act as electron receptors at the end of the **electron transport chain (ETC),** the step in respiration that produces the most ATP. In **anaerobic respiration**, other acceptors such as sulfate or nitrate are used in place of oxygen and less energy (ATP) is produced.

Yet another type of respiration, **fermentation**, takes place without the use of the electron transport chain. It can take place in both anaerobic and aerobic environments although it is more commonly used only when oxygen is not available for us in the ETC. For example, during exercise when muscles use up all the available oxygen, muscle cells use lactic acid fermentation to acquire energy. Yeast cells, on the other hand, will use fermentation even in the presence of oxygen.

### Photosynthesis

So where does the energy stored in the bonds of glucose come from? Glucose is made during the anabolic process of **photosynthesis**, which takes place in plants as well as in some protists and monerans. In photosynthesis, cells use energy from sunlight to turn carbon dioxide and water into glucose while producing oxygen as a waste product:

$$CO_2 + H_2O \rightarrow C_6H_{12}O_6 + O_2$$

Photosynthesis takes place in organelles called **chloroplasts**. Within the chloroplasts are molecules called **chlorophylls**; when sunlight strikes a chlorophyll molecule, one of its electrons is stimulated into a higher energy state. This higher-energy electron then passes that energy onto other electrons in other molecules, creating a chain that eventually results in glucose. Chlorophyll absorbs energy from red and blue light, but not green; green light is reflected off of plants, which is why plants appear green to us.

# Practice Drill: Metabolism

1. Plants appear green because chlorophyll:
A)    absorbs green light
B)    reflects red light
C)    absorbs blue light
D)    reflects green light

2. The compound that absorbs light energy during photosynthesis is:
A)    chloroform
B)    chlorofluorocarbon
C)    chlorinated biphenyls
D)    chlorophyll

3. What is the name of the sugar molecule produced during photosynthesis?
A)    chlorophyll
B)    glycogen
C)    glucose
D)    fructose

4. During aerobic respiration, the majority of ATP is produced by
A)    the electron transport chain
B)    the nucleus
C)    the chloroplast
D)    fermentation

Answers: 1) **D**  2) **D**  3) **C**  4) **A**

## Classification of Organisms

All of Earth's organisms have characteristics that distinguish them from one another. Scientists have systems to organize and classify all of Earth's organisms based on those characteristics; in fact, there's a whole branch of biology called **taxonomy** that's devoted to defining related groups of organisms. It should be noted that the system described below is not set in stone. As taxonomists discover new genetic techniques and learn more about the evolutionary relationships between organisms, taxonomic categories will continue to evolve as well.

### Levels of Classification

The biological classification system groups together organisms into eight levels based on organisms' shared characteristics and evolutionary history: domain, kingdom, phylum, class, order, family, genus, and species. As we move down the chain, characteristics become more specific, and the number of organisms in each group decrease.

Domains are the broadest biological classification. All life on earth can be placed in one of three *domains*: Archaea, Bacteria, and Eukaryota. The first two domains are prokaryotic microorganisms; the third contains all eukaryotic and multi-celled life. Each *taxon* below a domain includes smaller groups of increasingly closely related organisms until *species*, which is a single organism (except in the case of species that are further divided into sub-species).

Organisms are identified using a system called **binomial nomenclature**, which gives the (usually Latin) genus and species name of the organism (and sub-species if relevant). For example, humans are in the genus *Homo,* and our species name is *sapien*, so we are identified as *Homo sapiens*. Grizzly bears, which are a sub-species, are identified as *Ursus arctos horribilis.*

### Eukaryotic Kingdoms

Organisms in the domain Eukaryota are grouped into several kingdoms. The exact number and classification are often in dispute among scientists, but the four most commonly used kingdoms are described below. (The other two domains have one kingdom each, for a total of six kingdoms across all three domains).

The **Animal Kingdom** (Animalia) contains heterotrophic (meaning they eat for energy), multicellular organisms. Those heterotrophs that eat only plants are called herbivores; those that kill and eat other animals for food are called carnivores, and still other animals eat both plants and other animals—they are called omnivores.

The organisms in the Animal Kingdom have nervous tissue that has developed into nervous systems and brains; they are also able to move from place to place using muscular systems. The Animal Kingdom is divided into two groups: **vertebrates** (with backbones) and **invertebrates** (without backbones).

As you can guess from its name, the **Plant Kingdom** (Plantae) contains all plant life. Plants are autotrophic (meaning they produce their own food using photosynthesis), mostly multicellular organisms. Their cells are notable not only because they contain chloroplasts, but also because they have **cell walls**. There are a few organisms included in the Plant Kingdom which are not multicellular—certain types of algae which, while not multicellular, have cells with a nucleus. These algae also contain chlorophyll.

Except for algae, plants are divided into one of two groups: vascular plants (most crops, trees, and flowering plants) and nonvascular plants (mosses). **Vascular plants** have specialized tissue that allows them to transport water and nutrients from their roots to their leaves, and back again, even if they are several hundred feet tall. **Nonvascular plants** cannot do this, and, therefore, remain very small in size. Vascular plants can grow in both wet and dry environments; whereas nonvascular plants, since they are unable to transport water, are usually found only in wet, marshy areas.

The **Fungi Kingdom** contains organisms that share some similarities with plants but also have other characteristics that make them more animal-like. For example, they resemble animals in that they lack chlorophyll, meaning they cannot perform photosynthesis. They reproduce by spores, like some plants, and have cell walls, although their chemical composition is different from that of plants.

The bodies of fungi are made of filaments called **hyphae**, which in turn create the tissue **mycelium**. The most well-known examples of organisms in this Kingdom are mushrooms, yeasts, and molds.

The **Protista Kingdom** includes single-celled organisms that contain a nucleus. They are considered a simple cell, but still contain multiple structures and accomplish many functions. This Kingdom includes organisms such as paramecium, ameba, and slime molds. They often move around using hair-like structures called **cilia** or tail-like **flagellums**.

# Practice Drill: Classification of Organisms

1. Which of the following has the classification levels in the correct order, from most general to most specific?
A)      domain, kingdom, phylum, class, order, family, genus, species
B)      order, family, genus, species, class, phylum, kingdom, domain
C)      domain, species, genus, family, order, class, phylum, kingdom
D)      domain, kingdom, phylum, class, species, genus, family, order

2. Some members of the _____ have cell walls but do not perform photosynthesis.
A)      Animal Kingdom
B)      Plant Kingdom
C)      Fungi Kingdom
D)      Monera Kingdom

3. Which of the following kingdom's members are multicellular AND autotrophic?
A)      Fungi
B)      Animalia
C)      Protista
D)      Plantae

4. Which of the following kingdom's members has tissue called hyphae?
A)      Fungi
B)      Animalia
C)      Protista
D)      Plantae

5. Single-celled organisms with no nucleus belong to the domain
A)      Archaea
B)      Bacteria
C)      Eukaryota
D)      Archaea or Bacteria

Answers: 1) **A**  2) **C**  3) **D**  4) **A**  5) **D**

## Animals

Animals are multi-celled and unable to produce their own food internally, just like plants. As mentioned previously, the Animal Kingdom is divided into two large groupings: the **invertebrates** and **vertebrates.**

**Invertebrates** are multicellular organisms that lack a backbone or cell walls, reproduce sexually, and are heterotrophic. They make up approximately 97% of the animal population.

**Vertebrates**, on the other hand, have well-developed internal skeletons, highly developed brains, an outer, protective cellular skin, and an advanced nervous system. They make up the remaining 3% of the animals.

### What Is an Animal?

All animals, from sponges to human beings, share some fundamental characteristics. One such characteristic is cellular division. At the beginning of reproduction, an egg is fertilized and then undergoes several cell divisions (cleavages); this process quickly produces a cluster of cells. Cell division continues through many distinct stages before finally resulting in an embryo. The full, multi-celled organism then develops tissues and organ systems, eventually developing into its adult form.

All multicellular animals must come up with solutions to several basic problems:

- **Surface-area-to-volume issues**: Nutrients, air, and water must be able to enter an animal's body in order to sustain life. The surface area of an animal's body must be large enough to allow a sufficient amount of these elements to be consumed by the organism. In single-celled organisms, the cell size is limited to the amount of nutrients able to pass through the cell membrane to support the cell. In multi-celled organisms, specialized tissues and organ systems with very large surface areas bring in the necessary elements and then carry them to the cells. Those specialized tissues are found in the respiratory system, urinary system, excretory system, and the digestive system. These tissues and organs, along with the circulatory system, are able to support a large-sized body.

- **Body support and protection**: All animals have some form of support and protection in the form of their internal or external skeletal systems. These skeletal systems provide support for the animal's body and protect the internal organs from damage.

- **Mobility**: Animals are heterotrophs and must acquire food; this need, along with the need to mate and reproduce, requires the animal to move. Although plants move, they are considered stationary because they are rooted. Animals, on the other hand, move from place to place; this is called **locomotion.** Locomotion requires a muscular system. Muscles are found only in animals; they are not present in plants, fungi, or single-celled microorganisms.

- **Sensory integration**: Animals have many specialized sensory organs: eyes, ears, noses, etc. These organs make animals aware of the environment and give them the ability to respond to environmental stimuli. The integration and coordination of sense organs with other bodily functions requires an organized collection of specialized nervous tissue, known as a **central nervous system** (CNS).

**A Few Animal Phyla**

**Phylum Porifera**: Groups of individual cells that lack tissues or organs, a nervous system, or skeleton. Example include: sponges.

**Phylum Coelenterata**: Bodies symmetrical in a circular fashion with rudimentary organs and systems, but no skeleton. Examples include: coral, jellyfish, and sea anemones.

**Phylum Echinodermata**: Bodies have circular symmetry with five body parts arranged around a central axis. They have calcium spines or plates just under the skin. Examples include: sea stars and sea urchins.

**Phylum Mollusca**: These creatures have circulatory, nervous, and digestive systems that are well-developed; some, such as octopuses, also have well-developed brains. Examples include: octopi, snails, and clams.

**Phylum Arthropoda**: This phylum has more species than the other phyla. They have exoskeletons, and most undergo **metamorphosis** (a physical transformation that is a part of the growth process). Many have special body parts such as antennae or pinchers. Examples include: spiders, insects, and crustaceans.

**Phylum Chordata:** All animals from this group share four characteristics: a notochord that develops into a vertebral column in vertebrate animals, a nerve cord that runs along the spinal column, gills in development at some point, and a tail or vestigial tail (humans have a tailbone). : Examples include: mammals, birds, amphibians, reptiles, and fish.

# Practice Drill: Animals

1. Multicellular animals have developed respiratory and excretory systems to overcome which of the following issues?
    A) Weight versus mass.
    B) Surface-area-to-volume.
    C) Height to weight.
    D) Mass to volume.

2. The two categories of animals are:
    A) Single-celled and multi-celled.
    B) Autotrophic and heterotrophic.
    C) Those that live in water and those that live on land.
    D) Vertebrate and invertebrate.

3. Jellyfish and coral are related to:
    A) Octopi.
    B) Sea anemones.
    C) Sea urchins.
    D) Sponges.

4. Humans are classified under which of the following Phyla?
    A) Echinodermata.
    B) Chordata.
    C) Mollusca.
    D) Platyhelminthes.

Answers: 1) **B**  2) **D**  3) **B**  4) **B**

## Plants

Organisms within Kingdom Plantae are very diverse, but they usually share certain characteristics that make them recognizable as plants. Chlorophyll ensures that some, if not all, of a plants body will have a green color, and their root systems render plants incapable of locomotion. Remember photosynthesis? Plants are autotrophs; they create their own food through photosynthesis, which turns carbon dioxide and water into sugars and oxygen gas. This process takes place using chlorophyll in structures called **chloroplasts**. Plants also have hard cell walls made of the carbohydrate **cellulose**.

### Diverse Environments and Plants

Plants are found in nearly every place on Earth. Since plants need light to photosynthesize, their ability to survive in different environments depends upon their access to sources of light. Water is also an important part of a plant's growth and development, partly because the water contained within plant cells (by the cell wall) provide a plant with structure and support.

Land plants evolved from algae into two large groups: **bryophytes** (nonvascular plants) and **tracheophytes** (vascular plants).

### Tracheophytes

These plants have tubes (vessels) which provide both support and a means of transporting water and nutrients throughout their bodies. This support enables them to grow much larger than bryophytes.

The tracheophyte group is further broken down into two types: **seedless** and **seeded** vascular plants.

> **Seedless** vascular plants require moist environments because they need water to reproduce. Millions of years ago, seedless plants dominated the Earth; you can see many of them still today, such as club mosses, horsetails, and ferns.

> **Seeded** vascular plants have become dominant today because they have developed a reproductive system that includes pollen and seeds. In response to harsh and dangerous conditions, plants have developed **pollen** as a structure to protect sperm cells until they can safely reach the female part of a flower. Another structure that protects plants against the environment is a seed. **Seeds** contain and protect an immature plant in a state of dormancy until conditions are favorable. They then germinate and form a new plant.

> Since plants cannot transport themselves (remember: no locomotion), they depend on dispersal systems to establish themselves in new areas. Many systems help distribute seeds, including wind, water, and animals.

Seeded vascular plants are divided into two groups: **gymnosperms** and **angiosperms**.

**Gymnosperms** are seeded vascular plants that do not flower. They include plants such as pines, spruce, and cypresses. Gymnosperms are adapted to cold, dry areas. They have very thin, small leaves covered with a waterproof layer that keeps them from drying out; additionally, a biological antifreeze in their sap keeps them from freezing. Gymnosperms retain green leaves year-round and produce seeds in cones.

**Angiosperms** are seeded vascular plants that *do* form flowers. These plants have thrived. They dominate the Earth and are highly diverse, largely because they have developed flowers, fruits, and broad leaves.

> **Broad leaves** capture more sunlight and, therefore, produce more food than the narrow, thin leaves of the gymnosperms can produce.

> **Flowers** are the place in plants where sperm and egg cells are produced – they contain both the male and female sexual parts. A flower is designed to attract animals, which is why their structures are so colorful and fragrant. Animals assist in the pollination process by carrying pollen and other seeds to diverse locations; the animal often receives a "reward" from the plant in the form of nectar or pollen. Bees, for example, receive nectar and pollen for food from flowering plants.

> **Fruits** contain the fully developed seed of flowering seed plants. Animals are attracted to the plant, eat the fruit, and then disperse the seeds.

## Bryophytes

Quite different from tracheophytes, bryophytes lack roots, leaves and stems. Instead, structures called **rhizoids** (root-like hairs) absorb water and nutrients. Since they do not have a tubular system with which to move water throughout their bodies, bryophytes rely on diffusion to distribute water and nutrients. This process is slow, and not efficient enough to support large bodies, so bryophytes cannot grow very large. The largest types of bryophytes are liverworts and mosses.

# Practice Drill: Plants

1. Which of the following characteristics is NOT a characteristic of plants?
   A) They are able to engage in locomotion by moving from place to place.
   B) They use chlorophyll contained in chloroplasts.
   C) They produce sugars and oxygen.
   D) They use carbon dioxide and water in photosynthesis.

2. Which of the following is a bryophyte?
   A) Horsetail.
   B) Fern.
   C) Liverwort.
   D) Spruce tree.

3. Which plant group currently dominates the Earth in terms of quantity over other plant groups?
   A) Gymnosperms.
   B) Bryophytes.
   C) Seedless vascular plants.
   D) Angiosperms.

4. "Tracheophytes" is another name for:
   A) Nonvascular plants.
   B) Angiosperm plants.
   C) Gymnosperm plants.
   D) Vascular plants.

5. Rhizoids are similar to _____ in vascular plants?
   A) Leaves
   B) Chloroplasts
   C) Roots
   D) Stems

Answers: 1) **A**  2) **C**  3) **D**  4) **D**  5) **C**

## Ecology

### Biosphere and Biome

Life is possible due to the presence of air (**atmosphere**), water (**hydrosphere**), and soil (**lithosphere**). These factors interact with each other and the life on Earth to create an environment called a **biosphere**. The biosphere contains all of Earth's living organisms. Smaller living systems called **biomes** exist in large areas, both on land and in water; they are defined by the physical characteristics of the environment which they encompass, and by the organisms living within it.

### Ecosystem

Ecosystems are communities comprised of living and non-living things working in symbiosis. Ecosystems do not have a defined size; from large lakes and deserts to small trees or puddles. Everything in the natural world – water, water temperature, plants, animals, air, light, soil, etc. – all form ecosystems.

The physical environment of an ecosystem includes soils, weather, climate, the topography (or shape) of the land, and many other factors. If there isn't enough light or water within an ecosystem, or if the soil doesn't have the right nutrients, plants will die. If plants die, the animals that depend on them will die. If the animals are depending upon the plants die, any other animals depending upon those animals will also die. Regardless of the type of ecosystem they are in, all organisms – even microscopic ones – are affected by each other and their physical surroundings.

There are two components of an ecosystem. The **biotic** (biological) component includes the living organisms; nonliving factors – such as water, minerals, and sunlight – are collectively known as the **abiotic** (non-biological) component. While all ecosystems have different organisms and/or abiotic factors, they all have two primary features:

1. **Energy flows in one direction**. Beginning in the form of chemical bonds from photosynthetic organisms, like green plants or algae, energy flows first to the animals that eat the plants, then to other animals.

2. **Inorganic materials are recycled.** When taken up from the environment through living organisms, inorganic minerals are returned to the environment – mainly via decomposers such as bacteria and fungi. Other organisms called **detritivores** (such as pill bugs, sow bugs, millipedes, and earthworms), help break down large pieces of organic matter into smaller pieces that are handled then by the decomposers.

But since that's a lot of information to take in at once, here's a simple and complete definition of an ecosystem: a combination of biotic and abiotic components, through which energy flows and inorganic material is recycled.

### An Organism's Niche

The area in which an organism lives – and therefore acquires the many things needed to sustain their lives – is called a **habitat.** An organism's role within its community, how it affects its habitat and how it is affected by its habitat, are the factors that define the organism's **niche**. A niche is an organism's role within a community.

For instance, birds and squirrels both coexist in a tree habitat; however, they eat different foods, have different living arrangements, and have different food-gathering abilities. Therefore, the do not occupy the same niche.

---

### THE ECOLOGICAL ORDER OF LIFE

**Biosphere** - All ecosystems on the planet make up the biosphere.

**Ecosystem** – Large community of numerous communities, and the physical non-living environment.

**Community** - A group of populations in a given area.

**Population** - A group of organisms of the same species in a given area.

**Organism** - A living thing.

**Organ Systems** - A group of organs that perform certain functions to form an organism.

**Organs** - A group of tissues that perform a certain function to form organ systems.

**Tissues** - A group of cells that perform certain functions to form an organ.

**Cells** - The building blocks of life which form tissues.

**Organelles** - Small parts of cells that have specific functions.

---

One of the most important relationships among organisms exists between predators and their prey. You may have heard of this relationship described through **food chains** and **food webs**.

**Food Chains** represent the flow of energy obtained from the chemical breakdown of food molecules. When one animal (the predator) consumes another (the prey), the chemical bonds making up the tissues of the prey's body are broken down by the predator's digestive system. This digestive process releases energy and smaller chemical molecules that the predator's body uses to make more tissue. Prior to being the consumed, the prey obtains energy from foods for its own life processes.

Here's a basic example of a food chain:

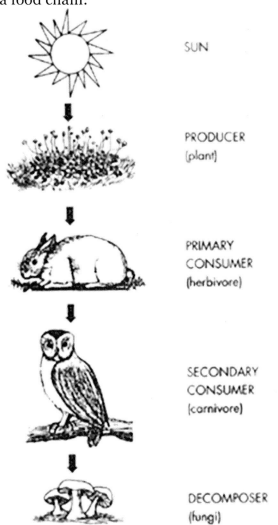

Food chains are a part of **food webs**, which offer a more complex view of energy transfer. They include more organisms, taking into account more than one predator-prey relationship. Each step along a food chain, or within a food web, is called a **trophic** (or feeding) level. Organisms at that first trophic level are known as **primary producers** and are always photosynthetic organisms, whether on land or in water.

At the second trophic level, herbivores (referred to as **primary consumers**) eat plants to produce the energy needed for their metabolism. A large portion of the energy that transfers from the first trophic level to the second level is not transformed into tissue. Instead, it is used for the digestive process, locomotion, and is lost as heat. As you move from one trophic level to another, it is estimated that roughly 10% of the available energy is transformed into body tissue at the next level up.

---

[1] Graphic from: http://www.king.portlandschools.org

The following is an example of a food web:

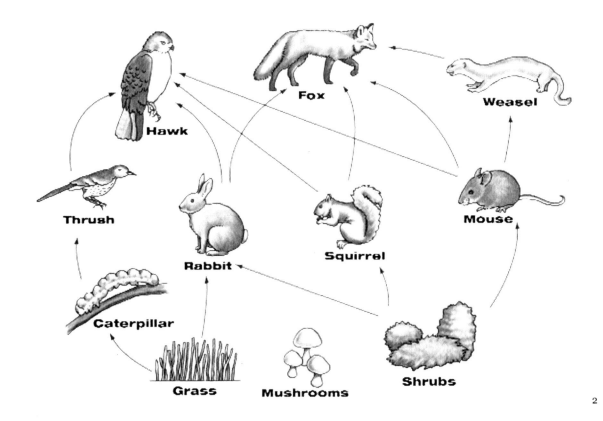

² Graphic from: http://www.education.com

# Practice Drill: Ecology

1. Ecology is the study of organisms interacting with:
   A) The physical environment only.
   B) The internal environment only.
   C) The physical environment and each other.
   D) Each other and the internal environment.

2. In terms of energy, an ecosystem is defined as:
   A) Moving energy back and forth between organisms.
   B) Moving energy in one direction from plants to animals.
   C) Not utilizing energy.
   D) Moving energy in one direction from animals to plants.

3. Decomposers are important because they:
   A) Recycle nutrients.
   B) Produce sugars.
   C) Produce oxygen.
   D) Engage in asexual reproduction.

4. Which of the following best describes the concept of an organism's niche?
   A) It is the organism's function, or "occupation", within an ecosystem.
   B) It is the organism's location, or "address", within an ecosystem.
   C) It is both an organism's function and location in an ecosystem.
   D) It is the binomial classification of an organism in an ecosystem.

5. Pill bugs are also known as:
   A) Decomposers.
   B) Detritivores.
   C) Producers.
   D) Autotrophs.

6. The steps in a food chain or food web are called _____ and represent the _____ of an organism.
   A) biome levels; energy level
   B) trophic levels; energy level
   C) trophic levels; feeding level
   D) energy levels; feeding level

7. Another term for herbivores is:
   A) Plants.
   B) Secondary consumers.
   C) Primary consumers
   D) Third trophic-level organisms.

8. Several interacting food chains form a:
   A) Food pyramid.
   B) Food web.
   C) Food column.
   D) Food triangle.

9. Herbivores are at the second trophic level, so they are:
   A) Primary producers.
   B) Primary consumers.
   C) Secondary consumers.
   D) Secondary producers.

Answers: 1) C  2) B  3) A  4) C  5) B  6) C  7) C  8) B  9) B

**General Physiology**

**Human Body Science**
Anatomy and physiology are the studies of body parts and body systems. This section will cover all necessary medical terms, prefixes, suffixes, and terminology as well as the anatomy and physiology of each body system.

**Terminology**

| STRUCTURE HIERARCHY | DIRECTIONAL TERMS | PREFIXES | SUFFIXES |
|---|---|---|---|
| organism | superior toward the head, or toward the upper body region | epi- on/upon | -coccus spherical bacterium |
| organ system | inferior toward the lower body region | hyper- over | -ia condition |
| organs | anterior (ventral) on the belly or front side of the body | hypo- under | -ectomy removal |
| tissues | posterior (dorsal) on the buttocks or back side of the body | intra- within | -malacia softening |
| cells | proximal near the trunk or middle part of the body | para- beside | -tome an instrument to cut |
| molecules | distal furthest away from the point of reference | per- through | -tomy to cut |
| atoms | medial close to the midline of the body | peri- surrounding | -rrhea discharge |
|  | lateral away from the midline of the body | sub- under | -plasty surgical repair |
|  |  |  | -opsy View of |

**Cranial cavity:** contains the brain

**Spinal cavity:** contains the spinal cord, and extends from the brainstem in the cranial cavity to the end of the spinal cord

**Thoracic cavity:** contains the lungs, heart, and large blood vessels, and is separated from the abdomen by the diaphragm

**Abdominal cavity:** contains the stomach, intestines, liver, gallbladder, pancreas, spleen, and kidneys, and is separated from the thoracic cavity by the diaphragm

**Pelvic cavity:** contains the urinary bladder, urinary structures, and reproductive organs

## Cells, Tissues, and Organs
All organisms are composed of microscopic cells, although the type and number of cells may vary. A **cell** is the minimum amount of organized living matter that is complex enough to carry out the functions of life. This section will briefly review both animal and plant cells, noting their basic similarities and differences.

## Cell Membranes
Cells are enclosed by the **cell membrane**, which separates the living cell from the rest of the environment and regulates the movement of molecules into and out of the cell. Cell membranes are composed of two layers of lipid molecules called the **lipid bilayer**, which acts as a barrier to most molecules. Embedded in the bilayer are other molecules that selectively transport substances across the membrane. Because the cell membrane allows some molecules to pass through while blocking others, it is considered **semipermeable**.

In additional to a cell membrane, plants and some fungi also have a **cell wall** that is necessary for structural support and protection. Animal cells do not contain a cell wall.

## Organelles
Cells are filled with a gelatin-like substance called **protoplasm** that contains various structures called **organelles**, so-called because they act like organs within the cell. Many organelles can be found in all cells, but there are also organelles that are particular to certain types of cells. Chloroplasts, for example, exist only in the cells of autotrophic organisms.

It can be helpful to think of the cell as being like a factory with each organelle serving a distinct purpose:

- The **nucleus** is the cell's main computer: it houses the blueprints for life in the form of DNA.
- **Mitochondria** are the cell's power plant: this is where respiration takes place and ATP (the cell's main power source) is made.
- **Ribosomes** are the cell's workers: they make proteins.
- The **endoplasmic reticulum** (ER) is the cell's assembly line: it's where ribosomes work, and it helps package proteins. ER can be either rough (when ribosomes are attached) or smooth (no ribosomes attached).
- The **Golgi apparatus** is the cell's shipping department: it packages and ships out proteins made by ribosomes.
- **Vacuoles** are the cell's warehouses: they serve as storage for many types of molecules.

- **Lysosomes** are the cell's janitors: they break down and dispose of waste in the cell.
- **Chloroplasts** are the power generators in plant cells: they house the molecules that make photosynthesis possible.

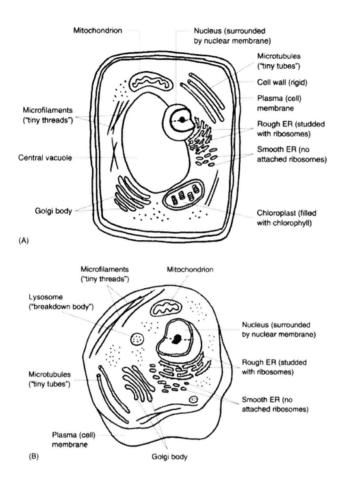

## Tissues

Single-celled organisms have only one cell to carry out all of their required biochemical and structural functions. On the other hand, multi-celled organisms—except for very primitive ones—have groups of cells organized into **tissues** that perform specific functions. There are four main types of tissues: epithelial, connective, muscular, and nervous.

**Epithelial tissue** is made up groups of flattened cells which are grouped tightly together to form a solid surface. Those cells are arranged in one or more layers to form an external or internal covering of the body or organs. Epithelial tissue protects the body from injury and allows for the exchange of gases in the lungs and bronchial tubes. There's also a form of epithelial tissue that produces eggs and sperm, an organism's sex cells.

**Connective tissue** is made of cells that support, connect, or separate other tissues and organs. Tendons, cartilage, and blood are all connective tissues.

**Muscular tissue** has the ability to contract. (For more on the types of muscle tissues, see "The Muscular System.")

**Nervous tissue** consists of cells called neurons (see "The Nervous System" above). Neurons specialize in making many connections with and transmitting electrical impulses to each other. The brain, spinal cord, and peripheral nerves are all made of nervous tissue.

Tissues are further organized into organs, which are grouped into organ systems. (For more on organs and organ systems, see Ch. 8 "Human Body Science.")

# Practice Drill: Cells, Tissues, and Organs

1. What organelle produces the majority of a cell's energy?
A)     chloroplast
B)     nucleus
C)     mitochondrion
D)     endoplasmic reticulum

2. Which of the following lists biological systems from least to most complex?
A)     cells, tissues, organ systems, organs
B)     cells, organs, organ systems, tissues
C)     cells, tissues, organs, organ systems
D)     cells, organ systems, organs, tissues

3. Cardiac muscle is an example of which type of tissue?
A)     smooth muscle
B)     nervous
C)     contractile
D)     connective

4. Which organelle has two forms: rough and smooth?
A)     mitochondrion
B)     Golgi apparatus
C)     nucleus
D)     endoplasmic reticulum

5. Which organelle produces proteins?
A)     mitochondrion
B)     Golgi apparatus
C)     nucleus
D)     ribosome

Answers: 1) **C**  2) **C**  3) **A**  4) **D**  5) **D**

**From DNA to Protein**

All the information that cells need to produce biological molecules is stored in nucleic acids (DNA or RNA). It's the use of this code that allows organisms to pass on complex information to the next generation, a process called **inheritance**.

**The Structure of Nucleic Acids**
Nucleic acids are long chain, polymeric molecules that encode protein sequences. These macromolecules are made up of monomers called **nucleotides**. There are two types of nucleic acids. DNA stores genetic information in most cells; in eukaryotic cells, the DNA is separated from the rest of the cell in the nucleus. DNA is a double-stranded helix constructed from the nucleotides **guanine** (G), **adenine** (A), **thymine** (T), and **cytosine** (C). The backbone of each strand in the helix is formed by the five-carbon sugars in the nucleotides. Each nucleotide also contains a nitrogenous base that bonds only to one other base: adenine and thymine always bond together while guanine and cytosine always pair up. The bonds between these bases make up the "ladder rungs" of the DNA helix.

Within the nucleus, DNA molecules are tightly packed around proteins called **histones** to make structures called **chromosomes**. Human beings have 23 pairs of chromosomes—46 total—in every cell except for germ cells. The sex chromosomes determine sex (XX for female, XY for male); the other chromosomes are called **autosomes**. Chromosomes are not normally visible under a microscope. It's only during mitosis that the chromosomes condense enough to be seen.

RNA is a single stranded nucleic acid that plays various roles in the production and decoding of DNA. It also serves as the primary genetic materials (as opposed to DNA) in some viruses. RNA is composed of the same nucleotides as DNA with one exception: RNA uses **uracil** (U), in place of thymine. The sugar of RNA is also slightly different from that of DNA.

**DNA Transcription & Translation**
The sequence of DNA that codes for a particular protein is called a **gene**. In order for that gene to be used to make a protein, the DNA must be "read" and its code used to put amino acids in the correct order. These two processes are known as transcription and translation, respectively.

In **transcription**, the double-stranded DNA is "unzipped" by the enzyme RNA polymerase, and a strand of **mRNA** (messenger RNA) is made when nucleotides line up with the now-free DNA nucleotide bases. mRNA is built from the 3' to 5' end of the DNA. Next, regions of the mRNA called introns, which don't code for anything, are removed by a complex called the spliceosome. The remaining exons (the coding regions) are spliced back together to get the final mRNA product.

During translation, the mRNA strand is carried out of the nucleus to a ribosome, a large complex of enzymes whose purpose is to read the mRNA and assemble a string of amino acids.  Later it will be folded into a protein. The mRNA strand is read in sets of three nucleotides, called **codons**, which correspond to specific amino acids. Some codons also code instructions such as *stop* and *start*.

| 1st base | 2nd base | | | | 3rd base |
|---|---|---|---|---|---|
| | U | C | A | G | |
| U | UUU {Phe/F} Phenylalanine | UCU {Ser/S} Serine | UAU {Tyr/Y} Tyrosine | UGU {Cys/C} Cysteine | U |
| | UUC | UCC | UAC | UGC | C |
| | UUA {Leu/L} Leucine | UCA | UAA Stop (Ochre) | UGA Stop (Opal) | A |
| | UUG | UCG | UAG Stop (Amber) | UGG {Trp/W} Tryptophan | G |
| C | CUU {Leu/L} Leucine | CCU {Pro/P} Proline | CAU {His/H} Histidine | CGU {Arg/R} Arginine | U |
| | CUC | CCC | CAC | CGC | C |
| | CUA | CCA | CAA {Gln/Q} Glutamine | CGA | A |
| | CUG | CCG | CAG | CGG | G |
| A | AUU {Ile/I} Isoleucine | ACU {Thr/T} Threonine | AAU {Asn/N} Asparagine | AGU {Ser/S} Serine | U |
| | AUC | ACC | AAC | AGC | C |
| | AUA | ACA | AAA {Lys/K} Lysine | AGA {Arg/R} Arginine | A |
| | AUG[A] {Met/M} Methionine | ACG | AAG | AGG | G |
| G | GUU {Val/V} Valine | GCU {Ala/A} Alanine | GAU {Asp/D} Aspartic acid | GGU {Gly/G} Glycine | U |
| | GUC | GCC | GAC | GGC | C |
| | GUA | GCA | GAA {Glu/E} Glutamic acid | GGA | A |
| | GUG | GCG | GAG | GGG | G |

A molecule called tRNA (transfer RNA) carries the amino acids and attaches at the correct spot on the mRNA using **anti-codons.** (e.g., the codon GGC is for glycine, so the tRNA carrying glycine has the anti-codon CCG) The amino acids then bond together and detach from both RNA strands.

Note that each amino acid is represented by three or more different codons. As a result, even if there is a small mutation in the DNA strand, often there will be no result because it may end up coding for the same amino acid anyway. However, some mutations may result in the incorrect amino acid being added to the new protein.

The proteins that are produced from the DNA transcription and translation process are then exported from the endoplasmic reticulum or freely released into the cytosol, where they can perform their work.

# Practice Drill: From DNA to Protein

1. Which of the following is true about DNA?
A)      All living organisms except viruses have DNA.
B)      DNA and RNA have the same sugar backbone.
C)      DNA is found only in sex cells.
D)      Humans have more chromosomes than any other species.

2. Given the sequence ATGAACT, what is the correct complementary DNA sequence?
A)      GTACCGT
B)      TACTTGA
C)      TTACCGA
D)      ATGAATC

3. Given the sequence GCCATATG, what is the correct complementary RNA sequence?
A)      CGGUAUAC
B)      CGUTAUTC
C)      AGTCCATC
D)      CGGTATAC

4. Which of the following is NOT a nucleotide found in DNA?
A)      uracil
B)      guanine
C)      cytosine
D)      thymine

5. Which of the following enzymes is responsible for making RNA from DNA?
A)      RNA ligase
B)      DNA polymerase
C)      RNA polymerase
D)      DNA helicase

6. When a ribosome reads an mRNA strand, how many base pairs are read at a time?
A)      1
B)      2
C)      3
D)      4

7. The RNA strand AUGCACAGG codes for which sequence of amino acids? (See Fig. X)
A)      M-H-V
B)      V-H-R
C)      M-H-R
D)      R-A-V

8. Which of the following statements is not true regarding RNA?
A)      RNA is produced using DNA as a template.
B)      RNA is read by a ribosome to produce proteins.
C)      RNA is non-degradable and exists permanently in the cell.
D)      RNA uses uracil rather than thymine as a nucleotide.

Answers: 1) **A**  2) **B**  3) **A**  4) **A**  5) **C**  6) **C**  7) **C**  8) **C**

**Mitosis and Meiosis**

New cells are created when **parent cells** divide to make **daughter cells**. Cells can undergo two different types of division. In **mitosis**, which takes place in **somatic** (body) cells, a single diploid parent cell results in two genetically-identical diploid daughter cells. Mitosis takes place in somatic (body) cells, allowing for growth in multi-cellular organisms. It is also a means of reproduction for single-celled organisms.

In **meiosis**, a single diploid parent cell results in four genetically diverse haploid cells. Meiosis takes place in **germ** (reproductive) cells and produces gametes (eggs in females and sperm in males). Both mitosis and meiosis are part of the larger **cell cycle**, which is a series of growth, rest, and division.

Mitosis
Before mitosis begins, the cell is in **interphase**, which is the period of growth that takes up the majority of the cell cycle. During interphase, the cell goes through normal cellular functions such as making proteins and organelles. During the synthesis (S) stage of interphase, the cell replicates its DNA to prepare for mitosis. During DNA replication, the DNA strand "unzips" so that the enzyme DNA polymerase can add complementary nucleotides to each strand of the double helix. The resulting two sets of DNA each contains half the original DNA and half new DNA, which is why the process is called **semiconservative replication**.

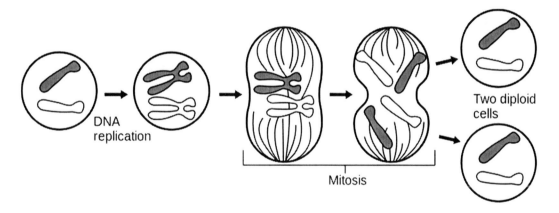

Mitosis properly begins during **prophase**, when the DNA condenses into chromatin and forms into chromosomes; it is during this phase that chromosomes become visible under a microscope. In this phase, the **centrioles** within the cell also migrate to opposite ends of the cell.

The cell them moves into **metaphase**, during which the centrioles are attached to individual chromosomes by actin filaments and then start pulling chromosomes to opposite ends of the cell. This pulling action lines up the chromosomes at the midline of the cell, which has itself begun to elongate and stretch.

In **anaphase**, the chromosomes cleave, creating two sets of diploid chromosomes that are then pulled to opposite ends of the cell. This is followed by **telophase**, during which a nuclear envelope reforms around each set of chromosomes and the chromosomes loosen.

Once the new nuclei have formed, mitosis is officially over. The cell then begins the process of **cytokinesis**, during which the cell divides into two complete daughter cells.

**Meiosis**

Like mitosis, meiosis is preceded by interphase, meaning cells enter meiosis having replicated their DNA to produce two complete sets of chromosomes. The replicated material stays attached at the centromere to the original chromosome, creating a four-chromatid group called a **tetrad**.

Meiosis takes place in two separate stages. During **meiosis I**, homologous chromosomes align in the middle of the cell. However, unlike in mitosis, here the homologous chromosomes line up side by side, allowing for a process called **crossing over**, in which DNA is exchanged between chromosomes. Crossing over is one of the primary generators of variation in sexually reproducing organisms.

After lining up, the homologous chromosomes are separated and pulled to opposite ends of the cell, meaning each new cell will contain only one version of each chromosome (either the maternal or paternal). The cell then divides, creating two haploid cells. Note that the sister chromatids are not separated as they are in mitosis, meaning that while each cell contains only one version of a chromosome, it still contains two copies of that chromosome attached as a tetrad. The chromosomes are **independently assorted** as well, meaning each cell contains a mix of maternal and paternal chromosomes.

During meiosis II, the cell divides again much as it does in mitosis with sister chromatids being pulled to opposite ends of the cell. The cells then divide, creating four daughter cells with a single copy of each chromosome. When these sex cells fuse during fertilization, the new cell will again be diploid.

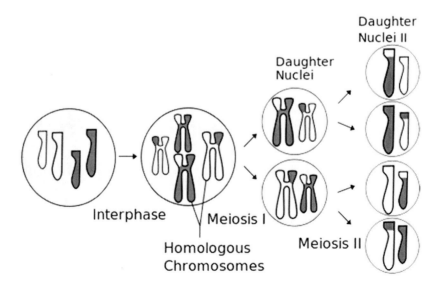

# Practice Drill: Mitosis and Meiosis

1. During which stage of the cell cycle is DNA replicated?
A)      interphase
B)      metaphase
C)      telophase
D)      anaphase

2. If a human cell undergoes mitosis, how many pairs of chromosomes will be present in each daughter cell?
A)      1
B)      2
C)      3
D)      4

3. A single cell undergoes mitosis every 20 minutes. How many cells will be present after 2 hours?
A)      8
B)      16
C)      32
D)      64

4. A haploid cell that is used in sexual reproduction is a:
A)      blastocoel
B)      gamete
C)      zygote
D)      Barr body

5. Which of the following species would not use meiosis as a cell process?
A)      elephant
B)      oak tree
C)      salmon
D)      E. coli

6. In DNA replication, what enzyme is responsible for copying the DNA?
A)      DNA helicase
B)      DNA polymerase
C)      DNA transcriptase
D)      DNA replicase

Answers: 1) **A**  2) **B**  3) **D**  4) **B**  5) **D**  6) **B**

# Genetics

**Genetics** is broadly defined as the study of how genes function and how they are passed from one generation to the next. When studying genetics, it's necessary to draw the distinction between an organism's **genotype**—its genetic sequence— and its **phenotype**, which is the physical appearance that results from its genotype. You can remember this differentiation by looking at the beginning of each word: genotype is genetic, and phenotype is physical.

Because expression of genes is controlled by many factors, including the environment, organisms with the same genotype may have different phenotypes. For example, twins raised in different environments may have different heights or weights.

## Mendelian Inheritance

Alternate forms of the same gene are called **alleles**. For example, if a gene codes for the color of a flower's petals, one gene might result in red petals and another in white petals. Diploid organisms will carry two copies of every gene—one maternal and one paternal. When the alleles of these two genes are identical, the individual is **homozygous** for that trait. When the alleles are different, the individual is **heterozygous** for that trait.

Two heterozygous alleles can interact in a number of different ways. If one allele is **dominant** (denoted with a capital letter), then it will be expressed while the other is not. The allele that is not expressed is then **recessive** (denoted with a lower-case letter). Alleles can also be **codominant**, meaning both are expressed, and the phenotype exhibits traits of both alleles (for example, a flower might have both red and white petals). In **incomplete dominance**, both alleles are expressed, and the resulting phenotype is a blend of both alleles (so, the heterozygous red and white flower would have pink petals).

Gregor Mendel was a 19th-century monk who did some of the first quantitative experiments on genetics. The modern study of genetics was founded on his work and his three laws of genetics.

Mendel's first law is the **law of segregation**, which states that every organism receives a pair of alleles for each gene (one from each parent). When gametes are produced, each gamete receives only one allele. The second law is the **law of independent assortment**. This law states that genes for separate traits are passed to the offspring independently. For example, the gene for black hair is independent of the gene for height; having one gene does not guarantee having the other. This assortment occurs during meiosis when maternal and paternal chromosomes sort independently (e.g., gametes end up with a random mix of maternal and paternal genes). The third law is the **law of dominance**, which states that recessive alleles will be masked by dominant alleles.

## Punnett Squares

**Punnett Squares** are a basic tool for looking at inheritance patterns. Alleles from one parent are placed along the top of the square (the x-axis), and alleles from the second parent on the left (y-axis). Crossing these alleles will show all the possible genotypes for the resulting offspring. This first generation is called the $F_1$ generation; the next generation is the $F_2$.

Let's look at an example. A sunflower plant has an allele that determines the roundness of the flower: R is dominant for roundness and r is recessive for oval. Two plants are mated together—one is RR and one is Rr. The results are shown below:

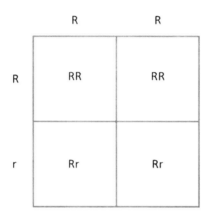

We see that the result is half the offspring have the genotype RR, and the other half have the genotype Rr. Because the R allele is dominant, all of the offspring flowers will be round, and none of them should be oval.

## Natural Selection and Evolution
**Natural selection** is a biological process in which certain heritable traits confer individuals with differential reproductive success, meaning organisms with those traits are more or less likely to reproduce. Organisms that carry traits increasing reproduction will obviously leave behind more offspring, increasing the appearance of those traits in the population. Traits that limit reproductive success will appear less frequently in the population or disappear altogether. For example, if a mutation in a gene for fur color in mice creates an allele for a brown color that allows the mice to hide better. Mice expressing that allele are less likely to be eaten by predators. Thus, those mice are more likely to reproduce and pass this allele on to their offspring.

Notice that in our example the environment did not create the new allele: the mouse did not become brown in order to fit in better with its surroundings. Changes in genetic code are created randomly through mutations. Most of these mutations will be meaningless, but every so often, a mutation will influence the fitness of an animal and thus will become responsive to the pressures of natural selection.

Natural selection is the mechanism through which **evolution** takes place. As environments change, and new genetic mutations appear, the forces of natural selection will gradually shift the genotype (and thus the phenotype) of species. If this pressure is great enough, a new species may be created. The theory of evolution was first advanced by Charles Darwin in his 1859 book *On the Origin of Species*.

# Practice Drill: Genetics

1. If an organism is heterozygous with one dominant and one recessive allele,
A)      only the dominant allele will be expressed.
B)      both alleles will be expressed.
C)      only the recessive allele will be expressed.
D)      the dominant allele will be passed down to all of the organism's offspring.

2. If both alleles of a gene are being expressed in an organism, those alleles are:
A)      dominant
B)      codominant
C)      incompletely dominant
D)      codominant or incompletely dominant

3. If a gene is sex-linked, and the recessive trait is mostly seen in males, but occasionally seen in females, then the trait is passed on through:
A)      the 22nd chromosome
B)      the X chromosome
C)      the Y chromosome
D)      the somatic cell DNA

4. A phenotype trait is the result of the:
A)      expression of a gene
B)      expression of a gene and the environment
C)      environment only
D)      dominant allele only

5. In roses, R is dominant for red, and r is recessive for white. When a gardener takes a red rose and crosses it with another red rose, a quarter of the offspring are white. This is because:
A)      Both parent roses were homozygous recessive.
B)      Both parent roses were homozygous dominant.
C)      Both parent roses were heterozygous.
D)      One parent rose was heterozygous and the other homozygous dominant.

6. Brown eyes are dominant in humans (B), and blue eyes are recessive (b). A family has three children, one of which has blue eyes. Which of the following must be true?
A)      One of the parents must have blue eyes.
B)      Both of the parents must have blue eyes.
C)      Only one parent carries the gene for blue eyes.
D)      Both parents must carry the gene for blue eyes.

7. Hemophilia is an X-linked recessive genetic disease. If a female has hemophilia, then:
A)      All of her female children will have hemophilia.
B)      All of her male children will have hemophilia.
C)      All of her children will have hemophilia.
D)      All of her children will have a 50% chance of having hemophilia.

8. The $F_2$ generation of a breed of roses was found to be all red in color. Red is dominant (R), whereas white is recessive (r). This means that:
A)      The parent generation was homozygous recessive.
B)      The F1 generation was heterozygous.
C)      The F1 generation was half homozygous dominant and half heterozygous.
D)      The parent generation was homozygous dominant.

9. A faster, or more rapid, rate of evolution will likely be seen in a species which:
A)      matures slowly and is able to reproduce after twenty years
B)      matures quickly and is able to reproduce after one week
C)      has a large number of genes
D)      has a small number of genes

10. Which of the following scenarios is most likely to lead to natural selection?
A)      An organism eats a high-fat diet and gains weight.
B)      An organism creates a tool that allows it to access a new food source.
C)      A mutation creates a new gene that allows an organism to forage for food more efficiently.
D)      A mutation which creates a debilitating disease that appears after the organism has passed reproductive age.

Answers: 1) **A**  2) **D**  3) **B**  4) **B**  5) **C**  6) **D**  7) **B**  8) 9) **B**  10) **C**

**The Circulatory System**

The **circulatory system** is composed of the cardiovascular and pulmonary systems. The **cardiovascular system** includes the heart, blood, and blood vessels. This is where circulation begins, ends, and begins again. The **pulmonary system** is made up of the lungs and muscles that allow breathing.

### The Heart

The cardiovascular system plays a vital role in the functioning of humans, as it distributes oxygen, nutrients, and hormones to the entire body. The whole system relies on the **heart**, a cone-shaped muscular organ that is no bigger than a closed fist. The heart must pump the blood low in oxygen to the lungs; once the blood is in the lungs, it is oxygenated and returned to the heart. The heart then pumps the oxygenated blood through the whole body.

The heart is located inside the rib cage. It can be found approximately between the second and the sixth rib from the bottom of the rib cage. The heart does not sit on the body's midline. Rather, two-thirds of it is located on the left side of the body. The narrower part of the heart is called the apex, and it points downwards and to the left of the body; the broader part of the heart is called the base, and it points upwards.

The cavity that holds the heart is called the **pericardial cavity**. It is filled with serous fluid produced by the pericardium, which is the lining of the pericardial cavity. The serous fluid acts as a lubricant for the heart. It also keeps the heart in place and empties the space around the heart.

The heart wall has three layers:

- **Epicardium**: the outermost layer of the heart, and is one of the two layers of the pericardium.
- **Myocardium**: the middle layer of the heart that contains the cardiac muscular tissue. It performs the function of pumping what is necessary for the circulation of blood. It is the most massive part of the heart.
- **Endocardium**: the smooth innermost layer that keeps the blood from sticking to the inside of the heart.

The heart wall is uneven because some parts of the heart—like the atria—don't need a lot of muscle power to perform their duties. Other parts, like the ventricles, require a thicker muscle to pump the blood.

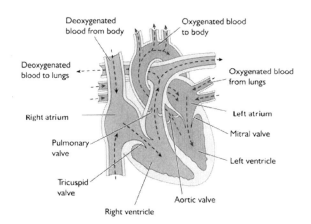

There are four **chambers** in the heart: the right and left atria, and the right and left ventricles. The **atria** (plural for atrium) are smaller than the ventricles, and they have thin walls, as their function is to receive blood from the lungs and the body and pump it to the ventricles. The **ventricles** have to pump the blood to the lungs and the rest of the body, so they are larger and have a thicker wall. The left half of the heart, which is responsible for pumping the blood through the body, has a thicker wall than the right half that pumps the deoxygenated blood to the lungs.

The heart has one-way valves allowing the blood to flow in only one direction. The valves that keep the blood from going back into the atria from the ventricles are called the **atrioventricular valves**. Theses valves that keep the blood from going back into the ventricles from the arteries are called the **semilunar valves**.

The pumping function of the heart is made possible by two groups of cells that set the heart's pace and keep it well coordinated: the sinoatrial and the atrioventricular node. The **sinoatrial node** sets the pace and signals the atria to contract; the **atrioventricular node** picks up the signal from the sinoatrial node, and this signal tells the ventricles to contract.

## The Blood Vessels

The **blood vessels** carry the blood from the heart throughout the body and then back. They vary in size depending on the amount of the blood that needs to flow through them. The hollow part in the middle, called the **lumen**, is where the blood flows. The vessels are lined with endothelium, which is made out of the same type of cells as the endocardium and serves the same purpose, to keep the blood from sticking to the walls and clotting.

**Arteries** are blood vessels that transport the blood away from the heart. They work under a lot more pressure than the other types of blood vessels; hence, they have a thicker, more muscular wall, which is also highly elastic. The smaller arteries are usually more muscular while the larger are more elastic.

The largest artery in the body is called the **aorta**. It ascends from the left ventricle of the heart, arches to the back left and descends behind the heart. Narrower arteries that branch off of main arteries and carry blood to the capillaries are called **arterioles**. The descending part of the aorta carries blood to the lower parts of the body, except for the lungs. The lungs get blood through the **pulmonary artery** that comes out of the right ventricle.

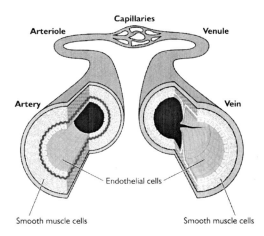

The arching part of the aorta (called the **aortic arch**) branches into three arteries: the brachiocephalic artery, the left common artery, and the left subclavian artery. The **brachiocephalic artery** carries blood to the brain and head. The brachiocephalic artery divides into the right subclavian artery, which brings the blood to the right arm.

The **left common carotid artery** carries blood to the brain; the **left subclavian artery** carries blood to the left arm.

**Veins** are blood vessels that bring the blood from to the body and then back to the heart. As they don't work under the same pressure as the arteries, they are much thinner and not as muscular or elastic. The veins also have a number of one way valves that stops the blood from going back through them.

Veins use inertia, muscle work, and gravity to get the blood to the heart. Thin veins that connect to the capillaries are called **venules**. The lungs have their own set of veins: the **left** and **right superior** and **inferior pulmonary veins**. These vessels enter the heart through the left atrium.

The two main veins are called the superior vena cava and the inferior vena cava. The **superior vena cava** ascends from the right atrium and connects to the head and neck, delivering the blood supply to these structures. The superior vena cava also connects to the arms via both subclavian and brachiocephalic veins. The **inferior vena cava** descends from the right atrium, carrying the blood from the lumbar veins, gonadal veins, hepatic veins, phrenic veins, and renal veins.

**Capillaries** are the smallest blood vessels, and the most populous in the body. They can be found in almost every tissue. They connect to arterioles on one end and the venules on the other end. Also, capillaries carry the blood very close to the cells, and thus, enable cells to exchange gasses, nutrients, and cellular waste. The walls of capillaries have to be very thin for this exchange to happen.

## The Blood

**Blood** is the medium for the transport of substances throughout the body. There are four to five liters of this liquid connective tissue in the human body. Blood is comprised of red blood cells, hemoglobin, white blood cells, platelets, and plasma.

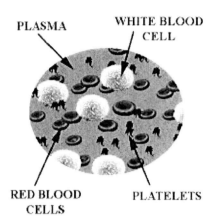

Also called **erythrocytes**, **red blood cells** (RBCs) are produced inside the red bone marrow and transport oxygen. **Hemoglobin** (HGB) is a red pigment found in the red blood cells, and it is rich in iron and proteins, which both allow these cells to transport the oxygen. Hemoglobin also has a biconcave shape, which means it is round and thinner in the middle. This shape gives them a larger surface area, making them more effective.

**White blood cells** (WBCs), also called **leukocytes**, are important for the human immune system. There are two classes of white blood cells: granular and agranular leukocytes. **Granular leukocytes** are divided into three types: the neutrophils that digest bacteria, the eosinophils that digest viruses, and the basophils that release histamine.

**Agranular leukocytes** are divided into two classes: the lymphocytes, which fight off viral infections and produce antibodies for fighting pathogen-induced infection and the monocytes, which play a role in removing pathogens and dead cells from wounds.

**Platelets**, also called **thrombocytes**, are vital for blood clotting. They are formed in the red bone marrow and serve many functions in the body. Finally, **plasma** is the liquid part of blood, and it forms 55 percent of the total blood volume. Plasma consists of up to 90 percent water, as well as proteins, including antibodies and albumins. Other substances circulating in the blood plasma include glucose, nutrients, cell waste, and various gasses.

## The Cardiac Cycle

The heart works by shifting between two states: systole and diastole. In **systole**, the cardiac muscles are contracting and moving blood from any given chamber. During **diastole**, the muscles are relaxing, and the chamber is expanding to fill with blood. The systole and diastole are responsible for the pressure in the major arteries. This is the **blood pressure** that is measured in a regular exam. The two values are systolic and diastolic pressures respectively, with the former being larger than the latter.

**A cardiac cycle** is the series of events that occur during one heartbeat. These events include:

- Atrial systole: The first phase of the cardiac cycle is atrial systole. With this, the blood is pushed by the atria through the valves into ventricles, which are in diastole during that event.
- Ventricular systole: After atrial systole, ventricular systole occurs. This pushes the blood from the ventricles to the organs, which occurs while the atria are in diastole.
- Relaxation phase: After ventricular systole, there is a pause called the relaxation phase. During this, all the chambers are in diastole, and the blood enters the atria through the veins.
- Refilling phase: When atria are at about 75 percent of their capacity, the cycle starts again. With the refilling phase, the atria are fully filled before atrial systole occurs again.

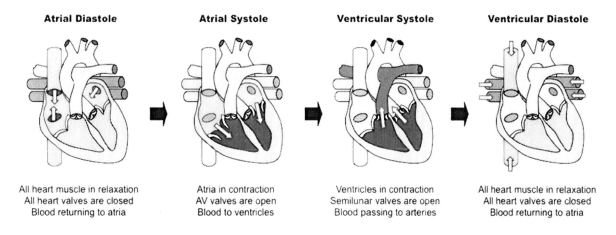

| Atrial Diastole | Atrial Systole | Ventricular Systole | Ventricular Diastole |
|---|---|---|---|
| All heart muscle in relaxation<br>All heart valves are closed<br>Blood returning to atria | Atria in contraction<br>AV valves are open<br>Blood to ventricles | Ventricles in contraction<br>Semilunar valves are open<br>Blood passing to arteries | All heart muscle in relaxation<br>All heart valves are closed<br>Blood returning to atria |

## Oxygenating the Blood

There are four steps to blood cell oxygenation:

1. The poorly oxygenated blood comes into the right atrium through the superior and inferior vena cava.

2. The blood is then passed to the right ventricle, which sends it through the pulmonary artery into the lungs where oxygenation occurs.

3. The oxygen-rich blood then comes to the left atrium through the pulmonary veins, and gets moved from the left atrium to the left ventricle.

4. By way of blood pressure, the blood is then sent from the left ventricle through the aorta and the aortic arch into the arteries in the whole body.

After leaving the left ventricle, the blood passes from the arteries to the arterioles and on to the capillaries, where the exchange of gasses, nutrients, wastes, and hormones occur. The blood then passes into venules and gets back to the heart through the veins. A healthy resting heart can pump around 5 liters per minute through this cycle.

The veins of the stomach and intestines don't carry the blood directly to the heart. Rather, they divert it to the liver first, through the hepatic portal vein, so that the liver can store sugar, remove toxins, and process the products of digestion. The blood then goes to the heart through the inferior vena cava.

# Practice Drill: The Circulatory System

1. At what rate does a healthy heart pump blood while resting?
A)      Around 3 liters per minute.
B)      Around 5 liters per minute.
C)      Around 8 liters per minute.
D)      Around 10 liters per minute.

2. Which of the layers of the wall of the heart contains cardiac muscles?
A)      myocardium
B)      epicardium
C)      endocardium
D)      All layers of the heart contain cardiac muscle.

3. The heart chamber with the thickest wall is:
A)      the left ventricle
B)      the right ventricle
C)      the right atrium
D)      the left ventricle

4. The blood from the left ventricle goes to:
A)      the right ventricle
B)      the vena cava
C)      the aorta and aortic arch
D)      the lungs

5. The blood vessels that carry the blood from the heart are called:
A)      veins
B)      venules
C)      capillaries
D)      arteries

Answers: 1) **B**  2) **A**  3) **D**  4) **C**  5) **D**

**The Respiratory System**

The human body needs oxygen in order to function. The system that is responsible for intake of the gas is called the **respiratory system**. It's also in charge of removing carbon dioxide from the body, which is equally important.

The respiratory system can be divided into two sections: the upper respiratory tract and the lower respiratory tract.

**The Upper Respiratory Tract**
The **upper respiratory tract** consists of the nose, nasal cavity, olfactory membranes, mouth, pharynx, epiglottis, and the larynx.

The **nose** is the primary body part for air intake and removing carbon dioxide. The nose itself is made out of bone, cartilage, muscle, and skin, and it serves as a protector of the hollow space behind it called the **nasal cavity**. The nasal cavity is covered with hair and mucus, which together serve an important function – they stop contaminants from the outside. Common contaminants include dust, mold, and other particles. The nasal cavity prevents the contaminants from entering further into the respiratory system; it also warms and moisturizes air.

The nose and the nasal cavity also contain **olfactory membranes**, which are small organs responsible for our sense of smell. They are located on the top of the nasal cavity, just under the bridge of the nose.

We can also breathe through the **mouth** although it is not the primary breathing opening. The mouth doesn't perform as well when it comes to the three functions of the primary opening: (filtering, moisturizing, and warming of air). However, the mouth does have its advantages over the nose when it comes to breathing, including its larger size and proximity to the lungs.

The next part of the respiratory system is the **throat**, which is also called the **pharynx**. The pharynx is a smooth, muscular structure lined with mucus and divided into three regions: the nasopharynx, the oropharynx, and the laryngopharynx.

Air comes in through the nose and then passes through the **nasopharynx**, which is also where the Eustachian tubes from the middle ears connect with the pharynx. The air then enters the **oropharynx**, which is where air from the mouth enters the pharynx; this is the same passageway used for transporting food when eating. Both air and food also pass through the **laryngopharynx**, where these substances are diverted into different systems.

The **epiglottis** is responsible for ensuring that air enters the trachea and food enters the esophagus. The epiglottis is a flap made of elastic cartilage, which covers the opening of one passageway to allow the air or food to go into the other one. When you breathe, the epiglottis covers the opening of the esophagus, and when you swallow, it protects the opening of the trachea.

The **larynx** is the part of the airway that sits between the pharynx and the trachea. It is also called the voice box, because it contains mucus membrane folds (vocal folds) that vibrate when air passes through them to produce sounds. The larynx is made out of three cartilage structures: the epiglottis, the thyroid cartilage (also called the Adam's apple), and the cricoid cartilage, a ring-shaped structure that keeps the larynx open.

## The Lower Respiratory Tract

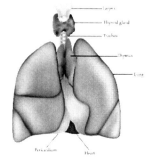

The **lower respiratory tract** consists of the trachea, bronchi, lungs, and the muscles that help with breathing.

The lower respiratory tract begins with the **trachea**, also known as the windpipe. The trachea is the part of the respiratory system between the larynx and the bronchi. As its name suggests, the windpipe resembles a pipe, and it's really flexible so it can follow various head and neck movements. The trachea is made out of fibrous and elastic tissues, smooth muscle, and about 20 cartilage rings.

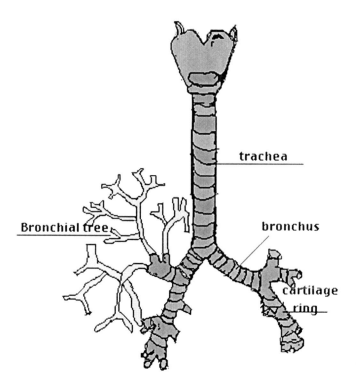

The interior of the windpipe is lined with mucus-producing cells called **goblet cells**, as well as cells that have small fringes that resemble hair. These hair-like structures, called **cilia**, allow air to pass through the windpipe, where it is further filtered by the mucus. The fringes also help to move mucus up the airways and out, keeping the air passage free.

Connecting to the trachea are the **bronchi. The primary bronchi,** consisting of many C-shaped cartilage rings, branch into the secondary bronchi. Two extend from the left primary bronchi, and three branch from the right, corresponding to the number of lobes in the lungs. The **secondary bronchi** contain less cartilage and have more space between the rings. The same goes for the **tertiary bronchi,** which are extensions of the secondary bronchi as they divide throughout the lobes of the lungs. Like the trachea, the bronchi are lined with epithelium that contains goblet cells and cilia.

**Bronchioles** branch from the tertiary bronchi. They contain no cartilage at all; rather, they are made of smooth muscle and elastic fiber tissue, which allows them to be quite small yet still able to change their diameter. For example, when the body needs more oxygen, they expand, and when there is a danger of pollutants entering the lungs, they constrict.

Bronchioles end with **terminal bronchioles**, which connect them with **alveoli**, which is where the gas exchange happens. Alveoli are small cavities located in alveolar sacs and surrounded by capillaries. The inner surface of alveoli is coated with the **alveolar fluid**, which plays a vital role in keeping the alveoli moist, the lungs elastic, and the thin wall of the alveoli stable. The wall of the alveoli is made out of alveolar cells and the connective tissue that forms the respiratory membrane where it comes into contact with the wall of the capillaries.

The **lungs** themselves are two spongy organs that contain the bronchi, bronchioles, alveoli, and blood vessels. The lungs are contained in the rib cage and are surrounded by the pleura, a double-layered membrane consisting of the outer **parietal pleura** and the inner **visceral pleura**. Between the layers of the pleura is a hollow space called the **pleural cavity**, which allows the lungs to expand.

The lungs are wider at the top, which is referred to as the **base**, and they are narrower at the bottom part, which is called the **apex**. The lungs are divided into **lobes**, with the larger lung (the right one) consisting of three lobes, and the smaller lung (the left lung) consisting of two lobes.

### Respiration
The muscles that play a major role in respiration are the diaphragm and the intercostal muscles. The **diaphragm** is a structure made of skeletal muscle, and it located under the lungs, forming the floor of the thorax. The **intercostal muscles** are located between the ribs. The **internal intercostal muscles** help with breathing out (expiration) by depressing the ribs and compressing the thoracic cavity; the **external intercostal muscles** help with breathing in (inspiration).

Breathing in and out is also called **pulmonary ventilation**. The two types of pulmonary ventilation are inhalation and exhalation.

During **inhalation** (also called inspiration), the diaphragm contracts and moves a few inches towards the stomach, making more space for the lungs to expand, and this movement pulls the air into the lungs. The external intercostal muscles also contract to expand the rib cage, and pull more air into the lungs. The lungs are now at a lower pressure than the atmosphere, (called negative pressure), which causes air to come into lungs until the pressure inside the lungs and the atmospheric pressure are the same.

During **exhalation** (in expiration), the diaphragm and the external intercostal muscles relax, and the internal intercostal muscles contract. This causes the thoracic cavity to become smaller, and the pressure in the lungs to climb higher than the atmospheric pressure, which moves air out of the lungs.

**Types of Breathing**

In shallow breathing, around 0.5 liters of air is circulated, a capacity called **tidal volume**. During deep breathing, a larger amount of air is moved, usually 3–5 liters, a volume known as **vital capacity**. The abdominal and other muscles are also involved in breathing in and out during deep breathing.

**Eupnea** is a term for the breathing our body does when resting, which consists of mostly shallow breaths with an occasional deep breath. The lungs are never completely without air—around a liter of air is always present in the lungs.

# Practice Drill: The Respiratory System

1. The primary opening for breathing in and out is:
A)      the nose
B)      the mouth
C)      the skin pores
D)      the pharynx

2. The air that we breathe in through the mouth enters the throat at the:
A)      nasopharynx
B)      oropharynx
C)      laryngopharynx
D)      larynx

3. For the air to go the lungs, the epiglottis needs to close the:
A)      bronchi
B)      pharynx
C)      larynx
D)      esophagus

4. How many lobes does the left lung have?
A)      1
B)      2
C)      3
D)      4

5. Bronchioles branch from the:
A)      primary bronchi
B)      secondary bronchi
C)      tertiary Bronchi
D)      quaternary bronchi

Answers: 1) **A**  2) **B**  3) **D**  4) **B**  5) **C**

**The Skeletal System**

There are a number of roles the skeletal system plays in the body. The bones and joints that make up the skeletal system are responsible for:

- providing support and protection
- allowing movement
- blood cell genesis
- storing fat, iron, and calcium
- guiding the growth of the entire body

The skeleton can be divided into two parts: the axial skeleton and the appendicular skeleton. The **axial skeleton** consists of 80 bones placed along the body's midline axis and grouped into the skull, ribs, sternum, and vertebral column. The **appendicular skeleton** consists of 126 bones grouped into the upper and lower limbs and the pelvic and the pectoral girdles. These bones anchor muscles and allow for movement.

**Bone Components**

On the cellular level, the bone consists of two distinctively different parts: the matrix and living bone cells. The **bone matrix** is the non-living part of the bone, which is made out of water, collagen, protein, calcium phosphate, and calcium carbonate crystals. The **living bone cells** (**osteocytes**) are found at the edges of the bones and throughout the bone matrix in small cavities. Bone cells play a vital part in the growth, development, and repair of bones, and can be used for the minerals they store.

Looking at a cross section of bone, you can see that it is made out of layers. These include the **periosteum**, which is the topmost layer of the bone, acting as a layer of connective tissue. The periosteum contains collagen fibers that anchor the tendons and the muscles; it also holds the stem and the osteoblast cells that are necessary for growth and repair of the bones. Nervous tissue, nerve endings, and blood vessels are also present in the periosteum.

Under the periosteum is a layer of **compact bone**, which gives the bone its strength. Made out of mineral salts and collagen fibers, it also contains many cavities where osteocytes can be found. Under the compact bone is a layer where the bone tissue grows in columns called **trabeculae**. The bone tissue forms a space that contains the red bone marrow. The trabeculae provide structural strength, even while keeping the bones light.

**Hematopoiesis and Calcification**

Inside the red bone marrow, which is located in the medullar cavity of the bones, a process called **hematopoiesis** occurs. In the process, white and red blood cells are made from stem cells. The amount of the red bone marrow declines at the end of puberty, as a significant part of it is replaced by the yellow bone marrow.

When we are born, we have three hundred bones. As we grow, the structure of the bones changes. In **calcification,** bones transform from mostly hyaline cartilage and connective tissue to the osseous tissue. They also fuse together, which is why adults have 206 instead of 300 bones.

## The Five Types of Bones

The **long bones** make up the major bones of the limbs. They are longer than they are wide, and they are responsible for the most of our height. The long bones can be divided into two regions: the **epiphyses**, located at the ends of the bone, and **diaphysis**, located in the middle. The middle of the diaphysis contains a hollow medullary cavity, which serves as a storage for bone marrow.

The **short bones** are roughly as long as they are wide, and are cube-shaped or round. Short bones in the body include the carpal bones of the wrist and tarsal bones of the foot. The **flat bones** do not have the medullary cavity because they are thin and usually thinner on one end regions. Flat bones in the body include the ribs, the hip bones, as well as the frontal, the parietal, and the occipital bones of the skull. The **irregular bones** are those bones that do not fit the criteria to be the long, the short, or the flat bones. The vertebrae and the sacrum, among others, are irregular bones.

There are only two **sesamoid bones** that are counted as proper bones: the patella and the pisiform bone. Sesamoid bones are formed inside the tendons located across the joints, and apart from the two mentioned, they are not present in all people.

## The Skull

Made out of twenty-two bones, the **skull** protects the brain and the sense organs for vision, hearing, smell, taste and balance. The skull has only one movable joint that connects it with the mandible – the jaw bone, which is the only movable bone of the skull. The other twenty-one are fused together.

The upper part of the skull is known as the **cranium**, which is the part that protects the brain while the lower and frontal parts of the skull form the facial bones. Located just under the mandible, and not a part of the skull is the **hyoid bone**. The hyoid is the only bone in the body that is not attached to any other bone. It helps keep the trachea open and is where the tongue muscles are anchored.

Other bones closely connected to, but not part of the skull, are the **auditory ossicles**: the malleus, incus, and stapes. These bones play an important role in hearing.

## The Vertebral Column

The **vertebral column**, or the spine, begins at the base of the skull and stretches through the trunk down the middle and to the back to the coccyx. It provides support for the weight of the upper body and protects the spinal cord. It is made up of twenty-four vertebrae, plus the **sacrum** and the **coccyx** (the tailbone). These twenty-four vertebrae are divided into three groups:

- the **cervical**, or the neck vertebrae (7 bones)
- the **thoracic**, or the chest vertebrae (12 bones)
- the **lumbar**, or the lower back vertebrae (5 bones)

Furthermore, each vertebra has its own name, which is derived from the first letter of the group it belongs (for example, *L* for lumbar vertebrae). The letter is placed in the group, followed by a number (the first of the lumbar vertebrae is thus called *L1*).

## VERTEBRAL COLUMN

### The Ribs and the Sternum

The ribs and the sternum are the bones that form the rib cage of the thoracic region. The **sternum**, also known as the breastbone, is a thin bone that goes along the midline of the thoracic region. Most of the ribs are connected to this bone via the **costal cartilage**, a thin band of cartilage.

The human skeleton has are twelve **ribs**. On the back side, they are attached to the thoracic vertebrae. On the front, the first seven of them attach directly to the sternum. The next three attach to the cartilage between the seventh rib and the sternum, and the remaining two do not attach to the sternum at all. Rather, they protect the kidneys, not the lungs and heart. The first seven ribs are known as the true ribs, and the rest are known as false ribs. Together, these bones form the **thoracic cage**, which supports and protects the heart and lungs.

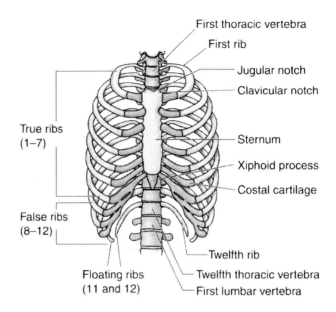

First thoracic vertebra
First rib
Jugular notch
Clavicular notch
Sternum
Xiphoid process
Costal cartilage
True ribs (1–7)
False ribs (8–12)
Floating ribs (11 and 12)
Twelfth rib
Twelfth thoracic vertebra
First lumbar vertebra

## The Appendicular Skeleton

The upper limbs, which belong to the **appendicular skeleton**, are connected with the axial skeleton by the **pectoral girdle**. The pectoral girdle is formed from the left and right **clavicle** and **scapula**. The scapula and the **humerus**, the bones of the upper arm, form the ball and socket of the shoulder joint. The upper limbs also include the **ulna**, which forms the elbow joint with the humerus, and the **radius**, which allows the turning movement at the wrist.

The **wrist joint** is formed out of the forearm bones and the eight **carpal** bones, which themselves are connected with the five **metacarpals**. Together, these structures form the bones of the hand. The metacarpals connect with the fingers, each made out of three bones called **phalanges**, except the thumb that only has two phalanges.
The lower limbs are connected to the axial skeleton by the **pelvic girdle**, which includes the left and right hip bone. The hip joint is formed by the hip bone and the **femur**, which is the largest bone in the body. On its other end, the femur forms the knee joint with the **patella** (the kneecap) and the **tibia**, which is one of the bones of the lower leg.

Of the two lower leg bones, the **tibia** is the larger, and it carries the weight of the body. The **fibula**, the other leg bone, serves mostly to anchor the muscle. Together, these two bones form the ankle joint with a foot bone called the **talus**. The talus is one of seven tarsal bones that form the back part of the foot and the heel. They connect to the five long **metatarsals**, which form the foot itself and connect to the toes. Each toe is made out of three phalanges, except the big toe, which has only two phalanges.

## The Joints

The **joints**, also known as articulations, are where the bones come into contact with each other, with cartilage, or with teeth. There are three types of joints: synovial, fibrous, and cartilaginous joints

The **synovial joints** feature a small gap between the bones that is filled with synovial fluid, which lubricates the joint. They are the most common joints in the body, and they allow the most movement. **Fibrous joints,** found where bones fit tightly together, permit little to no movement. These joints also hold teeth in their sockets. In a **cartilaginous joint, two bones are held together by cartilage; these joints** allow more movement than fibrous joints but less than synovial ones.

# Practice Drill: The Skeletal System

1. How many bones do adults have?
A)    201
B)    206
C)    222
D)    300

2. Stem cells can be found in the:
A)    red bone marrow
B)    periosteum
C)    compact bones
D)    cartilaginous joints

3. The long bones are the main bones of the:
A)    limbs
B)    thoracic cage
C)    scull
D)    vertebral column

4. The jawbone is called the:
A)    mandible
B)    cranium
C)    hyoid
D)    ulna

5. The second vertebra in the chest region is called:
A)    L2
B)    L3
C)    T2
D)    T3

Answers: 1) **B** 2) **A** 3) **A** 4) **A** 5) **C**

## The Muscular System

Movement is the main function of the **muscular system**; muscles are found attached to the bones in our bodies and allow us to move our limbs. They also work in the heart, blood vessels, and digestive organs, where they facilitate movement of substances through the body. In addition to movement, muscles also help support the body's posture and create heat. There are three types of muscle: visceral, cardiac, and skeletal.

### Visceral Muscle
**Visceral muscle** is the weakest type of muscle. It can be found in the stomach, intestines, and blood vessels, where it helps contract and move substances through them. We cannot consciously control visceral muscle – it is controlled by the unconscious part of the brain. That's why it's sometimes referred to as *involuntary muscle*.

Visceral muscle is also called **smooth muscle** because of its appearance under the microscope. The cells of the visceral muscle form a smooth surface, unlike the other two types of muscle.

### Cardiac Muscle
**Cardiac muscle** is only found in the heart; it makes the heart contract and pump blood through the body. Like visceral muscle, cardiac muscle cannot be voluntarily controlled. Unlike visceral muscle, however, the cardiac muscle is quite strong.

Cardiac muscle is composed of individual muscle cells called **cardiomyocytes** that are joined together by **intercalated discs**. These discs allow the cells in cardiac muscle to contract in sync. When observed under a microscope, light and dark stripes are visible in the muscle: this pattern is caused by the arrangement of proteins.

### Skeletal Muscle
The last type of muscle is **skeletal muscle**, which is the only type of muscle that contracts and relaxes by voluntary action. Skeletal muscle is attached to the bone by tendons. Tendons are formed out of connective tissue rich in collagen fibers.

Skeletal muscle is made out of cells that are lumped together to form fiber structures. These fibers are covered by a cell membrane called the **sarcolemma**, which serves as a conductor for electrochemical signals that tell the muscle to contract or expand. The **transverse tubes**, which are connected to the sarcolemma, transfer the signals deeper into the middle of the muscle fiber.

**Calcium ions**, which are necessary for muscle contraction, are stored in the **sarcoplasmic reticulum**. The fibers are also rich in **mitochondria**, which act as power stations fueled by sugars and providing the energy necessary for the muscle to work. Muscle fibers are mostly made out of **myofibrils**, which do the actual contracting. Myofibrils are made out of protein fibers arranged into small subunits called **sarcomeres**.

Skeletal muscle can be divided into two types, according to the way it produces and uses energy. **Type I** fibers contract slowly and are used for stamina and posture. They produce energy from sugar using aerobic respiration, making them resistant to fatigue. **Type II** muscle fibers contract more quickly. Type IIA fibers are found in the legs, and are weaker and show more endurance than Type IIB fibers, which are found mostly in the arms.

Skeletal muscles work by contracting. This shortens the length in their middle part, called the muscle belly, which in turn pulls one bone closer to another. The bone that remains stationary is called the **origin**. The other bone, the one that is moving towards the other, is called the **insertion**.

Skeletal muscles usually work in groups. The muscle mainly responsible for the action is called the **agonist**, and it's always paired with another muscle that does the opposite action, called the **antagonist**. If the two were to contract together at the same time, they would cancel each other out and produce no movement. Other muscles that support the agonist include **synergists**, which are found near the agonist, attach to the same bones, stabilize the movement, and reduce unnecessary movement. **Fixators** are other support muscles that keep the origin stable.

There are several different ways to name the more than six hundred skeletal muscles found in the human body. Muscles can be named according to:

- the region of the body in which they're located (e.g., transverse abdominis)
- number of origins (e.g., biceps)
- bones to which they are attached (e.g., occipitofrontalis)
- function (e.g., flexor)
- relative size (e.g., gluteus maximus)

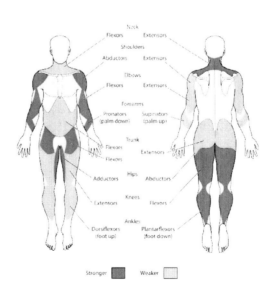

**Motor Neurons and Contractions**
The neurons that control muscles are called **motor neurons**. Motor neurons control a number of muscle cells that together are called the **motor unit**. The number of cells in the motor unit is larger in big muscles that need more strength, like those in the arms and legs. In small muscles where precision is more important than strength, like the muscles in fingers and around the eyes, the number of cells in motor units is smaller.

When signaled by motor neurons, muscles can contract in several different ways:

- isotonic muscle contractions: produce movement
- isometric muscle contractions: maintain posture and stillness
- muscle tone: naturally occurring constant semi-contraction of the muscle
- twitch contraction: a short contraction caused by a single, short nerve impulse
- temporal summation: a phenomenon in which a few short impulses delivered over time build up the muscle contraction in strength and duration
- tetanus: a state of constant contraction caused by many rapid short impulses

**Muscle Metabolism**
There are two ways muscles get energy: through aerobic respiration, which is most effective, and through **lactic acid fermentation**, which is a type of anaerobic respiration. The latter is less effective, and it only happens when blood cannot get into the muscle due to very strong or prolonged contraction.

In both these methods, the goal is to produce **adenosine tri-phosphate (ATP)** from glucose. ATP is the most important energy molecule for our bodies. During its conversion to **adenosine di-phosphate (ADP)**, energy is released.
Muscles also use other molecules to help in the production of energy. **Myoglobin** stores oxygen, allowing muscles to use aerobic respiration even when there is no blood coming into the muscles. **Creatine phosphate** creates ATP by giving its phosphate group to the energy-depleted adenosine di-phosphate. Lastly, muscles use **glycogen**, a large molecule made out of several glucose molecules, which help muscles make ATP.

When it runs out of energy, a muscle goes into a state called **muscle fatigue**. This means it contains little to no oxygen, ATP, or glucose, and that it has high levels of lactic acid and ADP. When a muscle is fatigued, it needs more oxygen to replace the oxygen used up from myoglobin sources and to rebuild its other energy supplies.

# Practice Drill: The Muscular System

1. Which type of muscle is found in the blood vessels?
A)      cardiac muscle
B)      skeletal muscle
C)      visceral muscle
D)      Type IIA

2. Cardiac muscle is:
A)      involuntary muscle
B)      voluntary muscle
C)      both
D)      neither

3. Tendons always attach skeletal muscle to bone:
A)      along the entire length of the bone
B)      at one end only
C)      at both ends
D)      at least one end

4. Myofibrils:
A)      store sugars
B)      are found only in smooth muscle
C)      make up the sarcolemma
D)      cause muscle contractions

5. Which is the strongest type of skeletal muscle?
A)      Type I
B)      Type II A
C)      Type II B
D)      Type III

Answers: 1) **C**  2) **A**  3) **D**  4) **D**  5) **C**

## The Nervous System

The **nervous system** consists of the brain, the spinal cord, the nerves, and the sensory organs. This system is responsible for gathering, processing, and reacting to information from both inside and outside of the body. It is divided into two parts: the central nervous system and the peripheral nervous system. The **central nervous system** (CNS) is made of the brain and spinal cord and is responsible for processing and storing information, as well as deciding on the appropriate action and issuing commands.

The **peripheral nervous system** (PNS) is responsible for gathering information, transporting it to the CNS, and then transporting commands from the CNS to the appropriate organs. Sensory organs and nerves do the gathering and transporting of information while the efferent nerves transport the commands.

### Nervous System Cells

The nervous system is mostly made out of nervous tissue, which in turn consists of two classes of cells: neurons and neuralgia. **Neurons** are the nerve cells. They can be divided into several distinct parts. The **soma** is the body of the neuron; it contains most of the cellular organelles. **Dendrites** are small, treelike structures that extend from the soma. Their main responsibility is to carry information to the soma, and sometimes away from it. Also extending from the soma is the long, thin **axon**. There is usually one axon per soma, but the axon can branch out farther. It is responsible for sending information from the soma, rarely to it. Lastly, the places where two neurons meet, or where they meet other types of cells, are called **synapses**.

Neurons can be divided into three classes. **Efferent neurons** are motor neurons responsible for transmitting signals from the CNS to the effectors in the body, while **afferent neurons** transmit signals from receptors in the body to the CNS. The third type of neuron—**interneurons**—form complex networks in the CNS. They integrate the signals received from the afferent neurons and control the body by sending signals through the efferent neurons.

Together, these three types of neurons perform the three main tasks of the nervous system:

1. Efferent neurons (also called motor neurons) signal effector cells in muscles and glands to react to stimuli.

2 Afferent neurons (also called sensory neurons) take in information from inside and outside the body through the sensory organs and receptors.

3. Interneurons transmit information to the CNS where it is evaluated, compared to previously stored information, stored or discarded, and used to make a decision (a process called integration).

**Neuralgia** are the maintenance cells for neurons. Neurons are so specialized that they almost never reproduce. Therefore, they need the neuralgia cells, a number of which surround every neuron, to protect and feed them. Neuralgia are also called the **glial cells**.

## Protecting the Central Nervous System

The CNS consists of the brain and spinal cord. Both are placed within cavities in protective skeletal structures: the brain is housed in the cranial cavity of the skull, and the spinal cord is enclosed in the vertebral cavity in the spine.

Since the organs that form the CINS are vital to our survival, they are also protected by two other important structures: the meninges and the cerebrospinal fluid. The **meninges** are a protective covering of the CNS made up of three distinct layers. The first is the **dura mater**, which, as its name suggests, is the most durable, outer part of the meninges. It is made out of collagen fibers-rich and thick connective tissue, and it forms a space for the cerebrospinal fluid around the CNS.

Next is the **arachnoid mater**, which is the thin lining on the inner side of the dura mater. It forms many tiny fibers that connect the dura mater with the next layer, the **pia mater**, which is separated from the arachnoid mater by the **subarachnoid space**. The pia mater directly covers the surface of the brain and spinal cord, and it provides sustenance to the nervous tissue through its many blood vessels.

The subarachnoid space is filled with **cerebrospinal fluid** (CSF), a clear fluid formed from blood plasma. CSF can also be found in the ventricles (the hollow spaces in the brain) and in the central canal (a cavity found in the middle of the spinal cord).

As the CNS floats in the cerebrospinal fluid, it appears lighter than it really is. This is especially important for the brain, because the fluid keeps it from being crushed by its own weight. The floating also protects the brain and the spinal cord from shock – like sudden movements and trauma. Additionally, the CSF contains the necessary chemical substance for the normal functioning of the nervous tissue, and it serves to remove the cellular waste form the neurons.

## The Brain

The nervous tissue that makes up the brain is divided into two classes. The **gray matter**, which consists mostly of interneurons that are unmyelinated, is the tissue where the actual processing of signals happens. It is also where the connections between neurons are made. The **white matter**, which consists mostly of myelinated neurons, and is the tissue that conducts signals to, from, and between the gray matter regions.

The brain can be divided into three distinct parts: the prosencephalon (forebrain), the mesencephalon (midbrain), and the rhombencephalon (hindbrain).

The **prosencephalon** is further broken down into two more regions: the cerebrum and the diencephalon. The outermost and the largest part of the brain, the **cerebrum** is divided through the middle by the longitudinal fissure into the left and the right hemisphere. Each of which is further divided into four lobes: the frontal, parietal, temporal, and occipital.

The surface of the cerebrum, called the **cerebral cortex**, is made out of gray matter with characteristic grooves (**sulci**) and bulges (**gyri**). The cerebral cortex is where the actual processing happens in the cerebrum: it's responsible for the higher brain functions like thinking and using language. Under the cerebral cortex, there is a layer of white matter, which connects the regions of the cerebrum with one another, and the cerebrum itself with the rest of the body. It contains a special band of white matter that connects the two hemispheres, which is called the **corpus callosum**. The regions located under the white matter are divided into two groups: the basal nuclei, which help control and regulate the movement of muscles, and the limbic system, which plays a role in memory, emotions, and survival.

The **diencephalon** is a structure formed by the thalamus, hypothalamus, and the pineal gland. Made out of two gray matter masses, the **thalamus** is located around the third ventricle of the brain. Its role is to route the sensory signals to the correct parts of the cerebral cortex. Under the thalamus is the **hypothalamus**, which plays a role in regulating hunger, thirst, blood pressure and body temperature changes, as well as the heart rate and the production of hormones. The **pineal gland** is located beneath the hypothalamus (and is directly controlled by it) and produces the hormone melatonin, which plays a vital role in sleep.

The **mesencephalon** is the topmost part of the brain stem. It is divided into two regions. The first is the **tectum**, which plays a role in reflex reactions to visual and auditory information. Second is the **cerebral peduncles**, which connect the cerebrum and thalamus with the lower parts of the brain stem and the spinal cord. It also contains the **substantia nigra**, which is involved in muscle movement, reward-seeking, and learning.

The **rhombencephalon** consists of the brain stem and the cerebellum. The brain stem is further broken down into the medulla oblongata and the pons. The **medulla oblongata** connects the spinal cord with the pons. It is mostly made out of white matter, but it also contains gray matter that processes involuntary body functions like blood pressure, level of oxygen in the blood, and reflexes like sneezing, coughing, vomiting and swallowing. The **pons** is located between the medulla oblongata and the midbrain, and in front of the cerebellum. It is in charge of transporting signals to and from the cerebellum, and the between the upper regions of the brain, the medulla and the spinal cord.

The **cerebellum** looks like a smaller version of the cerebrum—it has two spheres and is wrinkled. Its outer layer, called the **cerebellar cortex**, consists of gray matter, while the inner part, called the **arbor vitae**, consists of white matter that transports signals between the cerebellum and the rest of the body. The cerebellum's role is to control and coordinate complex muscle activities. It also helps us maintain posture and keep balance.

## The Spinal Cord

The **spinal cord**, located inside the vertebral cavity, is made out of both white and gray matter. It carries signals and processes some reflexes to stimuli. The spinal nerves stretch out from it.

## Peripheral Nerves

The nerves that form the PNS are made of bundled axons whose role is to carry signals to and from the spinal cord and the brain. A single axon, covered with a layer of connective tissue called the **endoneurium**, bundles with other axons to form **fascicles**. These are covered with another sheath of connective tissue called the **perineurium**. Groups of fascicles wrapped together in another layer of connective tissue, the **epineurium**, form a whole nerve.

There are five types of peripheral nerves. The **afferent, efferent,** and **mixed** nerves are formed out of the neurons that share the same name and perform the same roles. The **spinal nerves**—thirty-one pairs in total—extend from the side of the spinal cord. They exit the spinal cord between the vertebrae, and they carry information to and from the spinal cord and the neck, the arms, the legs and the trunk. They are grouped and named according to the region they originate from: eight pairs of cervical, twelve pairs of thoracic, five pairs of lumbar, five pairs of sacral, and one pair coccygeal nerves. Lastly, the **cranial nerves**—12 pairs in total—extend from the lower side of the brain. They are identified by their number, and they connect the brain with the sensory organs, head muscles, neck and shoulder muscles, the heart, and the gastrointestinal track.

## The Sense Organs

The sense organs include the specialized sense organs, which are responsible for the specialized senses: hearing, sight, balance, smell and taste. Sense organs also have sensory receptors for the general senses, which include touch, pain, and temperature. These senses are part of the PNS, and their role is to detect the stimuli and send the signal to the CNS when the detection occurs.

## The Divisions of the Peripheral Nervous System

The PNS is divided into two parts based on our ability to exert conscious control. The part of the PNS we can consciously control is the **somatic nervous system** (SNS), which stimulates the skeletal muscles. The **autonomic nervous system** (ANS) cannot be consciously controlled; it stimulates the visceral and cardiac muscle, as well as the glandular tissue.

The ANS itself is further divided into the sympathetic, parasympathetic, and enteric nervous systems. The **sympathetic nervous system** forms the fight or flight reaction to stimuli like emotion, danger and exercise. It increases respiration and heart rate, decreases digestion, and releases stress hormones. The **parasympathetic nervous system (PN)** is responsible for stimulating activities that occur when the body is at rest, including digestion and sexual arousal.

Lastly, the **enteric nervous system** (ENS) is responsible for the digestive system and its processes. This system works mostly independently from the CNS, although it can be regulated through the sympathetic and parasympathetic division.

## Practice Drill: The Nervous System

1. Which of the following forms the CNS along with the brain?
A)     the peripheral nerves
B)     the sensory organs
C)     the spinal cord
D)     the cerebral cortex

2. The part of the neuron that is mainly responsible for transporting information from the cell is called the
A)     soma
B)     axon
C)     dendrites
D)     sulci

3. The neurons that signal muscles to contract are called
A)     neuralgia
B)     afferent neurons
C)     interneurons
D)     efferent neurons

4. Cerebrospinal fluid can be found in all of the following except:
A)     arachnoid mater
B)     the central canal
C)     the ventricles
D)     the subarachnoid space

5.  The hypothalamus is located in the:
A)     mesencephalon
B)     rhombencephalon
C)     prosencephalon
D)     pineal gland

Answers: 1) **C**  2) **B**  3) **D**  4) **A**  5) **C**

**The Digestive System**

The **digestive system** is a system of organs in the body that is responsible for the intake and processing of food and the removal of food waste products. The digestive system ensures that the body has the necessary nutrients and the energy it needs to function.

The digestive system includes the **gastrointestinal** (GI) **tract**, which is formed by the organs through which the food passes on its way through the body:

1. oral cavity
2. pharynx
3. esophagus
4. stomach
5. small intestines
6. large intestines

Throughout the digestive system, there are also organs that have a role in processing food Even though food doesn't pass through them directly. These include the teeth, tongue, salivary glands, liver, gallbladder, and pancreas.

# DIGESTIVE SYSTEM

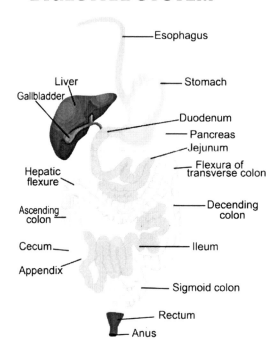

**The Mouth**

The digestive system begins with the **mouth**. Also known as the oral cavity, the mouth contains other organs that play a role in digestion. The **teeth** are small organs that cut and grind food. They are located on the edges of the mouth, are made out of dentin, which is a substance that resembles bone, and are covered by enamel. The teeth are very hard organs, and each of them has its own blood vessels and nerves, which are located in the matter that fills the tooth, called the pulp.

Also in the mouth is the **tongue**, which is a muscle located behind the teeth. The tongue contains the taste buds and moves food around the mouth as it is being processed by the teeth. It then moves food towards the pharynx when it's time to swallow. The **salivary glands**, located around the mouth, produce saliva. There are three pairs of salivary glands, and the saliva they produce lubricates and digests carbohydrates.

## The Pharynx

The **pharynx** is a tube that enables the passage of food and air further into the body. This structure performs two functions. The pharynx needs the help of the epiglottis, which allows food to pass to the esophagus by covering the opening of the larynx, a structure that carries air into the lungs. When you need to breathe in, the esophagus is closed, so the air passes only into the larynx.

## The Esophagus

The **esophagus** begins at the pharynx and continues to carry food all the way to the stomach. The esophagus is a muscular tube, and the muscles in its wall help to push food down. During vomiting, it pushes food up.

The esophagus has two rings of muscle, called **sphincters**. These sphincters close at the top and the bottom ends of the esophagus when food is not passing through it. Heartburn occurs when the bottom sphincter cannot close entirely and allows the contents of the stomach to enter the esophagus.

## The Stomach

The stomach is a round organ located on the left side of the body just beneath the diaphragm. It is divided into four different regions. The **cardia** connects the stomach to the esophagus, transitioning from the tube-like shape of the esophagus into the sack shape of the rest of the stomach. The cardia is also where the lower sphincter of the esophagus is located.

The **body** of the stomach is its largest part, and the **fundus** is located above the body. The last part of the stomach is the **pylorus**, a funnel-shaped region located beneath the body of the stomach. It controls the passage of partially digested food further down the GI tract through the **pyloric sphincter**.

The stomach is made out of four layers of tissue. The innermost layer, the **mucosa**, contains a smooth muscle and the mucus membrane that secretes digestive enzymes and hydrochloric acid. The cells that secrete these products are located within the small pores called the **gastric pits**. The mucus membrane also secretes mucus to protect the stomach from its own digestive enzymes.

The **submucosa** is located around the mucosa and is made of connective tissue; it contains nerves and the blood vessels. The **muscularis** layer enables the movement of the stomach; it's made up of three layers of smooth muscle. This layer enables the movement of the stomach. The outermost layer of the stomach is the serosa. It secretes

**serous fluid** that keeps the stomach wet and reduces friction between the stomach and the surrounding organs.

### The Small Intestine

The **small intestine** continues from the stomach and takes up most of the space in the abdomen. It's attached to the wall of the abdomen and measures around twenty-two feet long.

The small intestine can be divided into three parts. The **duodenum** is the part of the small intestine that receives the food and chemicals from the stomach. The **jejunum**, which continues from the duodenum, is where most of the nutrients are absorbed into the blood. Lastly, the **ileum**, which continues from the jejunum, is where the rest of the nutrients are absorbed.

Absorption in the small intestine is helped by the **villi**, which are small protrusions that increase the surface area available for absorption. The villi are made out of smaller microvilli.

### The Liver and Gallbladder

The **liver** is not a part of the GI tract. However, it performs roles that are vital for digestion and life itself. The liver is located just beneath the diaphragm and is the largest organ in the body after the skin. It's triangular in shape, and extends across the whole width of the abdomen.

The liver is divided into four lobes: the left lobe, the right lobe, the caudate lobe (which wraps around the inferior vena cava), and the quadrate lobe (which wraps around the gallbladder). The liver is connected to the peritoneum by the coronary, left, right, and falciform ligaments.

The liver is responsible for a number of functions, including detoxification of the blood, storage of nutrients, and production of components of blood plasma. Its role in digestion is to produce **bile**, a fluid that aids in the digestion of fats. After its production, bile is carried through the bile ducts to the **gallbladder**, a small muscular, pear-shaped organ that stores and releases bile.

### The Pancreas

The **pancreas** is another organ that is not part of the GI tract but which plays a role in digestion. It's located below and to the left of the stomach. The pancreas secretes both the enzymes that digest food and the hormones insulin and glucagon, which control blood sugar levels.

The pancreas is what is known as a **heterocrine gland**, which means it contains both endocrine tissue, which produces insulin and glucagon that move directly into the bloodstream, and exocrine tissue, which produces digestive enzymes that pass into the small intestine.

These enzymes include:
- pancreatic amylase: breaks large polysaccharides into smaller sugars
- trypsin, chymotrypsin, and carboxypeptidase: break down proteins into amino acid subunits
- pancreatic lipase: breaks down large fat molecules into fatty acids and monoglyceride
- ribonuclease and deoxyribonuclease: digest nucleic acids.

**The Large Intestine**

The **large intestine** continues from the small intestine and loops around it. No digestion takes part in the large intestine. Rather, it absorbs water and some leftover vitamins. The large intestine carries waste (feces) to the **rectum**, where it's stored until it's expelled through the **anus**.

# Practice Drill: The Digestive System

1. Food passes through all of the following organs except:
A)   stomach
B)   large intestine
C)   esophagus
D)   liver

2. How many pair(s) of salivary glands are in the human body?
A)   1
B)   2
C)   3
D)   4

3. The esophagus performs all of the following functions except:
A)   connecting the pharynx to the stomach
B)   preventing stomach acid from reaching the pharynx
C)   pushing food into the stomach
D)   moving food from the stomach to the small intestine

4. Which layer of the stomach contains blood vessels and nerves?
A)   the mucosa
B)   the submucosa
C)   the serosa
D)   the cardia

5. Bile is stored in the
A)   liver
B)   duodenum
C)   gallbladder
D)   pancreas

Answers: 1) **D**  2) **C**  3) **D**  4) **B**  5) **C**

**The Endocrine System**

The **endocrine system** consists of many **glands** that produce and secrete hormones, which send signals to molecules that traveling through the bloodstream. **Hormones** allow cells, tissues, and organs to communicate with each other, and they play a role in almost all bodily functions, including growth, sleeping, digestion, response to stress, and sexual functioning. The glands of the endocrine system are scattered throughout the body, and each has a specific role to play.

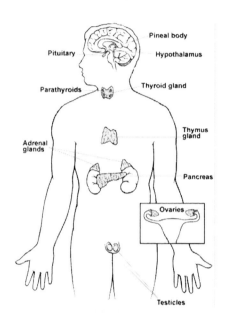

- The **pituitary gland** hangs from the base of your brain and produces the hormone that controls growth and some aspects of sexual functioning. (hormones: growth hormone, thyroid stimulating hormone, oxytocin, follicle-stimulating hormone)
- The **hypothalamus** is also located in the brain. Its main function is to control the pituitary gland, and many of the hormones it releases stimulate the pituitary gland to in turn release hormones itself. (hormones: dopamine, thyrotropin-releasing hormone, growth-hormone releasing hormone)
- The **pineal body**, located in the brain, releases melatonin, a hormone that induces drowsiness and lowers body temperature. (hormone: melatonin)
- The **thyroid gland** is found in the neck just below the Adam's apple. It controls protein production and the body's use of energy. (hormones: $T_3$ and thyroxine) The thyroid is regulated by the thyroid-stimulating hormone, which is released by the pituitary gland.
- The **parathyroid glands** are located behind the thyroid. They produce parathyroid hormone, which regulates calcium and phosphate levels in the body. (hormones: parathyroid hormone)
- The **pancreas,** discussed above, is located behind the stomach and releases hormones that regulate digestion and blood-sugar levels. (hormones: insulin, glucagon, somatostatin)
- The **adrenal glands** sit atop the kidneys. The adrenal glands have two regions that produce two sets of hormone: the adrenal cortex releases corticosteroids and androgens while the adrenal medulla regulates the fight-or-flight response. (hormones: cortisol, testosterone, adrenaline, noradrenaline, dopamine).
- The **testes** are glands found in males; they regulate maturation of sex organs and the development of secondary sex characteristics like muscle mass and growth of axillary hair. (hormones: testosterone, estradiol)
- The **ovaries** are glands found in females; they regulate the menstrual cycle, pregnancy, and secondary sex characteristics like enlargement of breasts and the widening of the hips. (hormone: progesterone, estrogen)

# Practice Drill: The Endocrine System

1. Which gland(s) indirectly controls growth by acting on the pituitary?
A)      hypothalamus
B)      thyroid
C)      adrenal glands
D)      parathyroid glands

2. Which hormone is primary responsible for the development of male secondary sexual characteristics?
A)      melatonin
B)      follicle-stimulating hormone
C)      estrogen
D)      testosterone

3. A patient experiencing symptoms such as kidney stones and arthritis due to a calcium imbalance probably has a disorder of which gland?
A)      hypothalamus
B)      thyroid
C)      parathyroid
D)      adrenal glands

Answer: 1) **A**  2) **D**  3) **C**

**The Reproductive System**

Reproductive systems are the groups of organs that enable the successful reproduction of a species. In humans, fertilization is internal, with sperm being transferred from the male to the female during copulation.

**The Male Reproductive System**
The male reproductive system consists of the organs that produce and ejaculate **sperm**, the male gamete. Sperm are produced in the **testes**, which are housed in the **scrotum**, which is located under the penis. During sexual arousal, the **vas deferens** carry sperm to the **urethra**, the tube that runs through the **penis** and carries semen (and urine) out of the body. Also emptying into the urethra is the **prostate gland**, which produces a nutrient-filled fluid that protects sperm and makes up the majority of **semen**. Before ejaculation, the **Cowper's gland** produces a thin, alkaline fluid that flushes any remaining urine from the urethra and makes up a small portion of the semen.

**The Female Reproductive System**
Sexual reproduction in animals occurs in cycles that depend on the production of an **ovule**, or egg, by the female of the species. In humans, the reproductive cycle occurs approximately once a month when an egg is released from the female's ovaries.

The female reproductive organs, or gonads, are called **ovaries**. Each ovary has a follicle that contains **oocytes**, or undeveloped eggs. The surrounding cells in the ovary help to protect and nourish the oocyte until it is needed. During the menstrual cycle, one or more oocytes will mature into an egg with help from the **corpus luteum**, a mass of follicular tissue that provides nutrients to the egg and secretes estradiol and progesterone.

Once it has matured, the egg will be released into the **fallopian tube** where fertilization will take place if sperm are present. The egg will then travel into the **uterus**. Unfertilized eggs are shed along with the uterine lining during **menstruation**. Fertilized eggs, known as **zygotes**, implant in the lining of the uterus where they continue to develop.

**Embryo Fertilization and Development**
After fertilization, the cell will start to divide and, after four to five days, become a ball of cells known as a **blastocyst**. The blastocyst is then implanted into the **endometrium** of the uterus. After the blastocyst has been implanted onto the endometrium, the placenta develops. The **placenta** is a temporary organ that attaches the embryo to the mother. It provides nutrients to the fetus, carries waste away from the fetus, protects the fetus from infection, and produces hormones that support pregnancy. The placenta develops from cells called the **trophoblast**, which come from the outer layer of the blastocyst.

In humans, the gestation period of the **embryo** (also called the **fetus**), is 266 days or roughly 8.8 months. The human development cycle in the womb is divided into three trimesters. In the first trimester, the organs responsible for the embryo's growth develop. This includes the placenta and umbilical cord. During this time, **organogenesis** occurs, and the various stem cells from the blastocyst differentiate into the organs of the body. The organs are not fully developed at this point, but they do exist.

In the second trimester, the fetus experiences rapid growth, up to about 25-30 cm in length. At this point, it is usually apparent that the woman is pregnant, as the uterus grows and extends, and the woman's belly becomes slightly distended. In the third trimester, the fetus finishes developing. The baby exits the uterus through the **cervix** and leaves the body through the **vagina**.

# Practice Drill: The Reproductive System

1. All of the following contribute material to semen except:
A)      the prostate
B)      Cowper's gland
C)      the penis
D)      the testes

2. Fertilization typically takes place in the:
A)      fallopian tubes
B)      ovaries
C)      uterus
D)      cervix

3. Which of the following statements about the placenta is not true?
A)      The placenta serves as part of the endocrine system because it releases hormones.
B)      The placenta provides nutrients to the fetus.
C)      The placenta develops from the outer layer of cells on the blastocyst.
D)      The placenta is expelled during the menstrual cycle if fertilization does not take place.

Answer: 1) **C**  2) **A**  3) **D**

**Physics**

Physics is the science of matter and energy, and of the interaction between the two. Physics is grouped into fields such as acoustics (the study of sound), optics (the study of light), mechanics (the study of motion), and electromagnetism (the study of electric and magnetic fields).

**Mechanics**

$$d = vt$$
$$v_f = v_0 t + at$$
$$p = mv$$

Newtonian mechanics is the study of masses in motion using five main variables. **Mass** ($m$), as discussed above, is the amount of matter in an object; it is measured in kilograms (kg). **Displacement** ($d$) is a measure of how far an object has moved from its starting point, usually given in meters (m). **Velocity** is the distance covered by an object over a given period of **time**, usually given in meters per second (m/s). Finally, the change in velocity over time is called **acceleration** ($a$) and is measured in meters per second squared (m/s²).

Velocity and displacement are both **vectors,** meaning they have a magnitude (e.g., 4 m/s) and a direction (e.g., 45°). **Scalars**, on the other hand, have only a magnitude. **Distance** is a scalar: it describes how far something has traveled. So, if you run 1000 meters around a track and end up back where you started, your displacement is 0 meters, but the distance you covered was 1000 meters. **Speed** is also a scalar; it is the distance traveled over the time the trip took.

Multiplying an object's mass by its velocity gives a quantity called **momentum** ($p$), which is measured in kilogram meters per second ((kg · m)/s). Momentum is always conserved, meaning when objects collide the sum of their momentums before the collision with each other will be the same as the sum after.

**Forces**

| force | formula |
|---|---|
| gravity | $F_g = mg$ (for falling objects) |
| | $F_g = \frac{Gm_1m_2}{r^2}$ (for the gravitational force between two masses) |
| electrostatic | $F = k\frac{q_1q_2}{r^2}$ |

Obviously, objects need a reason to get moving: they don't just start accelerating on their own. The "push" that starts or stops an object's motion is called a **force** ($F$) and is measured in Newtons (N). Examples of forces include gravity (created by mass of objects), friction (created by the movement of two surfaces in contact with each other), tension (created by hanging a mass from a string or chain), and electrical force (created by charged particles). The force needed to create circular motion is called the **centripetal force**. Note that all of these forces are vectors with a magnitude and direction. Gravity, for example, always points down toward the earth, and centripetal forces always point toward the center of the circular path.

Newton's three laws of motion describe how these forces work to create motion:

Law #1: An object at rest will remain at rest, and an object in motion will continue with the same speed and direction unless acted on by a force. This law is often called "the law of inertia."

Law #2: Acceleration is produced when a force acts on a mass. The greater the mass of the object being accelerated, the greater the amount of force needed to accelerate the object.

Law #3: Every action requires an equal and opposite reaction. This means that for every force, there is a reacting force both equal in size and opposite in direction. In other words, whenever an object pushes another object, it gets pushed back in the opposite direction with equal force.

## Energy

$$KE = \frac{1}{2}mv^2$$
$$PE_g = mgh$$

In simple terms, energy is the capacity to do work; in other words, it's a measurement of how much force a system could apply. There are two main categories of energy. The energy stored within an object is its **potential energy**: that object has the potential to do work. Potential energy can be created in a number of ways, including raising an object off the ground or compressing a spring. **Kinetic energy** is the energy possessed by an object due to its motion. The sum of an object's kinetic and potential energies is called the total **mechanical energy**.

Energy can be neither created nor destroyed; it can only be converted from one form to another. For example, when a rock is lifted some distance from the ground it has **gravitational potential energy**; when it's released, it begins to move toward the earth and that potential energy becomes kinetic energy. A pendulum is another example: at the height of its swing, the pendulum will have potential energy but no kinetic energy; at the bottom of its swing, it has kinetic energy but no more potential energy.

## Thermodynamics

While the terms are often used interchangeably, heat and temperature are actually two different things. **Temperature** is a measure of the average kinetic energy of the atoms or molecules of a substance. Substances with a higher temperature have more kinetic energy, meaning their molecules are moving at a higher velocity. Lowering the temperature of the substance will slow the speed of the molecules.

**Heat** is the transfer of energy between substances. When the air warms a block of ice, or a soda gets cold in the fridge, that transfer of energy is heat. Heat always moves from warmer substances to colder ones). Heat can be transferred in several different ways. One is **conduction**, which occurs when heat is transferred between neighboring molecules; conduction is what makes your hand cold when you hold an ice cube. During **convection**, heat is transferred away from an object by the movement of gases or fluids, for example when warm air rises from a radiator.

## Waves

A **wave** is a periodic motion that carried energy through space or matter. There are two main types of waves: mechanical and electromagnetic. **Mechanical waves** travel through a physical medium; ripples in a pond and sound waves traveling through the air are both examples of mechanical waves. **Electromagnetic waves** do not require a medium to travel because they consist of oscillating magnetic and electric fields. These waves are classified on the **electromagnetic spectrum** and include visible light, x-rays, and radio waves.

## Characteristics of Waves

$$v = \lambda f = \frac{\lambda}{T}$$

The four major characteristics of waves are wavelength, amplitude, period, and frequency. The **wavelength** ($\lambda$) is the distance from the peak of one wave to the next (or from the trough of one wave to the next). The **amplitude** ($A$) of a wave is the distance from the top of the wave to the bottom. Both wavelength and amplitude are measured in meters (the SI unit for distance).

The **period** ($T$) of a wave is the time it takes the wave to complete one oscillation; it is usually measured in seconds. The **frequency** ($f$) of a wave is the number of oscillations that occur per second; it is measured in $s^{-1}$. The period and frequency of a wave are inverses of each other: the shorter the period of a wave, the higher its frequency.

## Properties of Waves

Waves off all kinds exhibit particular behaviors. Waves can interact to either to create **constructive interference**, where the resulting wave is bigger than either original wave, or **destructive interference**, which creates a wave that is smaller than either original wave. Waves will also bend when passing through a slit, a process called **diffraction**. Waves will also **refract**, or bend, when they pass from one medium into another.

## Light

Light, which is an electromagnetic wave, has a number of special properties because it acts as both a particle and a wave—a phenomenon called the **wave-particle duality of light**. Light waves can experience both interference and diffraction like any other wave. Because light is made up of discrete packets of energy (called quanta), light also sometimes acts as a particle. For example, when light strikes a metal surface, the packets of energy can eject electrons from atoms in a process called the **photoelectric effect**.

# Practice Drill: Physics

1. An object that has kinetic energy must be:
A)    moving.
B)    falling.
C)    in an elevated position.
D)    at rest.

2. A moving object has
A)    velocity
B)    momentum
C)    energy
D)    all of these

3. _____ increases or decreases the rate of an object's motion or changes the object's direction of motion.
A)    force
B)    energy
C)    momentum
D)    inertia

4. _____is a measure of the average kinetic energy of the atoms or molecules of a substance.
A)    Specific heat
B)    Temperature
C)    Heat
D)    Force

5. Average speed is:
A)    A measure of how fast something is moving.
B)    The distance covered per unit of time.
C)    Always measured in terms of a unit of distance divided by a unit of time.
D)    All of the above.

6. Which of the following controls can change a car's velocity?
A)    The steering wheel.
B)    The brake pedal.
C)    Both A and B.
D)    None of the above.

Answers: 1) **A**  2) **D**  3) **A**  4) **B**  5) **D**  6) **C**

**Chemistry**

**Matter**
**Matter** is commonly defined as anything that takes up space and has mass. **Mass** is the quantity of matter something possesses (e.g., how much of something there is); it is usually measured in grams (g) or kilograms (kg). In addition to mass, it's possible to measure many other properties of matter, including weight, volume, density, and reactivity. These properties fall into one of two categories: **extrinsic properties** are directly related to the amount of material being measured (e.g., mass and volume), while **intrinsic properties** are those which are independent of the quantity of matter present (e.g., density and specific gravity).

Matter can undergo two types of change: chemical and physical. A **chemical change** occurs when an original substance is transformed into a new substance with different properties. An example would be the burning of wood, which produces ash and smoke. Transformations that do not produce new substances, such as cutting a piece of wood or melting ice, are called **physical changes**.

**The Atom**
An **atom** is the smallest particle of an element that is still identifiable as a part of that element; if you break down an atom any further, it is no longer an identifiable element.

An atom is made up of several subatomic particles. The three most important are **protons**; which have a positive charge; **electrons**, which have a negative charge; and **neutrons**, which are neutral. The protons and neutrons of an atom are located at its center in the nucleus; the electrons move in orbitals around the nucleus. Protons and neutrons both have mass that's measured in atomic mass units (amu); the mass of an electron is so negligible that it is usually not considered. The nucleus is only a small portion of the total amount of space an atom takes up, even though most of an atom's mass is contained in the nucleus.

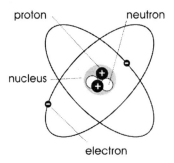

**Elements**
All atoms of the same **element** have the same number of protons (called that element's **atomic number**). For example, all carbon atoms have four protons. There are approximately 109 known elements; eighty-eight of these occur naturally on earth, while the others are synthesized (manufactured). The elements are grouped together on the Periodic Table, and each has its own one- or two-letter symbol.

While all atoms in an element have the same number of protons, they can have different numbers of neutrons and electrons. Atoms of the same element with different numbers of neutrons are called **isotopes** and can have different masses. Atoms of the same element that have different numbers of electrons are called **ions** and will have a charge (be positive or negative). If an atom has the same number of protons and electrons, it is neutral.

Hydrogen is the most abundant element in the universe: it's found in 75 percent of all matter known to exist. Helium is the second most abundant element, found in approximately 25 percent of all known matter. The Earth is composed mostly of iron, oxygen, silicon, and magnesium, though these elements are not evenly distributed. Ninety percent of the human body's mass consists of oxygen, carbon, hydrogen, nitrogen, calcium, and phosphorus. Seventy-five percent of elements are metals, and eleven are gases in their natural state.

## Molecules
A **molecule** is a group of atoms chemically bonded together; these atoms can be of the same or of different elements. The atoms can be held together by a number of different chemical bonds (see "Chemical Bonds" below). Chemical formulas are used to represent the atomic composition of a molecule. For example, one molecule of water contains two hydrogen atoms (H) and one oxygen atom (O), so its chemical formula is $H_2O$. Note

## The Mole
A **mole** is the amount of a substance that contains $6.02 \times 10^{23}$ particles. For example, a mole of copper is the amount of copper that contains exactly $6.02 \times 10^{23}$ atoms, and one mole of water contains $6.02 \times 10^{23}$ $H_2O$ molecules. This value is referred to as **Avogadro's number** and is based on the number of atoms in $^{12}C$ (Carbon 12). The weight of one mole of an element is called its **atomic weight**.

Because the weight of electrons is negligible, only the weight of protons and neutrons is considered when calculating atomic weight. The atomic weight of an element with isotopes is the average of the isotopes' individual atomic weights.

## Compounds and Mixtures
Substances that contain more than one type of element are called **compounds** (so a molecule that contains more than one element is also a compound). Compounds made up of identical molecules are called pure substances. Water, for example, is a pure substance made up only of identical water molecules.

A **mixture** consists of two or more substances that are not chemically bonded. Mixtures are placed in one of two categories. The components in a **homogeneous mixture** are uniformly distributed; examples include salt water and air. In a **heterogeneous mixture**, the components are not uniformly distributed. Vegetable soup, for example, is heterogeneous, as are rocks and soil.

A uniform, or homogenous, mixture of different molecules is called a **solution**. If the solution is a liquid, the material being dissolved is the **solute** and the liquid it is being dissolved in is called the **solvent**. Both solids and gases can dissolve in liquids. A **saturated solution** has reached a point of maximum concentration; no more solute will dissolve in it.

## Practice Drill: Matter

1. Which statement best describes an atom's nucleus?
A)      The nucleus takes up most of the atom's volume, but has little of its mass.
B)      The nucleus takes up very little of the atom's volume, and has little of its mass.
C)      The nucleus takes up most of the atom's volume, yet has most of its mass.
D)      The nucleus takes up very little of the atom's volume, yet contains most of its mass.

2. Which of the following is not a physical change?
A)      melting of aspirin
B)      lighting a match
C)      putting sugar in tea
D)      boiling antifreeze

3. The identity of an element is determined by:
A)      the number of its protons
B)      the number of its electrons
C)      its charge
D)      its atomic mass

4. An unsaturated solution:
A)      hasn't dissolved as much solute as is theoretically possible
B)      has dissolved exactly as much solute as is theoretically possible
C)      is unstable because it has dissolved more solute than would be expected
D)      is heterogeneous

5. A coffee solution is produced when a teaspoon of dry coffee crystals dissolves when mixed in a cup of hot water. The original crystals are classified as a:
A)      solute
B)      solvent
C)      reactant
D)      product

Answers: 1) **D**  2) **B**  3) **A**  4) **A**  5) **A**

## States of Matter

The physical states of matter are grouped into three main **states**:

**Solids** are rigid; they maintain their shape and have strong intermolecular forces. In solids, the molecules are closely packed together, and solid materials usually have a high density. In the majority of solids, called crystalline solids, the ions or molecules are packed into a crystal structure that is highly ordered.

**Liquids** cannot maintain their own shape; they conform to their containers but contain forces strong enough to keep molecules from dispersing into spaces.

**Gases** have indefinite shape; they disperse rapidly through space due to random movement of particles and are able to occupy any volume. They are held together by weak forces.

Two other states of matter include **liquid crystals**, which can maintain their shape as well as be made to flow, and **plasmas**, gases in which electrons have been stripped from their nuclei.

## Changes In State

Substances can change from one state to another when their temperature or the surrounding pressure changes. As a general rule, when the temperature increases, the matter will move from solid to liquid to gas. Changing the pressure will change the temperature at which these transitions will take place.

The changes between states each have their own specific terms. The **boiling point** is the combination of temperature and pressure at which matter moves from liquid to gas (vaporization). Bringing matter below the boiling point results in a change from gas to liquid (condensation). The heat or amount of energy needed to change the state of a particular substance from liquid to gas or vice versa is its **latent heat of vaporization**.

The **freezing point** (which is the same as the melting point) is the combination of pressure and temperature that results in a change from liquid to solid (freezing) or solid to liquid (melting). The heat required to change a substance's state from liquid to solid or vice versa is the **latent heat of fusion**.

Usually matter will pass from solid to liquid to gas, but matter can also change directly from solid to gas in a process called **sublimation**. The reverse process is called **deposition**.

The **critical point** is the temperature and pressure at which defined states do not exist. For example, at the critical point of water, which happens at 374°C and 218 atmospheres, there is no defined state for water. It is considered a plasma and behaves with properties of both liquids and gases.

**Phase diagrams** show the state of matter for a particular substance given different pressures and temperatures. Typically, as temperature drops, a substance is more likely to be a solid, and as pressure drops, a substance is more likely to be a gas. The point at which the three lines on a phase diagram meet is called the **triple point**, which is a state in which the material will exist in all three forms: solid, liquid, and gas.

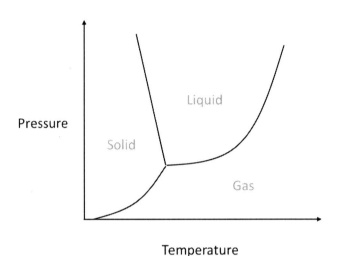

The **specific heat** of a substance is the amount of energy it requires to raise the substance by 1 unit of temperature. For example, the specific heat of water is about $4.19 \text{ J/g} \cdot \text{K}$. This means that you need 4.19 Joules of energy to heat 1 gram of water by 1 degree centigrade. The specific heat is a useful property that can be used to predict the amount of energy needed to heat up a substance. For example, if you want to warm a 100 mL (100 g) cup of water from 25 °C to 50 °C, you would need about 10,450 joules of energy.

**Gases**
The behavior of gases is described by a number of laws that relate to the volume ($V$), pressure ($P$), temperature ($T$), and number of molecules ($n$) in a sample of gas.

Boyle's Law: $P_1V_1 = P_2V_2$

Charles's Law: $\dfrac{V_1}{T_1} = \dfrac{V_2}{T_2}$

Avogadro's Law: $\dfrac{V_1}{n_1} = \dfrac{V_2}{n_2}$

Ideal Gas Law: $PV = nRT$ where $R = 8.314 \text{ J/mol} \cdot \text{K}$ and pressure is measured in Pascals. (Note that the value of $R$ changes when different units are used.)

The **kinetic theory of gases** assumes that gas molecules are very small compared to the distance between the molecules. Gas molecules are in constant, random motion; they frequently collide with each other and with the walls of whatever container they are in.

# Practice Drill: States of Matter

1. What is the correct term for the energy required for a solid to become a liquid?
A)    latent heat of vaporization
B)    latent heat of fusion
C)    latent heat of fission
D)    latent heat of condensation

2. Which of the following is not a state of matter?
A)    plasma
B)    liquid
C)    solid
D)    crystal

3. If the pressure is kept below water's triple point and the temperature is increased, ice will:
A)    turn to liquid
B)    turn to gas
C)    remain the same
D)    become more crystalline

4. Which of the following is likely to have the highest number of molecules?
A)    1 liter of water vapor
B)    1 liter of water
C)    0.5 liters of ice
D)    0.5 liters of an ice-water mixture

5. Which of the following is not true of a liquid?
A)    A liquid fills the volume of the container holding it.
B)    A liquid is fluid and can change shape.
C)    A liquid is always warmer than a solid.
D)    Molecules in a liquid can have attractive interactions.

6. The freezing point of a compound is the same as the:
A)    boiling point of the compound
B)    melting point of the compound
C)    triple point of the compound
D)    critical point of the compound

7. When the pressure is increased on a sample of gas with a constant temperature, its volume _____.
A)    stays the same
B)    increases
C)    decreases
D)    oscillates

8. A scientist has 1 mol of a sample of gas at 274°C and 1 atm of pressure. How much volume will it occupy? ($R = 0.0821$ L · atm/K · mol)
A)      18.5 liters
B)      19.9 liters
C)      22.4 liters
D)      25.2 liters

Answers: 1) **B** 2) **D** 3) **A** 4) **B** 5) **A** 6) **B** 7) **C** 8) **C**

# Periodic Table and Chemical Bonds

## The Periodic Table
The **Periodic Table of Elements** is a chart that arranges the chemical elements in an easy to understand way. Each element is listed in order of increasing atomic number and aligned so that the elements exhibit similar qualities. They are also are arranged in the same row, called a "period," or column often called a "group."

| H | | | | | | | | | | | | | | | | | He |
|---|---|---|---|---|---|---|---|---|---|---|---|---|---|---|---|---|---|
| Li | Be | | | | | | | | | | | B | C | N | O | F | Ne |
| Na | Mg | | | | | | | | | | | Al | Si | P | S | Cl | Ar |
| K | Ca | Sc | Ti | V | Cr | Mn | Fe | Co | Ni | Cu | Zn | Ga | Ge | As | Se | Br | Kr |
| Rb | Sr | Y | Zr | Nb | Mo | Tc | Ru | Rh | Pd | Ag | Cd | In | Sn | Sb | Te | I | Xe |
| Cs | Ba | 57-70 * | Lu | Hf | Ta | W | Re | Os | Ir | Pt | Au | Hg | Tl | Pb | Bi | Po | At | Rn |
| Fr | Ra | 89-102 ** | Lr | Rf | Db | Sg | Bh | Hs | Mt | Uun | Uuu | Uub | | Uuq | | | | |

| * Lanthanide series | La | Ce | Pr | Nd | Pm | Sm | Eu | Gd | Tb | Dy | Ho | Er | Tm | Yb |
|---|---|---|---|---|---|---|---|---|---|---|---|---|---|---|
| ** Actinide series | Ac | Th | Pa | U | Np | Pu | Am | Cm | Bk | Cf | Es | Fm | Md | No |

A few other notable trends in the periodic table:

- Elements within a group have the same outer electron arrangement. The number of the main group corresponds to the number of valence electrons in those elements; however, most of the transition elements contain two electrons in their valence shells.
- The horizontal rows correspond to the number of occupied electron shells of the atom.
- The elements set below the main table are the lanthanides (upper row) and actinides. They also usually have two electrons in their outer shells.
- In general, the elements increase in mass from left to right and from top to bottom.

## Electronic Structure of Atoms
The electrons of an atom have fixed energy levels called **shells** or principle energy levels. Shells are "filled" with electrons according to specific rules starting with the "inner" shells and working outward. The outermost shell, called the **valance shell**, includes the electrons usually involved in chemical bonding. The octet rule states that atoms of a low atomic number will share, gain, or lose electrons in order to fill the valence shell with eight electrons; this is achieved through different types of bonding. If this shell is full, then the element will be inert.

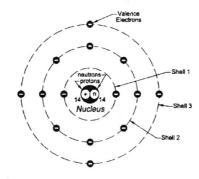

## Chemical Bonds

There are three main types of bonds that form between atoms: ionic, covalent, and metallic. In an **ionic bond**, one atom gains electrons to become a negatively charged **anion**, and the other loses electrons to become a positively charged **cations**. The oppositely charged **ions** then bond to each other.

A **covalent bond** forms when atoms share valence electrons. For example, in water, each hydrogen is sharing electrons with the oxygen atom. However, atoms do not always share electrons equally. Atoms that are more **electronegative** will pull electrons toward them more strongly than those that are less electronegative. This difference results in a **polar covalent bond**. A molecule where the electrons are shared equally is **nonpolar**. When atoms share more than one pair of electrons, they form a **double** (two pairs) or **triple** (three pairs) **bond**.

Electrons shared by two metallic atoms create a **metallic bond**. Those electrons participating in metallic bonds may be shared between any of the metal atoms in the region. Most metals have less than four valence electrons, which means they tend to lose electrons and form cations.

## VSEPR Bonding Theory

**VSEPR** (short for Valence Shell Electron Pair Repulsion) **theory** is a method for understanding the three-dimensional structure of covalently-bonded molecules. Because like charges attract, molecules will arrange themselves so that electrons are as far apart as possible. This fact allows us to determine the general shape of many molecules. A few of these are given below.

When there are 3 atoms in a molecule that have no high electronegativity differences, the molecule is **linear**.

$$X - A - X$$

Four atoms that have a lone pair on each end result in a **trigonal planar** molecule.

The **tetrahedral** molecule is the standard shape for a single central atom surrounded by four bonds. The bond angles between the different atoms may vary due to differences in electronegativity.

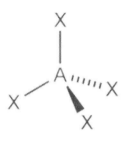

# Practice Drill: Periodic Table and Chemical Bonds

1. When cations and anions join, they form what kind of chemical bond?
A)      ionic
B)      hydrogen
C)      metallic
D)      covalent

2. In the periodic table of elements, generally speaking, how do the atomic masses vary?
A)      They decrease from left to right and increase from top to bottom.
B)      They increase from left to right and increase from bottom to top.
C)      They increase from left to right and increase from top to bottom.
D)      They increase from right to left and decrease from bottom to top.

3. The force involved in all chemical behavior is:
A)      electronegativity
B)      covalent bonds
C)      electromagnetism
D)      ionic bonds

4. Which one of the following is not a type of chemical bond?
A)      covalent bond
B)      VSEPR bond
C)      ionic bond
D)      metallic bond

5. Two atoms that do not share electrons equally will form what type of bond?
A)      metallic
B)      polar covalent
C)      ionic
D)      hydrogen

Answers: 1) **A**  2) **C**  3) **C**  4) **B**  5) **B**

**Chemical Reactions**

A **chemical reaction** occurs when there is a conversion of one set of chemical substances to another set. Chemical reactions are caused primarily by a change in bonding structure in these substances due to the exchange of electrons.

In a chemical reaction, the starting substances are called the **reagents** or **reactants**, and the ending substances are called the **products**. In the reaction below, the **reagents** sodium hydroxide (NaOH) and iron sulfate ($FeSO_4$) react to form sodium sulfate ($Na_2SO_4$) and iron hydroxide ($Fe(OH)_2$), the **products**. Note the **coefficient** of two in front of the sodium hydroxide; this tells you that for every one mole of the other reagents and products, the reaction requires two moles of sodium hydroxide.

$$2NaOH + FeSO_4 \rightarrow Na_2SO_4 + Fe(OH)_2$$

**Types of Reactions**
This reaction is known as a **double displacement reaction** because the ions in each reagent are displaced and trade places to form two new products. In a **single displacement reaction**, a lone atom or molecule displaces an ion in the second reagent, creating two new products, as shown below:

$$MgCl_2 + 2Na \rightarrow Mg + 2NaCl$$

In a **synthesis reaction**, two compounds combine to form a single product:

$$C + O_2 \rightarrow CO_2$$

The opposite reaction, when a single reactant breaks down into two or more products, is called a **decomposition reaction**.

Finally, a **combustion reaction** occurs when oxygen is reacted in the presence of heat to a combustible compound, usually an organic compound. The products of a combustion reaction are always water and carbon dioxide. For example, the reaction of methane with oxygen will proceed as follows:

$$CH_4 + 2\,O_2 \rightarrow CO_2 + 2H_2O$$

**Oxidation and Reduction**
In **oxidation/reduction reactions** (also called redox reactions), electrons are transferred between atoms. In a redox reaction, the total number of electrons shared by the reactants doesn't change—they are simply shifted around. The element that loses electrons is said to be **oxidized**, and the element that gains electrons is said to be **reduced**. The oxidized element is also called the **reducing agent** because has given electrons, or reduced, another element in the reaction. Similarly, the reduced element is called the **oxidizing agent** because it has oxidized, or taken electrons, from another element.

**Oxidation numbers**, which roughly correspond to the charge on an atom, can be used to find the oxidizing and reducing agents in a chemical reaction. Using the rule below, oxidation numbers can be assigned to each atom in the equation; those whose numbers change from one side of the equation to the other will have been oxidized or reduced.

Assigning oxidation numbers:

1. All elemental atoms, including diatomic gases like hydrogen ($H_2$), have an oxidation number of 0.
2. Oxygen in a compound has an oxidation number of −2.
3. Hydrogen in a compound has an oxidation number of +1.
4. The oxidation number for an ion is the charge on that ion.
5. The sum of the oxidation numbers of the atoms in a polyatomic ion sum to the charge on that ion.

# Practice Drill: Chemical Reactions

Identify the elements that are reduced and oxidized in the reaction shown below:

$$Cu_{(s)} + 2AgNO_{3\ (aq)} \rightarrow 2Ag_{(s)} + Cu(NO_3)_{2\ (aq)}$$

Answer:

Assign oxidation numbers for each atom on both sides of the equation:

|     | reactants | products |
| --- | --------- | -------- |
| Cu  | 0         | +2       |
| Ag  | +1        | 0        |
| N   | +6        | +6       |
| O   | −2        | −2       |

Copper is reduced because it loses two electrons; silver is oxidized because it has gained an electron. Note that there are two silver atoms each gaining one electron, the total number lost (two) is the same as the number gained.

## Energy of Reactions

Chemical reactions can either release or absorb energy as they progress. Those that absorb energy are **endothermic** and require an input of energy before the reaction can start. A chemical reaction that is **exothermic**, or heat releasing, will release energy during its course, forming lower-energy products. These reactions are often spontaneous, and do not require added energy.

## Balancing Equations

A chemical equation is considered balanced if the same amount of each element appears on both sides of the equation. This balance is important because atoms cannot be created or destroyed, so every atom included in the reagents must be accounted for in the products. For example, the combustion of methane includes one carbon, four hydrogen, and four oxygen on either side of the arrow.

$$CH_4 + 2\,O_2 \rightarrow CO_2 + 2H_2O$$

In order to balance an equation, you'll need to add the coefficients necessary to match the atoms of each element on both sides. In the reaction below, the numbers of bromine (Br) and nitrate ions ($NO_3^-$) do not match up:

$$CaBr_2 + NaNO_3 \rightarrow Ca(NO_3)_2 + NaBr$$

To balance the equation, start by adding a coefficient of two to the products to balance the bromine:

$$CaBr_2 + NaNO_3 \rightarrow Ca(NO_3)_2 + 2\,NaBr$$

This now gives you two sodium ions on the right, so you need to add another two on the left to balance:

$$CaBr_2 + 2\,NaNO_3 \rightarrow Ca(NO_3)_2 + 2\,NaBr$$

Notice that adding these two also balances the nitrate ions, so the equation is now complete.

## Reaction Stoichiometry

**Stoichiometry** is the use of the relative amounts of reagents and products in a reaction to find quantities of those reagents and products. Stoichiometry can be used to find a number of variables, including the quantities of products and reagents involved in a reaction and the identity of the limiting reagent (the reagent that gets used up first).

For example, in the single displacement reaction show below, 1 mol of magnesium chloride is needed for every 2 moles of sodium to complete the reaction. This reaction creates 1 mole of magnesium and 2 moles of sodium chloride.

$$MgCl_2 + 2Na \rightarrow Mg + 2NaCl$$

## Practice Drill: Energy of Reactions

1. In a furnace, natural gas (methane) is burned to produce heat to keep the house warm. What sort of reaction is this?
A)      acid base reaction
B)      combustion reaction
C)      single displacement reaction
D)      synthesis reaction

2. In chemistry class, a student mixes two unknown chemicals in a beaker. He notices that the beaker becomes hot to the touch. What type of reaction must be taking place in the beaker?
A)      exothermic
B)      endothermic
C)      combustion
D)      single replacement

3. Which of the following is a substance or compound that is entering into a reaction?
A)      mole
B)      reactant
C)      product
D)      chemical

4. Sulfur trioxide ($SO_3$) is produced when sulfur is burned. Which of the following is the correct general reaction for this process?
A)      sulfur + nitrogen $\rightarrow$ sulfur trioxide
B)      sulfur + oxygen $\rightarrow$ sulfur dioxide
C)      sulfur dioxide + oxygen $\rightarrow$ sulfur trioxide
D)      sulfur + oxygen $\rightarrow$ sulfur trioxide

5. In a balanced equation,
A)      the mass of the reactants equals the mass of the products.
B)      the number of moles of reactants equals the number of moles of the products.
C)      the size of each molecule in the reaction remains the same.
D)      None of the above are correct.

6. Balance the following equation: $KClO_3 \rightarrow KCl + O_2$
A)      $2KClO_3 \rightarrow KCl + 3O_2$
B)      $KClO_3 \rightarrow KCl + 3O_2$
C)      $2KClO_3 \rightarrow 2KCl + 3O_2$
D)      $6KClO_3 \rightarrow 6KCl + 3O_2$

Answers: 1) **B** 2) **A** 3) **B** 4) **D** 5) **D** 6) **C**

## Acids and Bases

There are a number of different technical definitions for acids and bases. In general, an **acid** can be defined as a substance that produces hydrogen ions ($H^+$) in solution while a **base** produces hydroxide ions ($OH^-$). Acidic solutions, which include common liquids like orange juice and vinegar, share a set of distinct characteristics: they have a sour taste and react strongly with metals. Bases, such as bleach and detergents, will taste bitter and have a slippery texture.

The acidity or basicity of a solution is described using its **pH** value, which is the negative log of the concentration of hydrogen ions. A neutral solution, which has the same concentration of hydrogen and hydroxide ions, has a pH of 7. Bases have a pH between 7 and 14, and acids have a pH between 0 and 7. Note that the pH scale is exponential, so a solution with a pH of 2 has one hundred times more hydrogen ions than one with a pH of 4.

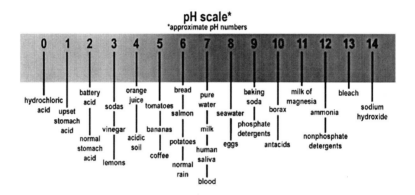

A **buffer** is a solution that does not exhibit much change in its pH when small amounts of an acid or base are added to it. An acidic buffer solution has a pH less than 7. Acidic buffer solutions are often made from a weak acid and one of its salts. On the other hand, an alkaline buffer solution has a pH greater than 7. Alkaline buffer solutions are often made with a weak base and one of its salts.

The human body contains many enzymes that only function at a specific pH. Once outside of this range, the enzymes are either unable to catalyze reactions or, in some cases, will break down. Our bodies produce a buffer solution that is a mixture of carbonic acid and bicarbonate in order to keep the pH of blood at 7.4.

# Practice Drill: Acids and Bases

1. One of the characteristic properties of an acid is that it increases the concentration of:
A)      hydrogen ions
B)      hydroxyl ions
C)      hydroxide ions
D)      oxide ions

2. A solution with a pH of 12 is:
A)      very acidic
B)      neutral
C)      very basic
D)      slightly acidic

3. Proper blood pH level for humans is:
A)      7.0
B)      7.2
C)      7.6
D)      7.4

Answers: 1) **A**  2) **C**  3) **D**

**Catalysts**

Reactions that require energy to activate need a minimum input of energy to get started, a value called the reaction's **activation energy**. **Catalysts**, substances that increase the rate of a chemical reaction, do so by lowering the reaction's activation energy. Catalysts can also bring two reactants closer together so that a reaction is more likely to occur.

Activation energy and the rate of the reaction can be influenced by a number of factors:

- Nature of the reactants: the electronegativity or electron structure of the reactants will affect how quickly they react.
- Concentration of the reactants: the more concentrated a reactive species is, the more likely they will come into contact with each other and react.
- Temperature: the temperature of the surrounding environment increases the internal energy of the reactants.

**Enzymes** are proteins found in living organisms that catalyze biological reactions. Unlike catalysts in a "typical" chemical reaction, enzymes are very specific to the reaction that they work on. For example, a platinum catalyst can be used in many different reactions, from decomposition of unburned hydrocarbons in your car to dehydrogenation of vegetable oils. On the other hand, an enzyme such as cellulase is specifically active for only one reaction: the breaking of the glycosidic bond between two glucose molecules in a cellulose chain.

# Practice Drill: Catalysts

1. Increasing the concentration of reactants will likely:
A)      decrease the rate of the reaction
B)      increase the rate of the reaction
C)      decrease the mass of the products
D)      increase the mass of the products

2. A reaction with a high activation energy will:
A)      require energy to begin
B)      require a catalyst to begin
C)      produce energy
D)      produce enzymes

3. A company is trying to make ammonia from the reaction of nitrogen ($N_2$) and hydrogen ($H_2$), but the reaction is progressing very slowly. Which of the following would be effective in increasing the reaction rate?
A)      increasing the temperature
B)      increasing the pressure
C)      adding a catalyst
D)      all of the above

Answers: 1) **B**  2) **A**  3) **D**

**Radioactive Decay**

The nuclei of some elements are unstable and will emit radioactive particles or energy in order to stabilize; together these emissions of particles and energy are called radiation. The three types of radiation that will be covered on the test include alpha, beta, and gamma radiation.

**Alpha particles** consist of two protons and two neutrons (i.e., a helium nucleus). They are written as $_0^2He$. In beta decay, high energy electrons or positrons are emitted from the nucleus. **Beta particles** are written as $_{-1}^0\beta$ (for electrons) and $_{+1}^0\beta$ (for positrons). Lastly, **gamma radiation** is a high frequency (and thus high energy) electromagnetic radiation written as $_0^0\gamma$. All three types of radiation can cause serious health issues ranging from nausea to cancer, both alpha and beta particles are relatively large and thus can be stopped by simple protective barriers. Gamma radiation, however, can travel through most substances, including concrete; lead is usually needed to provide protection from gamma rays.

# Geology

Geology is a branch of science, which deals with the materials that make up the Earth and the processes acting on them. A particularly important part of geology is the study of how these materials and processes have changed over time. Geology includes the study of features such as volcanoes, rocks, minerals, gemstones, earthquakes, fossils, fossil fuels, and tectonics.

## Earth's Structure

The Earth has a circumference of 40,075 kilometers, and is made of several—sometimes overlapping—layers. When the Earth first formed about 4.54 billion years ago, it was a soup of very hot rocks with different chemical elements, compounds, sizes, and weights. After a while, the heavier rocks sunk towards the center of the Earth, while the lighter rocks moved towards the Earth's surface. This separation of rocks took millions of years. The layers of the Earth can be classified in two ways: by chemical composition and by physical properties.

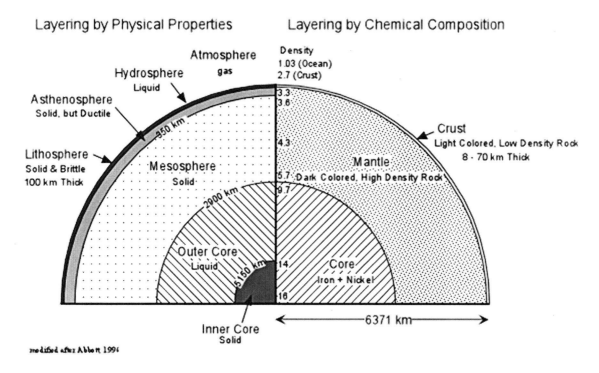

There are six levels to the Earth:
- Inner Core: Made of solid iron and nickel.
- Outer Core: Molten (hot liquid) iron and nickel, surrounding the inner core.
- Mantle (mesosphere): A large solid layer surrounding the core.
- Asthenosphere: The semi-fluid and flexible upper section of the mantle.
- Lithosphere: Includes the surface crust and the uppermost portion of the mantle.
- Hydrosphere: The liquid water component of the Earth.

**Rocks**

A mineral is a naturally occurring inorganic solid that has a definite chemical composition and crystal structure. Many processes form mineral deposits: separation by gravity, formation of placer deposits in streams (ex. gold) and lakes, chemical deposition of minerals in seawater, and more.

A rock is made up of minerals that are compacted together forming something solid. An example is quartz and feldspar (minerals) make up granite (rock). There are three different types of rocks, Igneous, Sedimentary, and Metamorphic.

- Igneous rocks are formed directly from molten magma, or lava.
- Sedimentary rocks are formed from sediments that are compressed or cemented together.
- Metamorphic rocks are formed when sedimentary, igneous, or metamorphic rocks are heated and compressed over long periods of time.

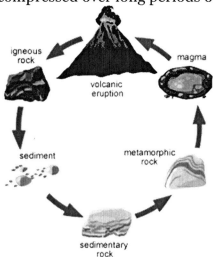

https://www.learner.org

Weathering is the deterioration of rock into small pieces, either through chemical or mechanical processes. Chemical weathering involves the direct effect of atmospheric or biologically produced chemicals on rocks. Mechanical (or physical) weathering involves the breakdown of rocks through atmospheric conditions such as temperature changes, biological processes, moving water, wind, and glaciers.

Erosion is the movement of small bits of rock and soil. Fossil fuel deposits are partially decomposed organic debris. Soil is a mixture of pulverized rock and organic debris. Soil conditions are regulated by humus: a complex mixture of compounds resulting from the decomposition of plant tissue (stems and leaves).

**Plate Tectonic Theory**

The Plate Tectonic Theory states that approximately 320 million years ago, the continents converged into a single land mass called Pangaea. Then, around 180 million years ago, Pangaea broke apart into seven tectonic plates: the African, North American,

South American, Eurasian, Australian, Antarctic, and Pacific plates. There are also several minor plates, including the Arabian, Nazca, Cocos, and Philippines plates. Tectonic plates make up the earth's lithosphere. The plates move about 2-10 cm per year. A plate boundary is where two plates meet. There are three different types of plate boundaries, convergent, divergent, and transform boundary. Convergent boundaries are when two plates come together. A divergent boundary is when two plates pull apart. Transform boundary is when two plates slide past each other.

Earthquakes generally occur where plates slip past each other; where one plate is subducted (pushed under another); or at mid-ocean ridges, where plates are separating. Volcanoes can also occur at these moments when magma rapidly rises to the surface. Mountain ranges are also formed through various processes – the Andes formed along a subduction zone, while the Himalayas were formed when two continental plates collided; the modern Rockies were formed by a compression followed by expansion.

### The Hydrologic Cycle
The movement of water on Earth is called the hydrologic cycle or water cycle. The process of the cycle consists of: evaporation, precipitation, and run off. The hydrologic cycle utilizes all three forms of water: vapor, liquid and solid.

## Water Cycle

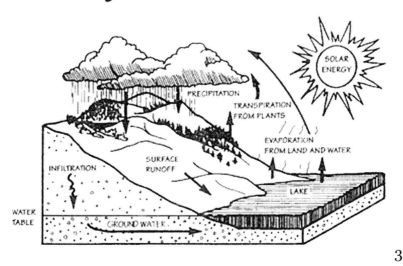

3

Evaporation is the transformation of liquid water to water vapor. Water can also vaporize through plant tissue, especially leaf surfaces. This process is known as transpiration.

Precipitation is the transformation from gas to liquid (rain) or solid (snow, sleet, or hail).

---

[3] Graphic from: greatswamp.org

Runoff is the flow of water back to bodies of water, either by land (rivers and streams) or through underground sources.

Ground water is found in spaces between soil particles underground (located in the zone of saturation).

Infiltration is the process by which groundwater accumulates and soaks into the ground. There it either replenishes shallow aquifers, or seeps into deep aquifers. Aquifers serve as underground beds of saturated soil or rock, which yield significant quantities of water. Shallow aquifers flow into and replenish rivers and streams, while deep aquifers represent large underground reservoirs of freshwater. Water can be present in deep water aquifers for centuries, while gradually moving towards and into the sea, where it eventually evaporates into the atmosphere.

### Tides

On the majority of earth it experiences two tides, low and high. The tides are directly linked to the amount of time it takes the earth to rotate one full rotation. The earth experiences these tides one of three ways. We have diurnal, semi-diurnal, and mixed. Diurnal tides consists of high and low tides occurring only once per day. Semi-diurnal tides consists of high and low tides occurring twice per day but with little difference in water level. Mixed tides occur when high and low tides occur twice per day with a significant change in water level.

An outgoing current or flow is known as an ebb current or tide. A slack tide occurs when there is little or no current between the tides. The incoming current, or tidal flow, is known as a flood current or tide.

Tides are significantly affected by the moon and lunar schedule. The tides are most affected during the new moon phase and the full moon phase. The tides are especially affected if the moon is aligned with the sun thus creating a high gravitational pull. When the moon does not align with the sun the force is weakened and the tides are not affected as greatly. A rip current or riptide may occur when the moon is aligned with the sun. A neap tide occurs when the sun and moon are out of alignment.

Tides are an important part of the ecological system and instrumental in the survival of many species. They can both create life and destroy it. Knowing and understanding tides is crucial for boaters, marine biologists and many others.

## Practice Drill: Geology

1. All of the following are types of plate boundaries except:
A)  Transform.
B)  Translational.
C)  Divergent.
D)  Convergent.

2. Which of the following situations would having a geologists be most beneficial?
A)  An oil and gas company is unsure what layer to drill into to maximize profits.
B)  A wastewater treatment plant is noticing a new mineral deposit in their water.
C)  An underwater canyon is spewing magma and affecting the local ecosystem.
D)  Geologists would likely be employed in all of these fields.

3. The most voluminous portion of the Earth is known to geologists as:
A)  The lithosphere.
B)  The mantle.
C)  The core.
D)  The crust.

4. On Earth the lithosphere is the portion where rocks act as:
A)  Metals
B)  Loose or Brittle Solids
C)  Pliable solids
D)  Fluids

5. Igneous, sedimentary, and metamorphic are:
A)  Three types of plate boundaries.
B)  Three divisions of Earth.
C)  Ways to describe soils.
D)  The three major classes of rocks.

6. All of the following are subdivisions of the earth's interior except:
A)  The magnetosphere.
B)  The lithosphere.
C)  The core.
D)  The mantle.

7. Transpiration can be described as:
A)  Process where water vapor enters the atmosphere when animals breathe.
B)  Process of water vapor leaving a plant through pores in the leaves.
C)  Process where water vapor forms clouds in the atmosphere.
D)  Process where water vapor enters the atmosphere from water evaporated on the ground.

8. What are the three states of water on Earth?
A)      Groundwater, lakes, and clouds.
B)      Liquid water, frozen water, and water vapor.
C)      Gas, steam, and vapor.
D)      Groundwater, oceans, and ice.

9. When a liquid turns into a gas, what change of state occurs?
A)      Eutrophication.
B)      Condensation.
C)      Evaporation.
D)      Precipitation.

10. Spring tides occur:
A)      At new moon and first quarter moon.
B)      At first quarter and third quarter moons.
C)      At new moon and full moon.
D)      At third quarter and full moons.

Answers: 1) **B** 2) **D** 3) **B** 4) **B** 5) **D** 6) **A** 7) **B** 8) **B** 9) **C** 10) **C**

# Meteorology

Meteorology, or the study of the changes in air pressure, temperature, wind currents, and moisture in the troposphere.

## The Atmosphere
Our atmosphere consists of a mixture of gases, but two make up 99% of it. Nitrogen and Oxygen occur in 78% and 21% of the air in our atmosphere. The other trace gases make up only 1% of the atmosphere but are still vital the life on earth. The most prominent gas is Argon, while carbon dioxide and the ozone, or ozone layer play tremendous roles in the survival of almost all species. Water vapor is also present in trace amounts and is vital to life as well.

## Energy Balance
The energy balance of the Earth is achieved by an opposition of energy flow to and from the ground level and all the atmospheric layers. Earth's tilt and shape play important roles in seasons and temperature across the globe.

## Pressure Systems
Pressure systems are an interesting and difficult occurrence to explain without a thorough understanding of physics. However, a simple explanation can help you understand at a level needed for this exam. Imagine the earth stopped rotating however the sun still heated it at the equator. While the poles remain cold because sunlight does not reach them. Because warm air rises and cool air stays low, the equator would have a low-pressure system, and the poles would have a high-pressure system. Now the caveat is that the earth does spin and thus creates two more zones of pressure. We see a low-pressure zone at 60 degrees latitude and a high-pressure system at 30 degrees. These occur because of wind currents and the earth's rotation.

These pressure systems are measured in barometers and conveyed in units called millibars or *mb*. There are two types of barometric measurements, mercurial, which is the most accurate but least available, and aneroid which is less accurate but portable.

## Atmospheric Structure
The atmosphere is divided into four layers based on temperature: the troposphere, the stratosphere, mesosphere, and thermosphere.

About 75% of the air in the atmosphere is compressed into the lowest layer, which is called the **troposphere**. In this layer, where clouds form and air masses continuously mix, the change of temperature in relation to height is relatively large. Within the troposphere, air consists of 78% nitrogen; 21% oxygen; and 1% argon, carbon dioxide, and minute amounts of other gases; this layer of air contains minute and trace amounts of dust, salt and other particles. The seasons determine how thick the troposphere layer is at any time.

The top of the troposphere is known as the **tropopause**. This zone between the troposphere and the stratosphere, the tropopause keeps a lid on the lower atmosphere below it. This lid contains occasional breaks and overlaps, which provide paths for high-velocity winds called jet streams. The jet streams or wind currents play a major role in our pressure systems. The strong winds cause pressure systems to mix thus leading to our ever changing weather conditions.

The layer directly above the tropopause is the **stratosphere**. The stratosphere is made up of two parts. The bottom half has a much more stable temperature and little to no cumuli or clouds. The upper portion sees temperatures rise as altitude increases. The stratopause layer the temperature is that of the earth's surface.

The Ozone Layer is responsible for absorbing the ultraviolet light produced by the sun and also gives the stratopause its warmth. Without the ozone layer and the barrier it creates between the earth's surface and the sun, life on earth would be all but impossible for most species.

Extending 50 to 80 km above the Earth's surface, the **mesosphere** is a very cold layer as temperatures typically drop as you increase in altitude. The air or atmosphere is very dense, is this is the layer responsible for slowing meteors down and sometimes completely disintegrating them before they reach the earth's surface.

The **thermosphere** extends from 80 km above the Earth's surface to outer space. The temperatures in this layer reach high extremes sometimes in the thousands of degrees Celsius. This layer like the ozone is responsible for toning down the effects of the sun on our planet.

The next layer is the ionosphere and is really an extension of the thermosphere; thus it's not known as another layer but more just as an extension. The ionosphere represents less than 0.1% of the total mass of the Earth's atmosphere. This small "layer" is very important to the earth as this is where ionization occurs because of the sun's extreme temperature.

The Atmosphere:

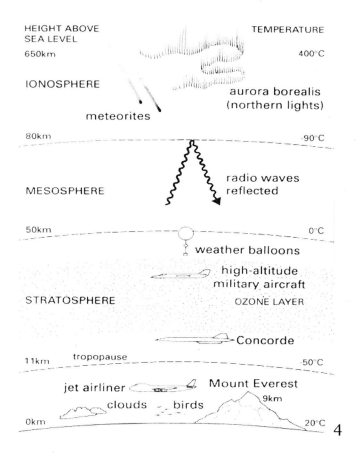

## The General Circulation of the Atmosphere

The earth includes two high-pressure systems and two low-pressure systems: high-pressure at the poles and 30 degrees latitude, and low-pressure at the equator and 60 degrees latitude.

Because of the rotation of earth we have three defined winds: easterlies which are between 60 degrees and the pole, are known appropriately as polar easterlies; and westerly winds from 30 to 60 degrees, known as the mid-latitude westerlies; and the tropical easterlies, most commonly known as trade winds. Doldrums occur where heated air is rising and fall at the horse latitudes. Many wind systems occur because of the suns affect on the temperature of the ocean.

## Clouds

Clouds are formed from the process of condensation. Condensation occurs when water vapor transforms into small drops of liquid water. This occurs under a few different scenarios; a decrease in pressure, temperature drop or an abundance of condensation. In order for clouds to form there must be something for the droplets of water to

---

[4] Graphic from: http://media.photobucket.com

condense upon. This is where the role of dust and other small particles play such an important role. Water vapor condenses on these trace elements and creates clouds. Some clouds produce moisture that makes it to the ground while others eventually evaporate. Sometimes clouds produce rain but it evaporates before it reaches the ground. This process is known as Virga.

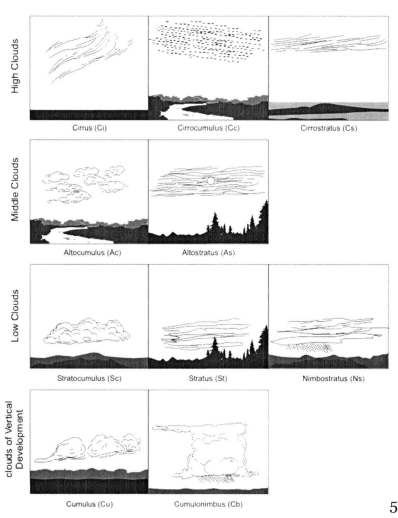

5

## Cloud Categories

When clouds form we tend to classify them by their shape. Cumuliform and stratiform are the two general categories into which all clouds fall. Cumulus clouds are formed when air currents are on the rise. Stratus clouds form when air is cooled below its saturation point. The thickness of these clouds varies greatly and often comes with continuous rainfall over an expansive area.

---

5 Graphic from: cmos.ca

## Cloud Classification

Clouds can also be classified in the following classes: towering, high, middle and low.
Towering Classification: These clouds reach the troposphere, but may descend as low as normal clouds.

High Classification: Clouds that appear above 6,000 meters and consist of ice crystals. These clouds are often delicate and can also be known as cirrocumulus or cirrostratus. These clouds appear as streaks or curls in the sky.

Middle Classification: Clouds exist between 2,000 and 6,000 meters and often get the prefix alto. Altocumulus or altostratus clouds make us the middle classification.
Low Classification: Clouds below 2000 meters above the earth's surface. Further classification occurs with these clouds. They can be either stratus or cumulus and if they produce rain they would receive a variation of the word "Nimbus." Cumulonimbus or Nimbostratus.

# Practice Drill: Meteorology

1. What are the two most abundant gases in the Earth's atmosphere?
A)     Nitrogen and oxygen.
B)     Oxygen and carbon monoxide.
C)     Water vapor and argon.
D)     Methane and hydrogen.

2.  Weather occurs in which layer of the Earth's atmosphere?
A)     Stratosphere.
B)     Mesosphere.
C)     Thermosphere.
D)     Troposphere.

3. Why is the mesosphere warmer than the layers around it?
A)     Trace elements absorb and hold heat in the mesosphere.
B)     Energetic particles hit the mesosphere to produce heat and aurorae
C)     Heat is transported into the ozone layer by convection from the troposphere.
D)     The ozone absorbs ultraviolet light which produces solar energy.

4. The thick, dense region of the atmosphere is known as:
A)     Ionosphere.
B)     Mesosphere.
C)     Stratosphere.
D)     Hydrosphere.

5. Of the clouds in the high-cloud classification, which word would you be most likely to see associated with them?
A)     Cirrus.
B)     Alto.
C)     Cumulus.
D)     Nimbus.

6. A cloud with some of the characteristics of both cumulus and stratus clouds is:
A)     Stratocumulus.
B)     Cirrus.
C)     Altostratus.
D)     Nimbostratus.

Answers: 1) **A**  2) **D**  3)**D**  4) **B**  5) **A**  6) **A**

## Astronomy

Astronomy is the scientific study of outer space. Scientist pay special attention to the positions of matter, dimensions, and distribution as well as the composition and motion of energy, and the development of celestial bodies and occurrences.

### Our Solar System

The earth is located in the Milky Way Galaxy, which is one of thirty plus galaxies in our local area or group. Our galaxy is known to have more than 200 billion stars some of which have already burned out but the light is still traveling. The Milky Way Galaxy is also part of a larger group called a super cluster that includes over 100 other galaxies. Scientists believe the super cluster, Virgo, which includes our galaxy is one of millions of other super clusters in our universe.

Our solar system, which is essentially everything that rotates around our sun, includes other planets, moons and meteors. Astronauts often encounter other debris, and rocks as they make their way into space. All of these objects have one thing in common, and that is they are in orbit around the sun.

The sun is currently in its "main sequence" or stage where it will remain for around 90% of its life cycle. The sun does not sit in the middle of our solar system but is actually 30,000 light years from the center of a solar system that spans between 80,000 and 120,000 light years in diameter. The sun which is a gaseous star rotates completely once every 26 days, while it takes more than 200 million years to rotate around the Milky Way Galaxy. The sun is currently in its fourth stage of six total stages. Fortunately for people on earth it'll be there for another five billion years.

### Planets

It is widely accepted by astronomers and scientists alike that we have eight planets that currently orbit our sun. The order of the planets currently is:

Mercury
Venus
Earth
Mars
Jupiter
Saturn
Uranus
Neptune

Each planet has very distinct characteristics. For example, Mars is often referred to as the "red planet" because when viewed through a telescope it gives off a reddish glow. Jupiter, a gaseous planet, is the largest in the solar system by millions of miles. Saturn is quite possibly the most pictured planet because of is beautiful orbital rings.
The solar systems are divided into the inner and outer planets both of which are very different from one another. The inner planets, from Venus to Mars, are made of rock and few or no moons in orbit around them. The outer planets, on the other hand, are

made mostly of a mixture of gases and will have many moons rotating in orbit around them. The outer planets include Jupiter-Neptune.

Further yet our solar system contains comets, asteroids and other small particles such as rocks and debris. Comets and asteroids are often confused . Comets are icy masses that orbit the sun and look like they leave a dusty tail behind them. Asteroids, called minor planets, consists of rock, debris, metals, and other materials. Similar to comets, asteroids orbit around the sun, but most are found in the "asteroid belt" between Jupiter and Mars.

Finally, meteors or meteoroids are small rocks made of metal and other debris that are traveling through space and not actually in orbit of the sun. They are small and occasionally make their way into the earth's atmosphere.

# Practice Drill: Astronomy

1. Which of the following objects make up Earth's solar system?
A)      Planets and comets
B)      Planets, asteroids and comets
C)      Sun, meteors and comets.
D)      Sun, Planets, comets, meteors.

2.  How many light years is in the sun from the middle of the solar system?
A)      80,000.
B)      120,000.
C)      30,000.
D)      0.

3. What planet is known as the largest in our solar system with a diameter two and half times that of all the other planets combined?
A)      Venus.
B)      Uranus.
C)      Saturn.
D)      Jupiter.

4. Often frozen and leaving a dusty tail, this object is in orbit of the sun:
A)      Comet.
B)      Meteoroid.
C)      Asteroid.
D)      Earth.

Answers: 1) **D**  2) **C**  3) **D**  4) **A**

# Chapter 10: Rotated Blocks

The Rotated blocks section is deceptively simple, which as you can probably tell by now is a recurring theme for the AFOQT exam. In this section, you have 13 minutes to complete 15 questions, so approximately 50 seconds per question.

The objective in the Rotated Blocks section is straight forward enough: you are given an image of a 3D "block" (or some shape or object) and must find the block that matches but is shown from a different angle. You'll be given 5 answer choices.

The trick is that the blocks are extremely similar, and the differences can be quite subtle. The general idea of the shape will be there for each answer choice, except one might be a little shorter on one side, or a little thicker, or the hole is placed slightly differently, etc.

This is one of those sections that is incredibly difficult to "study for". Frankly, most people either get it or they don't, depending on their innate ability to visualize three-dimensional objects. Even if you are not one of the lucky ones who are a natural at this, you can still do well with practice and using a systematic approach. Regardless of which category you might fall into, a good suggestion is to find a small detail of the shape and cull out any answer choices that don't match correctly. It might just be a single protrusion, the location of a hole, etc. What you want to avoid is getting distracted as you look through the answer choices. Review one aspect, then go back and look for another. If you get scatter brained and are trying to remember 5 different aspects at once, you'll never keep straight in your mind which ones were potential matches or not.

A final reminder, don't forget how similar the answer choices are. Even once you think you found the answer, look through the choices just one more time to be sure.
Those 50 seconds per question can go by quickly for some people, so do not forget about time management and give yourself enough time at the end to fill in guesses for any remaining questions.

With that, let's get started on some practice on the next page!

# Rotated Blocks Practice Test Questions

1)

A)      B)      C)      D)      E)

2)

A)      B)      C)      D)      E)

3)

A)      B)      C)      D)      E)

4)

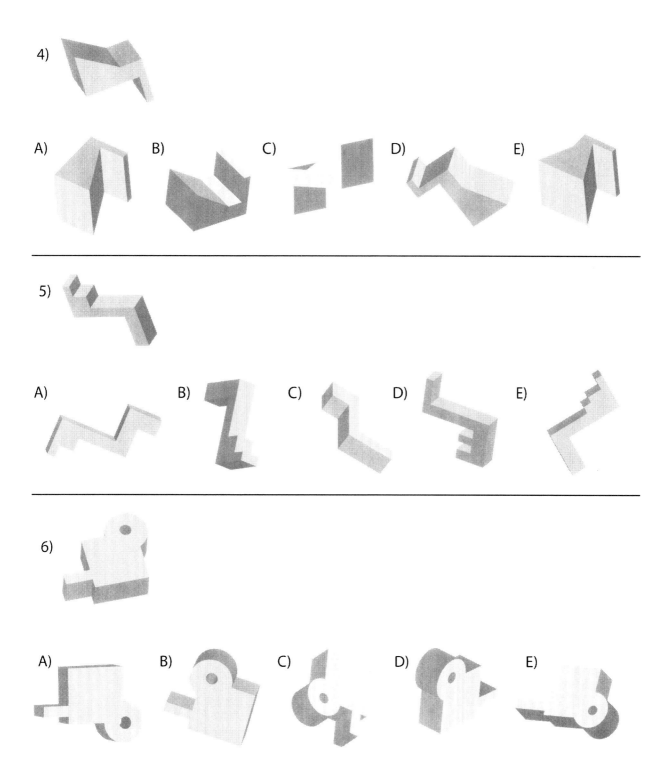

A)

B)

C)

D)

E)

5)

A)

B)

C)

D)

E)

6)

A)

B)

C)

D)

E)

7)

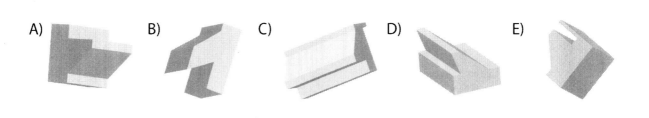

A)     B)     C)     D)     E)

8)

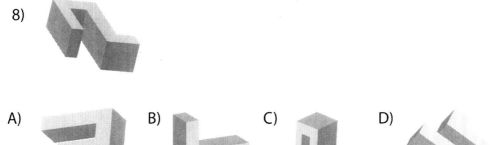

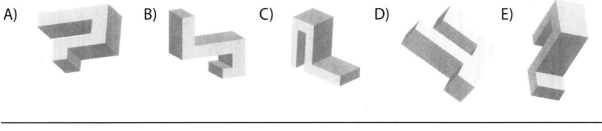

A)     B)     C)     D)     E)

9)

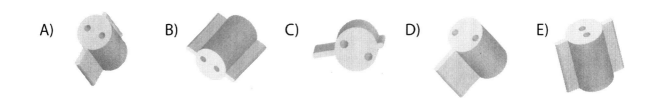

A)     B)     C)     D)     E)

10)

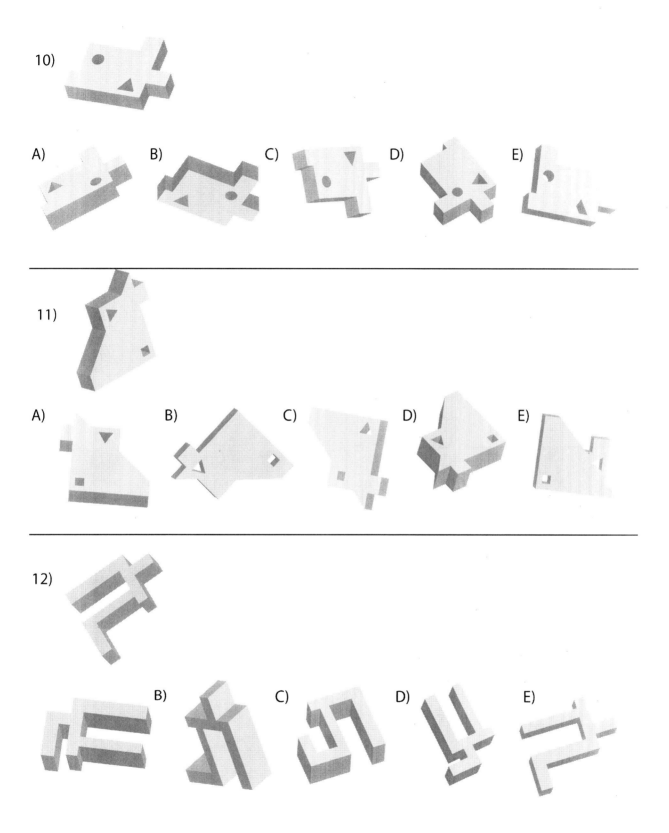

A)     B)     C)     D)     E)

11)

A)     B)     C)     D)     E)

12)

B)     C)     D)     E)

13)

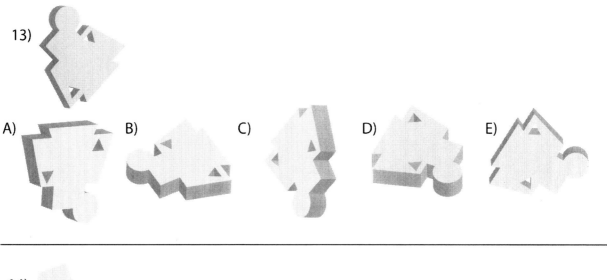

14)

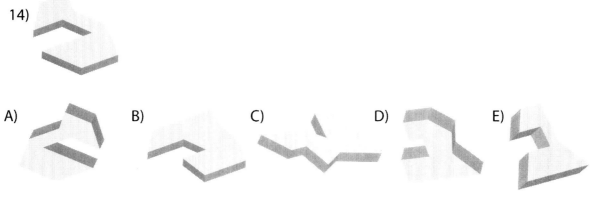

15)

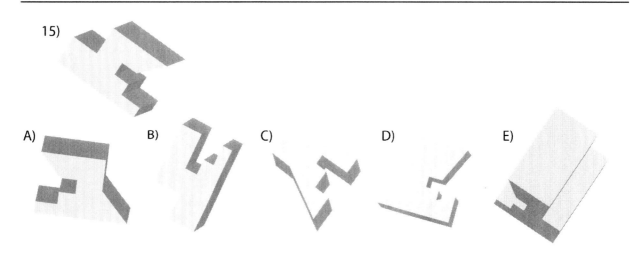

# Rotated Blocks Practice Test Answer Key

1. C
2. A
3. D
4. C
5. B
6. D
7. A
8. E
9. C
10. C
11. D
12. B
13. D
14. A
15. E

# Chapter 11: Hidden Figures

In the hidden figures section, you will have 8 minutes to complete 15 items. The first thing you will notice about this section is the formatting of the questions is totally different than any other section. You will be given 5 shapes with correlating answer choices A, B, C, D, & E. Below those answer choices, you will be presented the questions which is a box with a lot of zig-zagging lines in all directions. Somewhere in those zig-zagged lines is a shape that matches one of the 5 answer choices.

This section is straightforward enough, but a few things to remember that can help you:

- First and foremost, it is imperative to remember that the shape in the hidden figure will always match the same size, position, and orientation as shown in the answer choice selections. Do not over-analyze and think you see a figure that is rotated 90 degrees or slightly bigger or smaller because the AFOQT will never present questions that way on this section.
- Find a defining feature of the answer choices. That one long section or sharply angled protrusion can help you quickly ID the shape in many cases.
- Finally, this works for some and not for others, but if you squint and almost blur out the hidden figure image a little, sometimes the shapes will just kind of "appear" because there is a pattern to them, whereas the other lines in the box are just meant to distract and conceal. Not very scientific, we know, but this has been a life-saver for many people.

Let's get started with some practice on the next page. Do not let the hidden figure section overwhelm you. Even if you are struggling with it, just give it your best shot for a while, but focus your attention on the other sections as they are more important, require more study time, and you will see more results from your study effort elsewhere.

# Hidden Figures Practice Test Questions

For questions 1-5, use the below shapes as answer choices:

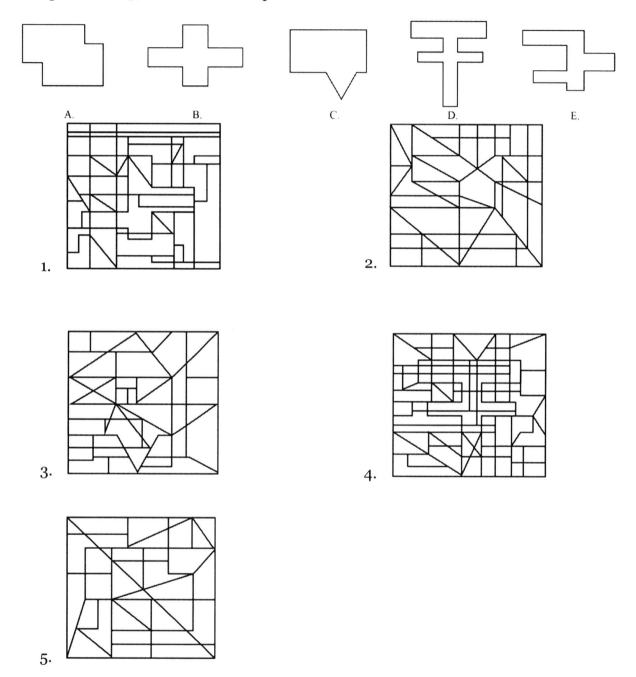

For questions 6-10, use the below shapes as answer choices:

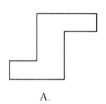
A.

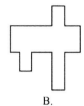
B.

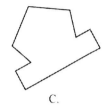
C.

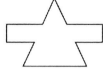
D.

E.

6.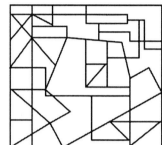

7.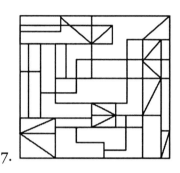

8.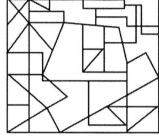

9.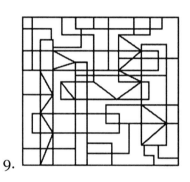

10.

For questions 11-15, use the below shapes as answer choices:

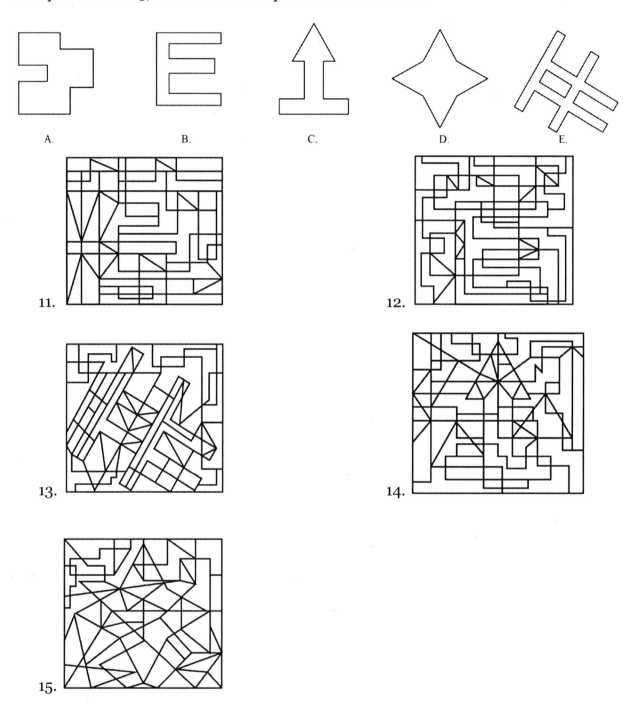

A.

B.

C.

D.

E.

11.

12.

13.

14.

15.

# Hidden Figures Practice Test Answer Key

1. E
2. B
3. C
4. D
5. A
6. C
7. A
8. B
9. E
10. D
11. A
12. B
13. E
14. C
15. D

## Conclusion

*At Accepted, Inc. we strive to help you reach your goals. We hope this guide gave you the information to not only score well but to exceed any previous expectations. Our goal is to keep it concise, show you a few test tricks along the way, and to ultimately help you succeed in your goals. Please let us know if we've truly prepared you for the exam and if don't mind including your test score we'd be thankful for that too! Please send us an email to feedback@acceptedinc.com.*

*Remember – Study Smarter. Score Higher. Get Accepted!*

*-Accepted, Inc.-*

CPSIA information can be obtained at www.ICGtesting.com
Printed in the USA
BVOW05s1620071015

421360BV00007B/81/P